Economic Development Through Entrepreneurship

NEW HORIZONS IN ENTREPRENEURSHIP

Series Editor: Sankaran Venkataraman
*Darden Graduate School of Business
Administration, University of Virginia*

This important series is designed to make a significant contribution to the development of Entrepreneurship Studies. As this field has expanded dramatically in recent years, the series will provide an invaluable forum for the publication of high-quality works of scholarship and show the diversity of issues and practices around the world.

The main emphasis of the series is on the development and application of new and original ideas in Entrepreneurship. Global in its approach, it includes some of the best theoretical and empirical work with contributions to fundamental principles, rigorous evaluations of existing concepts and competing theories, historical surveys and future visions. Titles include original monographs, edited collections, and texts.

Titles in the series include:

A General Theory of Entrepreneurship
The Individual–Opportunity Nexus
Scott Shane

Academic Entrepreneurship
University Spinoffs and Wealth Creation
Scott Shane

Economic Development Through Entrepreneurship
Government, University and Business Linkages
Edited by Scott Shane

Economic Development Through Entrepreneurship

Government, University and Business Linkages

Edited by

Scott Shane

Case Western Reserve University, USA

NEW HORIZONS IN ENTREPRENEURSHIP

Edward Elgar

Cheltenham, UK • Northampton, MA, USA

Published by
Edward Elgar Publishing Limited
Glensanda House
Montpellier Parade
Cheltenham
Glos GL50 1UA
UK

Edward Elgar Publishing, Inc.
136 West Street
Suite 202
Northampton
Massachusetts 01060
USA

A catalogue record for this book
is available from the British Library

Library of Congress Cataloguing in Publication Data
Economic development through entrepreneurship : government, university and
    business linkages / edited by Scott Shane.
        p. cm.
    Includes bibliographical references and index.
    1. Economic development—Effects of education on—Congresses. 2.
    Universities and colleges—Government policy—United States—Congresses.
    3. Industrial policy—United States—Congresses. 4. Regional
    planning—United States—Congresses. I. Shane, Scott Andrew, 1964–

    HD75.7.E27 2006
    338.9—dc22
                                                                2005046194

ISBN 1 84376 855 0 (cased)

Printed and bound in Great Britain by MPG Books Ltd, Bodmin, Cornwall

To Lynne, for supporting all my research efforts

Contents

Figures

Tables

Contributors

Eric Bettinger, Case Western Reserve University and National Bureau of Economic Research
John Butler, University of Texas
Bo Carlsson, Case Western Reserve University
Ben Craig, Federal Reserve Bank of Cleveland
Irwin Feller, American Association for the Advancement of Science
Michael Fogarty, Portland State University
Susan Helper, Case Western Reserve University
William Jackson, University of North Carolina, Chapel Hill
Michael Luger, University of North Carolina, Chapel Hill
Daniel Luria, Michigan Manufacturing Technology Center
Hunter Morrison, Youngstown State University
Richard Pogue, Jones Day Reavis and Pogue
Casey Porto, Oakridge National Lab
Erin Riley, Harvard University
William Seelbach, Ohio Aerospace Institute
Scott Shane, Case Western Reserve University
Robert Sheehan, University of Toledo
Marcus Stanley, Case Western Reserve University
Robert Strom, Ewing Marion Kauffman Foundation
James Thomson, Federal Reserve Bank of Cleveland

Acknowledgments

This book would not have been possible without the support and participation of a number of entities. The Office of Advocacy of the US Small Business Administration funded the conference itself. The SBC Foundation provided much of the financial support for the Center for Regional Economic Issues at Case Western Reserve University that helped host the conference. This conference and many of the activities of the Center would not be possible were it not for the generous support of the SBC Foundation. The Dean's office of the Weatherhead School at Case Western Reserve University provided access to the wonderful facility in which the conference took place, the Peter B. Lewis Building.

Several individuals helped greatly to organize the conference. Ed Morrison, the Executive Director of the Center for Regional Economic Issues, helped to line up participants for the conference and helped to shape the agenda, making sure it reflected the dual goals of providing scholarly insight and being useful to practitioners. Betsey Merkel and Susan Altshuler, staff members of the Center, did much of the hard work to make the conference happen, ensuring that participants were fed and housed, their transportation arranged, and their materials distributed. The conference and the resulting book would not have been possible without the contribution of these people.

Lastly, I would like to thank all of the participants in the conference for their contribution to the discussion that ensued after the presentation of the initial drafts of the papers contained in this volume. The feedback provided by many helped to shape the final drafts of the contributions to this volume in a variety of important ways. While many people contributed to this discussion, two stand out in their importance. David Morgenthaler of Morgenthaler Ventures and Chad Moutray of the US Small Business Administration both provided significant valuable feedback to the authors of virtually all of the chapters contained in this book. Without their participation, the output of this conference would have been much less.

Introduction

Scott Shane

THE PURPOSE

Entrepreneurship is often seen by policy makers as a key mechanism for enhancing economic development, particularly in regions where entrepreneurial activity was once vibrant and is now lagging. To policy makers, entrepreneurship is a good solution because it provides a relatively non-controversial way to increase the proverbial pie, creating jobs and enhancing per capita income growth. Therefore government officials frequently search for mechanisms to enhance entrepreneurial activity in their regions, whether those mechanisms are tax policies, financing subsidies or other tools.

Universities are also seen as valuable institutions for economic development. Perhaps because the primary mission of universities is education, and education is viewed by virtually everyone as good, and perhaps because universities are among the most geographically stable entities in existence, rarely relocating to other locales, policy makers often look to ways to turn universities in their regions into engines of economic development. Mechanisms to enhance technology transfer from universities, to reduce brain drain out of a region, and policies to create linkages between universities and industry are among the many efforts chosen by policy makers to use universities to enhance regional economic development.

Recently anecdotal evidence has begun to emerge to suggest that these two economic development efforts are not independent. Policy makers are beginning to examine the role of universities as entities to enhance economic development in regions through their effect on entrepreneurial activity. Whether the anecdotes focus on the creation of university spin-off companies to exploit intellectual property created at universities to create jobs and enhance productivity in a region, or they focus on ways to use universities to attract and train women and minority entrepreneurs who otherwise would not settle in a region, the message is clear. Policy makers are beginning to think about universities as facilitating economic development through entrepreneurship, and are searching for policy levers to enhance that activity. However, despite a wealth of efforts to examine both the role of entrepreneurs in economic development and the role of universities in economic development, no systematic effort has been made to examine the intersection of these two sets: the role of universities to enhance economic development through entrepreneurship.

This book seeks to fill this gap. The result of a workshop at Case Western Reserve University in which scholars were invited to present their views on the linkages between government, university and business efforts to promote economic development through entrepreneurship, the book aims to provide a systematic review of what we know about effective policies in this area. Each chapter focuses on a linkage in a different domain, such as technology transfer, education and so on. The authors present both best practices and problematic strategies for joint efforts by governments, industries and universities to promote economic development through entrepreneurship.

Many chapters are followed by commentary presented by a 'thoughtful practitioner'. The idea behind the commentaries is to present an evaluation of the academic's arguments from the perspective of someone directly involved in government–university–industry partnerships.

The chapters are non-technical and summarize existing knowledge and research on the topic rather than produce new primary research. The goal of the book is to help government policy makers, foundations, university officials, business leaders and other stakeholders interested in figuring out how to create partnerships between universities and governments to encourage economic development through entrepreneurship.

THE CHAPTERS

The first chapter, 'An historical perspective on government–university partnerships to enhance entrepreneurship and economic development', by Irwin Feller, traces the history of two important efforts by American universities to enhance economic growth: university–government–industry programs in research and development, and academic programs to foster entrepreneurship. The chapter traces the history of government–university–industry partnerships to promote economic development from the colonial period to the present, focusing on the major shifts in those efforts, including the creation of the land grant system, the role of universities to the war effort in World War II, and the Bayh–Dole Act. The main conclusions of Feller's historical review are that government–industry–university research and development partnerships appear to be working effectively, but could face challenges from federal budget deficits and state boom and bust policy shifts. These programs also remain a relatively small part of research and development efforts of both industry and universities. University funding of research and development at American universities may even decline further as conflict emerges over ownership of intellectual property.

The second chapter, 'Government policies to encourage economic development through entrepreneurship: the case of technology transfer', by Scott Shane, reviews the effects that university spin-offs have on economic development, as well as policies that federal and state governments have employed successfully to enhance the development of these companies. The chapter explains that many important high-technology companies were spin-offs from universities, that spin-offs commercialize many technologies that otherwise would go uncommercialized, induce greater amounts of investment than other licensees, and tend to locate close to the universities that spawn them. The chapter points to six policies that enhance spin-off company creation: (1) intense federal funding of academic research, (2) awarding of property rights to universities rather than inventors, (3) awarding the ownership of federally funded inventions to universities, (4) subsidizing new technology creation through incubators or other institutional mechanisms, (5) financing pre-market stage investment in technology development by new companies, and (6) creating policies, such as those that support leave of absence from academic positions, and ownership of equity in spin-off companies, to encourage academic participation in spin-off company creation.

The third chapter, 'Creating innovation networks among manufacturing firms: how effective extension programs work', by Susan Helper and Marcus Stanley, examines component manufacturing firms of fewer than 500 employees to determine the sources of their productivity and policies that help them enhance that productivity. The authors find that firms in urban areas are more productive, but that productivity benefits accrue to workers, not firms. Social networks increase the productivity of firms, and firms that do more engineering gain more from being in urban locations. Moreover urban location appears to help high wage–high skill manufacturing firms weather adverse trends. The authors recommend three categories of policies to help enhance the productivity of these small manufacturing firms: tax reduction, subsidies for training or research and development, and changing the way firms produce goods. The authors are largely agnostic on whether government programs should focus more on helping small firms than large firms, but offer several reasons why a focus on small firms might be beneficial. External ideas have greater effects on small firm productivity than on large firm productivity and small firms are more likely than large firms to stay in the region. However small firms may not benefit the most from government programs because of their lower wages and relative lack of technical skills.

The fourth chapter, 'Investing in the MEMS regional innovation networks and the commercialization infrastructure of older industrial states', by Michael Fogarty, examines the case of microelectrical mechanical systems as a case study of value to a locality in developing a systems approach to economic development, combining public and private sector innovation to enhance economic development. The chapter asks how localities with a disadvantaged technological position can improve that position. It answers that the locality must analyze the situation using a systems approach and then use the analysis to focus investment in key areas.

The fifth chapter, 'Buying Ohioans loyalty? How state financial aid affects brain drain', by Eric Bettinger and Erin Riley, addresses the issue of brain drain. It identifies the mechanisms through which college financial aid increases the probability that students will stay in a state. The chapter shows that the main mechanism is keeping students in the state longer so that life events, which reduce the probability of departure, occur in the state.

The sixth chapter, 'On SBA-guaranteed lending and economic growth', by Ben Craig, William Jackson and James Thomson, examines whether SBA-guaranteed loans to small business enhances local economic growth. Arguing that SBA guarantees might reduce information problems in small business finance, thereby reducing credit rationing, the authors find that the level of SBA loan guarantees across counties is positively related to growth in personal income in those counties.

The seventh chapter, 'Smart places for smart people: cluster-based planning in the 21st-century knowledge economy', by Michael Luger, describes the effort by the state of North Carolina to use an industry clustering process to identify industries for policy makers to focus their attention upon, not just on the basis of industry codes, but also on the basis of occupations and technologies. The chapter shows how industries can expand on more traditional methods of industry clustering to identify where to invest for new, knowledge-based, industries.

The eighth chapter, 'Regional wealth creation and the 21st century: women and "minorities" in the tradition of economic strangers', by John Butler, reviews the literature on the contribution of women and minority entrepreneurs to economic development. Drawing on the theoretical lens of in-group and out-group membership, Butler explains that women and minority entrepreneurs enhance economic development because they are often strangers to the existing social and economic system in a region. By bringing in new skills and knowledge, these groups enhance economic development within the region.

The final chapter, 'Universities, entrepreneurship and public policy: lessons from abroad', by Bo Carlsson, compares entrepreneurial activities in the United States and other countries. The chapter explains that the legal and economic environment for such activity differs between the USA and elsewhere. As a result, the focus of this activity in the USA is on technology transfer, whereas elsewhere it is on regional innovation systems and spillover mechanisms. The main policy implications of the chapter are that institutional arrangements matter a great deal, in particular the ownership of intellectual property by universities in the USA. The other major policy implication is that one needs a systems approach incorporating both supply and demand, to understand the phenomenon, with the USA providing the major lessons on the supply side, and Europe the major lessons on the demand side.

1. An historical perspective on government–university partnerships to enhance entrepreneurship and economic development

Irwin Feller

INTRODUCTION

This chapter offers an historical perspective on two highly visible recent developments in the efforts of American research universities to contribute to national and regional economic growth. The developments are, first, the advent, or what might be more correctly termed the rebirth and expansion, of university–industry–government R&D programs (Mowery and Rosenberg, 1993; Cohen *et al.*, 1994), and, second, the rapid growth of academic programs intended to foster entrepreneurship. The first section opens with exegesis on the multiple meanings and uses of the term 'entrepreneurship'; frequent as such treatments are, yet another one is necessary here as the chapter's level of analysis is funneled down from broad historical themes to its narrower focus on the modern panoply of university–industry–government/small business R&D/academic entrepreneurship programs. The second section presents an overview of facets of America's economic history. The third section describes the economic and policy conditions in the United States in the 1980s and 1990s; these decades are seen as setting the more immediate stage for current interest in university–industry–government R&D partnership and entrepreneurship programs. The last section opens with a summary assessment of evaluation-based findings about the impacts of government–university R&D partnerships and concludes with a statement of unresolved policy issues and, thus, research questions.

OVERVIEW AND LIMITATIONS

The chapter's focus is on what Audretsch *et al.* (2002) have termed public/private technology partnerships, or what in related policy and research streams are alternatively termed government–university–industry R&D partnerships or strategic research partnerships (National Science Foundation, 2001). Major examples of these partnerships include the National Science Foundation's Industry–University Cooperative Research Centers Program and Engineering Research Centers Program, National Institute of Standards and Technology's (NIST) Advanced Technology Program (ATP) and Ohio's Thomas Edison Program. Cohen *et al.*'s estimates for 1990 provide the single most comprehensive estimate of the number, spread and funding sources of financing for such undertakings (1994). As of that date, they reported 1056 university–industry research centers located at more than 200 campuses, with more than half of these centers established since 1980. The Federal government and state governments provided 34 per cent and 12 per cent, respectively, of their funding. (The balance came from industry (31 per cent) and the universities themselves (18 per cent).) By 1994, all 50 states had technology-based development initiatives, most involving some form of cooperative R&D partnership between universities and firms, initiated or partially subsidized by state funds (Berglund and Coburn, 1995, p. 9).

Collectively, these partnership programs (1) extend across a spectrum of research and development activities, ranging from support of basic research to commercialization of university-based research, (2) allow for the participation of small and large firms, and (3) have been initiated and continue to be funded by both the federal and state governments.

For the purposes of this chapter, the thread binding the above programs together is that they each involve governmental efforts more closely and effectively to link universities and firms in the performance and transfer of academic R&D. As variously phrased in several research and policy streams, these programs are intended to exploit, leverage or reap the economic benefits of academic R&D and of the public sector's investment in supporting these activities. (Total academic R&D expenditures are estimated at $33bn in FY 2002 in constant 1996 dollars, or $33bn in current year dollars.) Of the $33bn total, the federal government provided $19bn, or 59 per cent, academic institutions $6.7bn, state and local governments $2.2bn, industry $2.1bn, and other sources $2.4bn (National Science Foundations, 2004).

This wide focus has the drawback, though, of complicating both an historical narrative and a contemporary stocktaking, as the number of influences and range of outcomes are too numerous to compress findings readily into the textual equivalent of sound bites. The specific illustrative programs cited above are essentially components of the larger set of federal and state government legislative, regulatory, and funding strategies and policy actions directed towards promoting a faster and higher rate of technological innovation. Thus, while it is a relatively straightforward if not always simple matter to assess the impact of a specific program, it is far more difficult to assess the importance of interaction effects among them or of generic structural and policy changes in the American innovation system.

But the chapter does have boundary markers, albeit at times somewhat overstepped. It does not consider various government-funded, university-based technical assistance and advisory programs for business, such as the Economic Development Administration's University Centers Program (Mount Auburn Associates, 2001). Nor does it consider R&D partnerships involving only firms. Also, although it makes passing note of the increasing numbers and diverse objectives and curricular content of academic entrepreneurship programs (Cooper, 2003; Newton and Hendricks, 2003) and indeed concludes by posing questions about the connection of these programs to public/private R&D ventures, it does not enter into a sustained discussion of their impacts (Newton and Hendricks, 2003; Hopkins, 2004). Finally its exploration of selected aspects of the resurgent interest in and use of the concept of entrepreneurship is highly selective, and by no means intended as another entry into the burgeoning field of entrepreneurial research.

This selective emphasis is partly a matter of sticking to one's (scholarly) last, but it also stems from a finely parsed analytical perspective about the distinctions that need to be drawn among the theoretical, empirical and policy underpinnings of public/private technology partnership programs and those underpinning university-based entrepreneurship programs. The basis of these distinctions is briefly noted below.

EXEGESIS ON THE MEANINGS OF ENTREPRENEURSHIP

Historically, the term 'entrepreneur' has had two different if at times overlapping meanings (Hebert and Link, 1988; Pollards, 1994). The first, stemming from the works of Cantillon and Say in the late 18th and early 19th centuries, defines and conceptualizes the entrepreneur as the individual, or class of individuals, who assemble various factors of production – land, labor, capital – and then directs them to the production of goods and services, old or new (Casson, 1987). The second meaning, associated with Schumpeter's theory of economic growth under capitalism, sees the entrepreneur as responsible for producing innovation: the introduction of new products, processes, markets, or modes of organizing firms.[1] Innovation, in turn, is presented as the propelling force of growth and change in capitalist economies. Significantly, whereas the noun form of the word 'entrepreneur' connotes performance of a well-defined set of prescribed tasks, the adjective 'entrepreneurial' connotes creativity, innovativeness and risk taking – in effect, the dauntless courage associated with the Lewis and Clark exploration.

As an adjective, the word's use extends well beyond the economic activities of firms alone. It is now applied broadly to any putatively major (that is, discontinuous, disruptive) change in policy or practice. For example, Eisinger (1988) used the term 'entrepreneurial state' to describe the changed character of state economic development policies in the 1980s from 'supply-side', smokestack chasing to 'demand-side' creation of the knowledge base and capital base for spawning new technologies, firms and industries. In a similar vein, Clark (1998) selected the title *Creating Entrepreneurial Universities* to describe the transformation of a number of European universities, using the term both as a synonym for innovation and to convey the overtones of risk taking, energy and heightened aspirations.

Moreover, used as an adjective, quite different normative implications surround the word 'entrepreneurial'. Its use by the National Consortium of Entrepreneurial Centers, for example, carries a far more positive tone than that suggested when used by Slaughter and Leslie (1997) to describe the behaviors of entrepreneurial universities in establishing science/research/ innovation parks and becoming equity holders (and at times investors) in start-up firms based on the inventions of their faculty.

The two seemingly contradictory meanings of the term – assembler and coordinator of economic activity and source of disruptive activity – do have common underpinnings. They each relate to the actions of profit-seeking individuals to obtain and combine resources for market-oriented activity. They differ, however, in the emphasis attached by the former, classical definition to the entrepreneur's search to optimize existing means–end relationships and by the latter in its Schumpeterian mode to discover new means–end relationships (Shane and Venkataraman, 2000). The difference is seen clearly in Pollard's juxtaposition of the Schumpeterian entrepreneur and his rivals:

> Entrepreneurship in the Schumpeterian theory ... involved being different, engaging in deviant behavior, trusting one's judgment against that of the herd, upsetting and reorganizing exist structures, making worthless some old invested capital or some of the old transmitted skills. It was above all the action of the individual, not the class as a whole, and it was the mainspring of progress and growth in the world's capitalist economies. (Pollard, 1994, pp. 63–4)

Further complicating the descriptive and analytical sections that follow is the need to call attention to differences in the origins, histories, rationales, funding arrangements, participants and impacts of public/private R&D partnerships, on the one hand, and entrepreneurship programs, on the other. For the former, at least in the context of debates at the national level about the need for and impacts of partnership-type programs, the framing issues typically center on competing theories of market failure and government failure (Wolf, 1988). Government-funded university–industry R&D partner-ship programs are typically presented as means of addressing markets rife with appropriability problems, spillovers and information asymmetries – in sum, settings that are held to lead to socially suboptimal investments in 'basic' or 'high-risk' research. (Alternatively, they can be perceived as forms of technology pork barrels, involving premature and excessive investments in technologically and economically 'innovative' enterprises that would fail carefully thought through private tests; see Cohen and Noll, 1991.) At times, too, such programs are advanced on the grounds of achieving selected national distributional objectives (for example, participation by small firms, underrepresented groups, geopolitical regions). Finally, a relatively recent but influential argument on behalf of these partnership programs is that they are needed to overcome institutional and cultural barriers that impede the optimal degree of interaction between universities and federal laboratories, on the one hand, and firms, on the other.

Although public/private technology partnership programs are clearly intended to foster a higher and more rapid rate of technological innovation, implicitly thereby encouraging the entry of new individuals and firms, they are not, per se, justified on the grounds of a socially inadequate supply of entrepreneurs. Nor does one tend to find the words 'entrepreneurship' or 'entrepreneurial' widely used in mainstream evaluations of federal or state government R&D partnership programs.

This absence largely mirrors the absence for several decades of the concept of entrepreneurship from the mainstream of economics, political science, R&D management, geography, program evaluation and policy analysis — in short, the major academic and practitioner fields that have shaped the dialogue about public/private technology partnerships. As Casson has noted in his review of the way economists have conceptualized and studied the entrepreneur, by the turn of the 19th century, the term 'had almost disappeared from the theoretical literature' (Casson, 1987, p. 151),[2] existing at most as a niche area of interest to a few scholars at a few institutions.

This absence may be interpreted in different ways. One is to treat entrepre-neurship as so obviously a part of the policy and programmatic objectives of R&D partnerships (it is difficult to think of the SBIR program or the Bayh–Dole Act's emphasis on small firms without implicitly at least invoking images of innovative, risk-taking behavior) that there was no need explicitly to interject the 'E' word. Entrepreneurship thus may have been akin to the astonished realization of Molière's character, Monsieur Jourdain, that for more than 40 years he had been speaking prose without knowing it. Another perspective is that it is precisely the silence on the subject in science and technology policy and regional economic development discussions that speaks the loudest. To shift from Molière to Arthur Conan Doyle, in the same sense that Sherlock Holmes, in 'The Adventure of Silver Blaze', answered the question about the curious incident of the dog that did nothing in the night-time by responding that this absence obviously meant that the 'midnight visitor was someone whom the dog knew well', the absence of specific language (and programmatic activities) connecting the set of government–university R&D partnerships with other programs directed at promoting entrepreneurship also may speak loudly about the pervasive if in specific periods unspoken belief that entrepreneurial behavior geared to technological innovation, although subject to cyclical fluctuations, is a basic component of the historic dynamics of the American economy and culture. As T. Hughes has stated this proposition: 'inventors, industrial scientists, engineers, and system builders have been the makers of modern America' (Hughes, 1989, p. 4).

Starting from the latter perspective, the emergence and upsurge in academic entrepreneurship programs – with more than 1500 colleges and universities currently offering some form of entrepreneurship training, according to the Kaufman Foundation – reflects a contemporary belief in the economic importance of firm formation and innovativeness (as well, obviously, as that the skills necessary to overcome the technical, managerial and financial risks associated with new businesses can be taught). Although variation in objectives, curriculum and student populations involved in academic entrepreneurship programs can be expected given their large number, the programs that are of relevance here are those that seek to bridge knowledge gaps between the 'technological' and 'business' compartments of faculty and student interests and skills. The major thrust of these programs appears to be to the cross-training of students from business with those from engineering, life sciences and the physical sciences, so that each group has the skills necessary to commercialize a proto-invention that may have emerged from the student's own research as well as inculcating a spirit of entrepreneurship among students by exposing them to 'real-life' success stories and inserting them into networks of funding and technical support services, thus increasing the likelihood that the student will participate in the formation of a new firm rather than seek employment in an existing firm. Or, to adopt a framework offered by Baumol, these programs may help the 'entrepreneur with innovative propensities' to overcome 'lack of types of rather elementary knowledge that are particularly critical for successful and innovative firms', such as guidance on different sources of funding (Baumol, 2004, pp. 26–7).

The rationales, audiences and contents of these programs, however, connect only in the most general way to the rationales or program activities of public/private technology partnerships. Thus funding for academic entrepreneurship programs appears to derive mainly from (current or projected) student enrollment demand, foundations that have made entrepreneurship their special domain of activity, and a mix of state government and occasional Federal agency grants. The latter, in turn, are tied more to economic development than to science and technology portions of larger agencies; thus they derive support from the US Department of Commerce's Economic Development Administration and Small Business Administration rather than its Technology Administration, which administers the Advanced Technology Program (ATP) and the Manufacturing Extension Partnership (MEP) program.

To summarize the points at which the two subjects covered in this chapter do and do not connect, one can be entrepreneurial and contribute to national or regional economic development without necessarily being involved in the scientific or technological work that enters into the generation of new technologies, new firms or new high-tech industries. In a parallel manner, one can be a faculty member or student engaged in a university–industry–(government)-funded R&D project, file an invention disclosure, work with the university's technology transfer office in seeking the right firms to license and commercialize the embryonic technology, receive equity in the firm, take on full responsibility for commercializing the technology in cases where the university waives its ownership rights back to the inventor, and either take temporary leave or permanently leave the university to become part of the firm's senior management – any or all of this without becoming involved in any of the university's entrepreneurship programs.

HISTORICAL OVERVIEW

One has choices of multiple starting points and multiple paths to follow in preparing a brief, summary history of government–university partnerships to enhance entrepreneurship and economic development. One can start with the settling of the American colonies, which after the failures of the joint stock company mode of economic and political arrangements, were by the mid-1600s mainly Crown or proprietary colonies (McDougall, 2004; Walton and Shepherd, 1979) and thus geared to profit-seeking strategies. One could track the history of colonial legislation and policies to supporting manufacturing from the specific proposals in Hamilton's 1791 *Report on the Subject of Manufactures*, to the role of federal land grants to underwrite infrastructure development, as in the construction of the transcontinental railroad, emphasizing, as Bingham has done, that 'industrial policy ideas' American style have not moved much in over 200 years (1998, p. 21). Of course, no historical account of government–university R&D relationships would be complete without some reference to the development of the land-grant university system established under the Morrill Act (1862), Hatch Act (1887), Adams Act (1906) and Smith–Lever Act (1914). The programs created by these acts provided for a linked set of education, research and dissemination activities, becoming the historic (if more contemporaneously, at times mythic) exemplar both of an integrated university-based technology delivery system and of a university–federal–state government R&D partnership (Feller, 1990).[3] An alternative starting perspective is to leap over much of American economic history to the 'modern' period of Federal government and state government initiatives directed at the promotion of university–industry–government R&D partnerships beginning approximately in the 1980s and continuing to the present. (In making this leap, however, one would also have to note that the 'modern' post-World War II period of large Federal investments in non-defense R&D, both basic and applied, has been marked by periodic attempts to foster civilian technologies, in terms both of specific industries and of specific technologies, with these efforts typically involving some form of collaborative undertakings between and among industry, universities and federal laboratories; see Mowery and Rosenberg, 1993; Smith, 1990.)

Starting from the colonial and early national period contributes long-range perspective and frees one from preoccupation with the funding and programmatic vicissitudes of specific federal, state or local government programs. Starting from the contemporary period, which has been characterized by intense concerns about international economic competitiveness and attendant subtexts of flagging American technological innovativeness and resurgent state and local government initiatives to foster technology-based economic growth, has the advantage of immediately connecting to current policy debates: for example, the future of the ATP and MEP programs, or those that continue about the effectiveness of Small Business Innovation Research (SBIR) (Audretsch *et al.*, 2002; Wallenstein, 2000). The approach taken here is a time-span compromise: a quick glance backwards to identify themes relevant to the present (and future) consideration of university–industry R&D partnerships; a jump to the 1980s, which as noted is viewed as setting the stage for current debates; a pause to take stock of and comment on findings from assessments of the post-1980 portfolio of activities; and a forward-looking posing of selected policy-oriented research questions that will affect the future connections, if any, between R&D partnerships and academic entrepreneurship programs.

Both entrepreneurship and government support of economic activity are as American as apple pie; indeed, without entrepreneurship, there would not have been as many apple trees to plant or apples to harvest. Nor would these apples have been transformed into a commercial product, readily available from bakeries, supermarket shelves or fast food restaurants.[4] Government intervention to support, direct and control economic activity also is a grand American tradition – a 'habit' in Jonathan Hughes' words (1977) – that our colonial forebears brought with them from Europe, and which in various incarnations and levels of intensity over time constitute an integral feature of America's economic history. Finally, American universities, especially state-supported institutions but also private universities, have a long tradition, dating back to at least the mid-19th century, of active involvement in national and state-level activities directed at economic development (Feller, 1999; Rosenberg and Nelson, 1994).

If by entrepreneurship we mean market-oriented, risk-taking behavior directed at improving one's material condition, then this trait has been nurtured by the economic and political conditions that have shaped America's history from the colonial period onwards. Thus, without gainsaying the search by our Puritan (Massachusetts), Catholic (Maryland) and Quaker (Pennsylvania) ancestors for political and religious freedom, settlement was extensively motivated by the desires of land-grant holders to draw profit from populating uninhabited and hopefully resource-rich territories, and thereby they were required to offer prospective immigrants liberal land terms and political and economic environments conducive to individual initiative.

Consider here the influence of the colonial period in shaping this worldview, as described in de Crevecoeur's *Letters from an American Farmer*, an account of how European immigrants became Americans, written in 1782:

> He is hired, he goes to work, and works moderately; instead of being employed by a haughty person, he finds himself with his equal, placed at the substantial table of the farmer, or else at an inferior one as good; his wages are high, his bed is not like that bed of sorrow on which he used to lie … he begins to feel the effects of a sort of resurrection; hitherto he had not lived, but simply vegetated; he now feels himself a man because he is treated as such; the laws of his own country had overlooked him in his insignificancy; the laws of this cover him with their mantle…
>
> He looks around and sees many a prosperous person who but a few years before was as poor as himself. This encourages him much; he begins to form some little scheme, the first, alas, he ever formed in his life. If he is wise, he thus spends two or three years, in which time he acquires knowledge, the use of tools, the modes of working the land, felling trees, etc…. His good name procures him credit. (1925 edn, pp. 82–3)

Similarly, without too much of a stretch in analysis and recasting of language, one could portray the history of federal land policies, at least through the Homestead Act of 1862, not only as manifestations of the Jeffersonian ideal of encouraging independent yeomanry but also as efforts to assist small business start-ups in the dominant economic sector of the period.[5] In a related manner, one could explore the catalogue of state and local government subsidies to industrial firms and railroads throughout much of the 19th century (V. Clark, 1929), noting the vulnerability of governmental bodies to being whipsawed by private sector actors into underwriting via bonds and tax concessions major forms of economic infrastructure: the canals and railroads of the period being precursors of today's sports stadiums and convention centers.

To compress what might otherwise be an extended narrative along these lines, but more importantly to cast the narrative in the form of a set of testable propositions about why the connection of government–university partnerships and entrepreneurship and economic development seems so intuitively obvious today, I would advance the following set of propositions.

Given that, throughout American history, the bulk of economic activities have been shaped by market forces (North, 1961), government involvement, whether at the national or state government level, has tended to be directed at perceived bottlenecks to economic growth or vectors of economic opportunity at a specific point in time. Thus, variously, from the colonial period onward, government attention has focused on the adequacy of the labor supply, the stimulation of 'critical' industries, provision of capital, development of a flexible but stable monetary and banking system, insulation from foreign competition, and physical infrastructure (or social overhead capital). In the colonial period, for example, bounties, premiums and subsidies were readily offered to increase the supply of selected raw materials, for example hemp and flax, in order to stimulate domestic (home) manufactures of cloth, and land grants, loans and lotteries were used to provide both raw materials and capital for a host of consumer and producer goods (for example, salt, bricks, glass, iron) (Clark, 1929). Historically, too, modes of government support, once introduced, have often proved difficult to displace, for example the continuation of farm price supports now into their seventh decade, thus producing the prolix and often contradictory mix of economically effective and special interest subventions that now characterize the 'mixed' American economy.

THE (RE)EMERGENCE OF GOVERNMENT–INDUSTRY–UNIVERSITY R&D PARTNERSHIPS

As the US economy shifted towards what is now referred to as a 'knowledge economy', the emphasis of federal and state economic policies also shifted, this time towards the support of basic research, technology transfer/

commercialization, and the adequacy of the national supply of the scientifically and technically trained workforce (National Science Board, 2003). Incorporated in this shift was new attention to intrasectoral and intersectoral R&D partnerships and the need to break down, or at least modulate, analytical and policy dichotomies between public and private sector activities.

This trend became noticeable in the late 1970s and early 1980s. As Dimanescu and Bodkin, writing in 1986, observed, 'The 1980s might be called 'America's R&D consortia years'. Collaborative research agreements between industry, government and universities have proliferated' (1986, p. 1). These partnerships were of many forms and involved various combinations of entities: consortia of firms, only; firm–federal laboratory partnerships (under Cooperative Research and Development Agreements), between single firms and single universities, as reflected in the increased absolute and relative amount of industrial funding of academic R&D, among firms, universities and federal government and/or state governments (typically providing federal or state funds to universities, contingent upon the securing of counterpart funds from industry).

This increased attention arose from a number of technological, economic and political factors. The attention to high technology arose from pervasive beliefs that new technologies were the source of first-mover advantages in entering new, now global, markets, given rapid rates of both technological and economic obsolescence caused, in turn, by the internal dynamics of specific technologies: Moore's Law and the doubling of chip computer power every 18 months. It also stemmed from new, often painful recognition of the impacts of globalization, which in the context of the jeremiads of the 1970s and 1980s highlighted the diffusion of technical and scientific capabilities among an increasing number of nations – especially those in southeast Asia – to search, filter, comprehend, reengineer, adapt, and manufacture (often at lower unit cost) new science-based technologies.

It also reflected the increasing dependence of major technological advances on fundamental research, coupled with the view that both the upfront costs and technical uncertainties surrounding discontinuous technological advances were becoming too high for any single firm to accept, thereby making a national economy organized about the R&D activities of single firms, however large, vulnerable to being leapfrogged by firms in nations where cooperation among firms was permitted and/or where the government underwrote a substantial portion of the initial R&D. On a more pragmatic, bottom-line calculus, R&D partnerships, especially with universities, became a means by which firms could 'outsource' their basic R&D operations, closing down central corporate laboratories or redirecting their efforts towards laboratories to shorter-term projects more closely linked to the specific marketing and operational needs of divisional lines of business.

It arose, too, from specific comparisons with the political economy of major international economic competitors and the assessment that one of the competitive advantages of other nations was the closer integration of sectors, specifically government and industry (and publicly funded research institutes), than was possible in the United States (US Congress Office of Technology Assessment, 1990). US economic competitiveness was seen as constrained by archaic antitrust regulations that limited cooperation and coordination among firms, at least at what was termed the pre-competitive stage of research, by legal, administrative and cultural impediments to cooperation between industry and Federal laboratories, and finally by a combination of 'impedance' problems and inertia in relationships between firms and universities.

Many of the same observed events concerning America's loss of international economic competitiveness, especially in technology-intensive sectors, also undergird the resurgence of attention to entrepreneurship. Frequent laments, popularized in DeLorean and Wright's 1980 tell-all tale, *On a Clear Day You Can See General Motors*, were voiced that the risk-taking ethos of American industry was being smoothed by a combination of conservative managers too long accustomed to America's economic dominance to react swiftly to the rise of new, more nimble ways of just-in-time and flexible manufacturing, the displacement of risk-taking owner–managers with backgrounds and experience in engineering and R&D by cadres of MBAs trained in computing discounted rates of return but not in the inherent (but potentially profitable) risks of radical technological innovations, executive compensation systems tied to short-term movements in company share prices, and pervasive fears within corporate boardrooms of hostile takeover lest short-term financial metrics not be met.[6] The combined impact of these factors was held to weigh against investments in long-term (basic) R&D or in attempting major technological leaps (Dertouzos *et al.*, 1989).

Contemporary analysis of this waning of leadership at times took on the tones of Schumpeterian dirges, as the decline of mature capitalist economies, such as the United States and the United Kingdom, was seen as brought about by the loss of esprit and élan of each nation's entrepreneurs. The comparison with the UK was especially disturbing because it highlighted how world industrial leaders could indeed lose their technological and economic preeminence to newcomers. Intonations of what is referred to as a 'climacteric' in UK economic history, the period from approximately 1870 to 1913, when Britain saw itself experiencing decline both in traditional industries (shipbuilding, steel) and in new industries (chemicals, automobiles) relative to Germany and the USA (Floud, 1994) in part because of the (alleged) failure of the British businessmen to behave entrepreneurially in the face of new technologies and markets, thus losing out to those who acted more assertively in capitalizing on the market opportunities offered by scientific and technological advances (Pollard, 1994), began to be seen as unwelcome harbingers of America's future. Paul Kennedy's book, *The Rise and Fall of the Great Powers*, published in 1987, likewise offered a sober, scholarly reminder that economic hegemony was transitory and that erstwhile leaders tended to lose the dynamism that had character-ized their rise, causing them to experience decline relative to 'younger and leaner' newcomers.

An especially troublesome source of concern was that not only were established industries fast losing market shares to overseas competitors, but America seemed to be lagging in its ability to convert its national invest-ments in basic science into commercial products and processes. America may have been preeminent in world science, but the technological fruits of this investment seemed to be picked off by foreign rather than US firms. American firms were seen as suffering from a breakthrough illusion – the myth that innovation was synonymous with technological breakthrough – thus failing to follow through on the transformation of new ideas into commercially competitive products (Florida and Kenney, 1990). Relatedly, America's technology policies were seen as having a mission orientation (Ergas, 1987) that focused on 'big science deployed to meet big problems' (pp. 52–3). The technology policies of major international competitors, however, had a diffusion orientation, that is, they were directed at diffusing 'technological capabilities through the industrial structure, thus facilitating the ongoing and mainly incremental adaptation to change' (p. 52).

A widely prescribed new regime following these diagnoses saw that the United States had to improve its capacity to link research and technology transfer if it was to compete effectively in emerging high-tech industries. The result was the by now familiar set of legislative acts and government programs – the Stevenson–Wydler Technology Innovation Act (1980), Bayh–Dole Act (1980), National Cooperative Research Act (1984) and the Omnibus Trade and Competitiveness Act (1988) – as well as a set of counterpart state government programs. Indeed, as federal action appeared stalemated between a Republican Administration and a Democratic-controlled Congress, initiative in policy innovation shifted to state governments more pragmatically attuned to dealing with economic conditions, not theories.

The accumulating pressures to intertwine R&D and economic develop-ment policies at both the national and state government levels soon became wrapped within the hallowed imagery of Schumpeterian entrepreneurship. How this melding occurred is itself an interesting and important story in its own right, for it is not axiomatic. Indeed, in reviewing the economic competitiveness discourse of the late 1970s and 1980s, it is important to note that the above diagnosis can readily lead to dirigiste prescriptions that involve considerable participation by government officials in the direction of sector, industry, firm and regional investments. Relatedly industrial policy can lead to a concentration on the revitalization of established sectors and (large) firms, regions and occupational groups, not necessarily to investments in 'sunrise' industries or technologies. Indeed concerns about the inexorability of both these tendencies were (and remain) part of the opposition to extensive federal government involvement in supporting the development and commercialization of civilian technologies.

Much of the analytical and political opposition to the R&D, innovation and technology transfer proposals of the 1980s ran exactly along these lines: almost any new initiative was cast as 'statist'. In part, in response to this line of opposition, a dominant trait of many of the post-1980 program portfolio has been its incorporation of 'market' tests, reflected typically in requirements for industrial contributions, and a modicum of competitive, peer review of the technical and economic features of contending proposals. These program design elements have muted somewhat the directed thrust of federal and state government initiatives in public/private R&D ventures, although it is difficult not to see in the choice of 'clusters' 'strategically' chosen for development in some state technology development programs, attention to traditional sectors and the geopolitical regions in which they are located.

The connection of all this to current interest in entrepreneurship and the role of universities as both sources of commercially relevant research and education is through the heightened attention given to the role of small, and especially high-tech, start-up firms as sources of technological innovation, firm formation (including spin-offs from academic research) and job creation. The longstanding (and continuing) debate about the methodological or empirical soundness of the early estimates about the dominant role of small firms as sources of new job creation (for example, Birch, 1987; David *et al.*, 1996) is less important here than are the empirical studies such as the US Small Business Administration's 1994 survey that highlighted the importance of small firms as sources of technological innovation (Acs and Audretsch, 1990).

This emphasis on small firms as important sources of technological innovation is seen most visibly in the initial establishment and subsequent expansion of the SBIR program, both in terms of the increase in the number of federal agencies with SBIR programs and in the congressionally mandated increase in the percentage of its R&D funding, from an initial level of 0.2 per cent to its current level, authorized in 1992, of 2.5 per cent, that a federal agency must set aside for the program (Wessner, 1999; Brown and Turner, 1999).[7]

Programs to stimulate high-tech initiatives, such as SBIR and ATP, make it possible for new men and women to try new things; they thus stimulate and nurture entrepreneurship. There is a certain analytical irony, however, in coupling intertwining the importance of small firms to technological innovation with Schumpeterian imagery of entrepreneurial behavior because it flies in the face of another of Schumpeter's well-known, if long disputed, contentions that bigness and fewness were essential for the conduct of R&D and thus of technological innovation (Cohen, 1995).

PAST IMPACTS AND FUTURE PROSPECTS

We live in an evaluative society that is imposing increasing demands on all levels of government for documented evidence of program effectiveness. These demands stem from many sources, not the least of which is the continually politically contested nature of federal government technology development and transfer programs of the 1980s. Confronted annually by threats to their very existence by some combination of executive and/or congressional opposition, programs such as ATP and MEP, as a matter of a political (budgetary) survival, have from their very establishment sought to document their impacts and efficiency. Similar pressures have existed at the state government level, where changes in party control, especially in the governor's office, have led to swings in state economic development strategies, including recurrent questions about the effectiveness of cooperative technology development programs. Out of this mix of influences has come a large, if diverse and at times methodologically problematic, set of evaluations of various forms of government–university–industry R&D partnerships.

Surveying the topography and productivity of government–university partnership so as to tease out impacts or lessons learned is not simple. As noted in an earlier such review by Mowery and Rosenberg, 'There is a vast array of forms of research collaboration between universities and industry, making generalizations virtually impossible' (1993, p. 53). Much the same argument has been made recently by Bozeman and Dietz (2002), who have pointed to the various arrangements subsumed within the broad term of R&D partnership. Included, for example, in their typology are (a) joint research ventures and cooperative research agreements, (b) collaborative research centers, (c) research consortia, (d) R&D limited partnerships, and (e) research subcontracting.[8] Inclusion and review of selected programs that have the term 'R&D partnerships' in the title of course are relatively straightforward: for example, the National Science Foundation's Industry–University Cooperative Research Program or Pennsylvania's Ben Franklin Partnership program. But there are a host of other public sector programs that are clearly intended to use government funds or other legislative inducements to foster closer collaboration in both research and technology transfer between firms and universities that do not constitute formal partnerships. The Bayh–Dole Act, for example, which gives universities the right to patent inventions generated under federally sponsored research, is not per se a partnership program, but clearly has had an impact upon the magnitude and content of university–industry firm relationships. Relatedly SBIR, which can be interpreted as a major governmental stimulus to technology-based entrepreneurship, is not in the main a government–university partnership, although awardees frequently enter into subcontract collaborations with universities (Tibbetts, 1999). Finally ATP also may be seen as a mixed case because, although most of the awards involve firms only, either singly or in consortia, there are a number that formally involve universities as subcontractors.[9]

Not only do organizational arrangements differ among the various types of partnerships, but so too do the anticipated benefits that each of the various parties to the partnerships – firms, universities, government sponsors – expects when they enter into these partnerships. Firms, for example, frequently report that their primary interest in entering into R&D partnerships with universities, whether through sponsored research grants, university–industry consortia, or university–industry–government programs, such as NSF-funded Engineering Research Centers or state-funded centers of advanced technology, is to gain access to students and a 'window' on emerging technologies, not readily commercializable innovations (Feller, 1990). Thus performance measures that emphasize patents, licenses, or even spin-offs, while possibly of importance to the universities or others, do not capture what firms most want for their membership fees or sponsored research grants (Feller *et al.*, 2002).

Similar differences may be found in the outcome variables that are featured in evaluations of various federal and state government programs. As an approximate guide, federally funded R&D partnerships have tended to be measured in terms of 'upstream' 'knowledge' and 'technological' indicators (for example, patents, publications, patent publication citations, new/improved products/processes), whereas state-funded programs have tended to emphasize downstream economic indicators (jobs, sales) and indeed at times have been impatient with or dismissive of the saliency of the upstream measures when considering continued support of, say, university-based centers of excellence. Layered atop these complexities are yet other analytical and empirical layers relating to the influences of technological fields, industrial sectors, size distribution of firms, 'quality' of academic institution, and more, that make findings 'context'-dependent. There is good reason, then, why generalizations about generic R&D partnerships are often presented in guarded terms.[10]

CONCLUSIONS

Mindful of all these caveats, I would offer the following summary assessment. Government–university–industry R&D 'partnerships' may be said to be working and to have become an accepted and established part of the US national innovation system, as follows:

- A sufficiently 'robust' series of evaluation findings, addressing different partnership forms, emphasizing different outcome variables, employing different criteria for success, and employing a diverse set of methodologies, exists that points to the social benefits of public/private technology partnerships. (In addition to the individual studies and review articles already cited, see Feller and Anderson, 1994; Ruegg and Feller, 2003.) As phrased succinctly by Scott, 'SRPs (strategic research partnerships) are socially useful because they expand the effective R&D resources applied in innovative investment' (Scott, 2001, p. 195).
- Retention of industrial membership in several of the longer-standing R&D partnership programs (for example, NSF's Industry–University Cooperative Research Center Program) has remained high (Gray *et al.*, 2001).
- Universities continue aggressively to seek industrial sponsorship of faculty research, to invest in research/innovation parks, and increasingly to enter into equity relationships with start-up firms (Feldman *et al.*, 2002).

But this summary also leads to a number of analytical and policy questions about the form, staying power and future of R&D partnership arrangements. Overall, they no longer represent major policy or organizational innovations. Instead, they appear to be experiencing incremental modification both quantitatively (number and relative importance) and qualitatively (characteristics of partners, range of activities). Indeed some curtailment may occur. To employ the familiar metaphor of the S-shaped logistic function to describe the diffusion of an innovation, my conjecture is that, after a period of policy and interorganizational trial and error in the 1970s and early 1980s and a period of accelerated adoption from the late 1980s to the 1990s, the first decade of this new century may be one of maximum penetration, consolidation and marginal changes for various forms of university–industry–government R&D partnerships.

Several factors point in this direction. They include the uncertain prospects for future funding from federal and state governments and what appears to be the ceiling to industry's investment in academic R&D (or, more precisely, US universities) as part of its diversified portfolio of internal and external sources of new scientific and technological knowledge, and increasingly vocal industry displeasure about aspects of university patent and licensing practices. Some brief observations may be made about each of these trends.

First, 'Nothing ever gets settled in this town. It's a seething debating society in which the debate never stops, in which people never give up', observed former Secretary of State George Schultz (as quoted in H. Smith, 1989, p. 566). Much the same may be said about the ATP and MEP programs established under the 1988 Omnibus Trade and Competitiveness Act. The continuing ideological battle about the rectitude of government support of private sector R&D activities means that evaluation studies that demonstrate that a program has positive impacts is no guarantee of program growth or survival. (Nor, for that matter, do evaluations that point to the inefficiency of programs necessarily mean that they are terminated or even kept from increasing in size.) As noted, few federal technology programs, for example, have been examined as systematically and rigorously as the MEP or ATP programs. Findings from these evaluations consistently point to the economic gains (value added, sales, employments) of firms that participate in these programs (relative to a comparison group). These findings, however, have been no protection against administration and congressional decisions to reduce drastically the program's budget in FY2005 (from $109m. to $36m.). The ATP is in a similar situation: a compendium of studies that show positive impacts consistent with legislative intent (Ruegg and Feller, 2003) have provided little protection against the Bush Administration's efforts to terminate the program. Current and looming sizeable federal budgetary deficits can be expected to exert further downward pressures on domestic discretionary expenditures, weakening yet further the parlous political setting in which these and related domestic R&D programs find themselves. Indeed, of these various R&D programs, the SBIR seems to be the best positioned to withstand budgetary strictures, but this is more a comment on the program's political base of support than evidence demonstrating its relative economic or technological impact.

Second, state government support of R&D partnerships continues to exhibit roller coaster tendencies: strong support in one administration, abrupt termination in the next. Thus, almost coincidentally in time, as the

National Governors Association issues *A Governor's Guide to Strengthening State Entrepreneurship Policy* (2004), a number of states, including Alaska, Michigan, New Jersey and Texas (the last three being leaders in the state cooperative technology movement of the 1980s) have terminated or severely reduced the magnitude of their programs. In part, these cutbacks reflect the dire fiscal conditions of many states in recent years, with the technology component of economic development programs being one of a set of 'discretionary' programs (support of higher education being another) that have experienced sharp reductions. In part, too, they reflect dissatisfaction (or impatience) with the trickle of tangible, downstream, firm- and job-creation benefits flowing from these programs. But the cutbacks also have a deeper source in their rejection of governmental responsibility for engendering entrepreneurial behavior. As stated by Jim Clark, Chief of Staff to Alaska's Governor, 'funding entrepreneurship is not an essential function of government' (as quoted in Geiger and Sa, 2004, p. 12). On the other hand, reports in the State Science and Technology Institute's bulletins throughout 2004 point to budgetary increases for some programs and the relaunching (often in new directions) of erstwhile state programs.

A special problem also arises in assessing the impact of state R&D partnership programs. The impacts of national programs are typically measured in terms of variables related to macroeconomic conditions, long-term growth rates and international competitiveness. From these vantage points, more detailed questions about the spatial location of the new firms and jobs within a country are second-order considerations. Location of benefits, however, is the essence of state programs. In terms of conventional shift-share analysis, states may be seen as competing for a larger share of the new industries and employment opportunities associated with the shift in the structural characteristics of the national economy. States, however, differ in the scale of their R&D partnership programs and the strategies embedded in these programs. Thus, even if a state program satisfies selected efficiency criteria, say a high benefit–cost ratio or a high rate of return, it does not follow that the state's share of the new economic sector will necessarily grow. Indeed, given the ubiquitous and imitative character of much of what the states are doing – 41 states were reported to be investing in biotechnology initiatives in 2001 (Battelle, 2001) – these initiatives are equally well viewed as maintenance as much as expansionary undertakings.

Third, for all of the attention paid since the 1980s to the formation of university–industry and university–industry–government R&D partnerships, these partnerships remain modest parts of the R&D activities of both universities and firms. More importantly for the future, they appear to have peaked. Industrial funding of academic R&D grew rapidly over the past three decades, reaching an estimated 8 per cent of total academic R&D

in 2000 (but down to 6.8 per cent in 2001: National Science Foundation, 2003). Even with this rate of growth, industry funds accounted for one of the smallest shares of academic R&D. Viewed from the perspective of industry, 'funding of academic R&D has never been a major component of industry-funded R&D ... Since 1994, the share has steadily declined from 1.5 per cent to 1.2 per cent' (National Science Foundation, 2002, pp. 5–13).

Further leading to conservative projections about the future course of industry willingness to enter into cooperative university–industry R&D partnerships is that one of the major reported motivations for a firm to participate in such programs is the opportunity to leverage the far larger federal government investment. Deceleration of rates of federal expenditures for some of these programs coupled with terminations and sharp reductions in funding for others is likely to be matched by smaller industry commitments.

Fourth, industry's interest and willingness to outsource its R&D activities to American universities under any of a variety of funding mechanisms may be lessening as a result of what are perceived to be excessive claims for ownership of intellectual property rights flowing from industry-funded research and excessive compensation for licensing university-held patents (Industrial Research Institute, 2001). Globalization of R&D capabilities in universities and research institutes in other countries has opened up new sources of expertise in basic research for many R&D-intensive industries. The logic of industry–university R&D partnerships may continue; it is just that industry's partners will be non-US universities.

Again the tenor with which these observations are offered must be emphasized. University–industry–government R&D partnerships are presented here as having yielded benefits to each of the partners and of becoming an established, if in places thinly rooted, part of the US national technology development and commercialization system. But these partnerships also are 'mature' policy and program innovations, with what appear to be modest prospects for future growth. Indeed, at the risk of stretching the analysis to its limits, it may be that the recent attention to entrepreneurship, especially the emphasis on firm formation, represents a search for the next potent growth-stimulating policy prescription.

Finally, to return to the theme broached in this chapter's opening about the problematic connections, analytically and programmatically, between university–industry–government R&D partnership programs and academic entrepreneurship programs, one question that emerges from this review is this: what in fact is their relationship? Each set of activities has its roots in the same general analytical and policy ground, namely, the dependence of national and state-level economies on the birth and growth of technology-intensive firms, the need for (or legitimacy of) public sector subventions to encourage this birth and growth, and the contention (buttressed by various evaluation studies) that some goodly number of these subventions are effective and efficient.

But little is known about the extent to which there is overlap among the participants in each set of programs, or the extent to which there is overlap, whether the performance of those who participate in both activities exceeds that of those who participate only in one. Of course, performance of either group must then be compared with that of like individuals who participate in neither. Evidence of the 'value-added' of entrepreneurship education programs is found in the Charney–Libecap study of graduates from the University of Arizona's program (2003). They found that graduates of the entrepreneurship program, on average, were three times more likely to be involved in the creation of a new business venture than were their non-entrepreneurial business school cohorts, were more likely to be employed with firms that license new technology or that license technology to others, and that, among self-employed entrepreneurship graduates, were more likely to own a high-technology firm than non-entrepreneurship graduates who owned their own firm. Missing from this analysis, however, is any information about the connection between the careers of the entrepreneurship graduates, either as employees of high-tech firms or as owners of such firms, and government–university–industry R&D partnerships, either in absolute terms or relative to the non-entrepreneurship graduates.

Embedded here are an increasingly more complex set of evaluative and thus policy evaluative questions. For example, to what extent do participants in academic entrepreneurship programs become high-tech entrepreneurs? To what extent do those individuals who first participate in academic entrepreneurship programs and then go on to launch R&D firms perform differently from a comparable set of firms that participate in none of the above? In short, a whole new agenda of research, evaluation and policy questions awaits.

NOTES

1. Thus Winter writes of an 'entrepreneurial regime' as one 'that is favorable to innovative entry and unfavorable to innovative activity by established firms; a routinized regime is one in which the conditions are the other way around' (1984, p. 122).
2. My own professional experience in part reflects this ebb and flow. My first published academic article, an extraneous chapter from my dissertation, was published in the 1960s in *Explorations in Entrepreneurial History*, Second Series. The journal, a modest affair at the time, printed in offset with stapled bindings, was housed at the University of Wisconsin, which had taken it over and revived it after its short initial life at Harvard University, where it was linked to the Research Center in Entrepreneurial History, a legacy

of Joseph Schumpeter's tenure as a faculty member. Reflecting the advent of cliometrics, or the new economic history and the appointment of new editors, the journal underwent, first, a major shift in content, physical form and, most importantly, name, becoming *Explorations in Economic History* in 1970. Consequently, the journal has become one of the major academic outlets for modern research in economic history, especially that authored by American scholars.

3. Historically, until relatively recently, the land-grant university-based system of agricultural research and transfer has differed in important ways from that subsumed under contemporary models of university–industry–government R&D partnerships. As described by Buttel *et al.*, under the land-grant university/state agricultural experiment station model, 'the bulk of new technology was technology transferred in the form of production advice from extension agents rather than in the form of purchased inputs. Relationships with *private industry* were quite decentralized', and occurred largely through 'small, largely development-oriented grants from an industry to a particular land-grant university researcher', and through land-grant universities 'delivering public-domain commodity products ... to private firms and quasi-private organizations such as seed improvement associations' (Buttel *et al.*, 1986, p. 297). This characterization no longer holds, given the rise of R&D-intensive agribusiness firms and academic patenting.

4. Walter McDougall, in *Freedom Just Around the Corner*, advances somewhat of the same argument, albeit with a broader purpose and more normatively laden terminology, in describing what he considers to be the distinctive theme in his recounting of US history. McDougall writes, 'It is the American people's penchant for hustling – in both the positive and negative senses' (2004, p. xvi).

5. Land, although not free until after the passage of the Homestead Act in 1862, was readily and cheaply available throughout most of the 19th century in the less densely settled areas of the United States and especially on the frontier. It promised economic and personal independence and proved an irresistible attraction to millions (Atack and Bateman, 1987, p. 6). Again, without straining historical parallels, one can see in academic entrepreneurship programs and state government seed capital funds efforts to offset one of the historic shortcomings of American land/agricultural policy, namely the provision of one factor of production without providing the knowledge or capital to make its economic use viable in a globally competitive environment.

6. Flagging entrepreneurial spirits appear to be a staple explanation of periods of economic retardation or 'relative' decline and, of course, are featured centrally in Schumpeter's doleful forecast for capitalist economies. For an earlier effort to give some empirical flesh to this analytical superstructure covering the period 1929–57, see Denison (1962, pp. 163–6).

7. The Bayh–Dole Act's emphasis on small firms, though, has been interpreted as less a belief in the comparative innovativeness of small firms as opposed to large firms than a political tactic intended to dampen criticism of the proposal that it would allow large firms to secure monopolies based on public sector investments in academic R&D (Mowery *et al.*, 2004, pp. 204–5).

8. They also have argued that 'most of our assumptions about their impact on the US economy are really nothing more than anecdotal or based on folk wisdom or based on research that employs diverse indicators and unclear conceptualizations' (ibid., p. 207).

9. The presence or absence of university participation in several of the major federally funded technology development and transfer programs (SBIR, ATP and MEP) affects the relevance of evaluations of these programs to this chapter, which, again, is centered on university-based activities. For example, Audretsch *et al.*'s evaluation of the impacts of the Department of Defense's SBIR program points to the program's contributions in 'stimulating technological innovation and increasing private sector commercialization of innovations derived from Federal research and development' (2002, p. 157). The study, however, contains no reference to universities as R&D partners or variables accounting for their presence, and thus cannot be considered to be a test of the effectiveness of university–industry–government R&D partnerships. Likewise evaluations by Jarmin

(1999) and Shapira (2003) of the MEP program contain few references to the role of universities as hosts or participants in MEP center operations.

10. The same holds true for programs related to encouraging entrepreneurship. Programmatically, as sketched above, 'entrepreneurial' has become the proverbial big tent that now accommodates a diverse set of activities, participants and economic sectors. It can as easily be used to describe the rise of Amazon as of Apple or Amgen. For example, referring to A.E. Hotchner, who founded the Newman's Own Food company with Paul Newman, a recent *New York Times* news item notes that 'Mr Hotchner, a playwright, biographer and novelist, probably never thought he would be a successful entrepreneur so late in life' (*New York Times*, 21 March 2004, Section 3, p. 2.) This diversity makes it difficult to make analytical sense of what is being attempted under the heading of entrepreneurship: educational programs are not incubators, are not early-stage sources of funding for new technologies, and are not university-based science/research/innovation parks. Findings relating to the effectiveness of one such set of programs need not imply anything about the effectiveness of others.

COMMENTARY

Richard Pogue

I am honored to have been asked by Ed Morrison and Scott Shane to supplement Professor Feller's learned paper.

On the general subject of government/university partnerships to enhance economic development through entrepreneurship, Scott Shane has asked me to comment from the local and regional perspective in Cleveland and Northeast Ohio. Just as Professor Feller covered 400 years in 19 1/2 minutes, so I will try to mention nine quick observations in ten minutes.

First, the definition. In the main I am using the broader definition of entrepreneurship to which Professor Feller referred, that is, that an entre- preneur is a person who organizes, operates and assumes the risk for a business venture, with emphasis on the word 'risk'. So, in my remarks, I am not limiting the concept of entrepreneurship to startling new innovations or creativity.

Second, local focus. My focus is on partnerships that have affected Cleveland, Greater Cleveland and/or Northeast Ohio. Some of the local public/private partnerships that helped this area over the last 25 years have drawn national attention; in the early 1980s, when we were coining the then-new term 'public/private partnership', Mayor George Voinovich used the slogan 'Together we can do it!'

As far as substantial involvement by the academic community in economic development in that quarter century is concerned, I would say that it is far more evident today than it was in 1980. Back in those days, the sleeping giant of Academy was, I would suggest, rather somnolent.

Third, non-federal. Although our conference is sponsored in part by the US Small Business Administration, I would have to say that where there has been government/university collaboration in recent years to support economic development through entrepreneurship in our area of the country, it has been primarily state and local government, rather than federal participation. Of course there has been substantial federal support of local activities in various areas, such as programs administered by the Small Business Administration (SBA), the National Institutes of Health (NIH), the National Aeronautics and Space Administration (NASA), the Department of Commerce, and so forth, and we are all tremendously grateful for that support, but in the main that support has furthered national policies as opposed to being responsive to locally articulated needs and programs. In terms of active participation in locally driven entrepreneurial and economic development activities, we – and here I include the local academic community – have tended to emphasize programs with the state, county and municipal governments.

Fourth, timing. In at least five places in his contribution, Professor Feller referred to 1980 as roughly a watershed date as the beginning of a new era for government interest in technology-intensive activities, university incubators, publicly supported venture capital funds and university–industry–government R&D partnerships. I believe that 1980 had another special significance in Greater Cleveland: it was the beginning of what became the brilliant Cleveland comeback, a phenomenon which endured roughly from 1980 to 1996, the year of the Cleveland Bicentennial celebration. This was a 17-year period during which there was much national doom and gloom but the Cleveland public/private partnership model became a national and, indeed, international standard to which to repair. As I indicated earlier, it is my belief that universities had a relative minor role in the early part of that comeback period, and that their role has increased over time, with recent acceleration.

Fifth, regionalism. Like the business community, academia is typically unshackled by arbitrary political boundaries such as city or county lines of demarcation, and this freedom from geographic restraint has enabled colleges and universities to contribute to the growing forces of regionalism as a factor in economic development through entrepreneurship.

Sixth, NOCHE. NOCHE is an example of this regional approach. Way back in the 1950s leaders in Cleveland's business community established an organization which has expanded over the intervening 50 years to become known today as NOCHE (the Northeast Ohio Council on Higher Education). NOCHE's board of trustees consists of the presidents of 23 colleges and universities in a 13-county area of Northeast Ohio and a like number of business leaders. NOCHE's current strategies include advocacy for the role of higher education in the region, workforce development and technology transfer: three important aspects of economic development. NOCHE in turn has been physically housed and has collaborated, with TeamNEO, a business-supported marketing organization that works closely with the state, and various counties and municipalities in the region to stimulate economic development through entrepreneurship.

Seventh, regional economics. If we go back to the early 1980s, we note that one aspect of the Cleveland comeback was the emergence on the economic scene of what is now the Center for Regional Economic Issues at the Case Weatherhead School of Management. While this important entity for collection and analysis of regional economic data was sired by a foundation, The Cleveland Foundation, rather than government, in fact the concept of REI, and indeed for several of its early years its landlord, was The Federal Reserve Bank of Cleveland. Interestingly the first home of REI was the College of Urban Affairs at Cleveland State University (CSU). REI moved on from there to the Fed, and ultimately to the Weatherhead School at Case. But even after REI left the Urban College at CSU, that college continued to assemble and utilize large quantities of important regional economic data on its own. I understand that today REI and the Urban College at Cleveland State are collaborating on certain projects in support of economic development through entrepreneurship, and I believe that this is a wonderful development for entrepreneurship support in the region.

Eighth, technology transfer. Another important, indeed some would say crucial, issue involving government/academic collaboration for the benefit of economic development through entrepreneurship is technology transfer. Professor Feller has referred to the Bayh–Dole Act, which gave universities the right to patent inventions that emerge from federally sponsored research; this very important federal legislation has stimulated various universities to upgrade substantially their technology transfer capability. As a longtime suffering member of the Case Board's Technology Transfer Committee, I was ecstatic when Dr Wagner, Case's interim president, made the decision a few years ago to invest heavily in this function and bring in some real experts. The result has been dramatically positive, and has led to a number of effective partnerships in the local entrepreneurial arena.

Ninth, miscellaneous. I would like to state three short points that I believe are relevant to my assignment. My recent experience as Chairman of Ohio Governor Bob Taft's Commission on Higher Education & the Economy leads me to say that leaders of higher education, that is, key presidents of various colleges and universities around the state of Ohio, seem more interested now than at any previous time in history in using their institutions to stimulate and support economic development.

A new day has also arrived in the interest of philanthropic foundations (perhaps, to some extent, in lieu of government) in economic development. This emerging realization of an extremely effective use of philanthropic dollars is, I would venture to say, somewhat historic. A dramatic illustration is the proposed $30 million Fund for Our Economic Future which was recently announced by a group of 28 foundations in a nine-county area of Northeast Ohio to promote and sustain economic development in the region. This wonderful new development was characterized in a *Cleveland Plain Dealer* headline as follows: 'Private groups take on a role usually played by government'.

While the emphasis here has been on universities, we should all remember that, in this area of government/academia partnerships to enhance economic development, the community colleges of the state are playing a tremendous role. The catalytic contributions of Lorain County Community College and Cuyahoga Community College to economic development through entrepreneurship are well known locally.

So I would say overall that partnerships between government and academic institutions, in partnership with business and philanthropic foundations, have played an important role in the region's economic development through entrepreneurism over the last 25 years, and the potential for the future is immense. This, along with the revitalization of REI, is exciting. In a time of economic doldrums, it is a strong source of optimism.

2. Government policies to encourage economic development through entrepreneurship: the case of technology transfer

Scott Shane

INTRODUCTION

The federal and state governments in the United States have long partnered with universities to promote economic development through entrepreneurship. In fact, even the land grant system that led to the formation of many American universities is, itself, based on the idea that universities should be established so as to create knowledge that entrepreneurs could use to improve local agriculture and manufacturing (Golub, 2003; Rosenberg and Nelson, 1994).

Over the past 25 years, American universities have become even more important contributors to economic development through entrepreneurship. Moreover several policies that have been put in place to encourage the formation of companies to exploit new knowledge created in academia by faculty, staff and students of research universities (university spin-offs) over this period have contributed to this increase in the contribution of university entrepreneurship to economic development. This chapter reviews many of the policies adopted by federal and state governments to enhance economic development through the creation of university spin-off companies to identify some best practices for the enhancement of economic development through the encouragement of university entrepreneurship.

The chapter is divided into three parts. The first section reviews evidence that the creation of spin-off companies indeed enhances economic development. The second section reviews the policies designed to promote economic development through the creation of new companies to exploit academic inventions to evaluate the case for the value of different policies. The third section offers some implications from the review of policies about best practices to encourage economic development through the creation of university spin-offs.

UNIVERSITY SPIN-OFFS ENHANCE ECONOMIC DEVELOPMENT

University spin-offs are some of America's best known technology companies, including such household names as Cirrus Logic, Genentech, Hewlett Packard, Lycos, and Yahoo! Given the prominence of these companies, even casual observation would suggest that the formation of spin-off companies is an important contributor to economic development. However, perhaps surprisingly, systematic study of the effect of university spin-off companies on economic development has never been undertaken, making an assessment of the importance of spin-off companies to economic development difficult to ascertain.

Nevertheless, taken together, the fragmentary evidence on this topic does suggest that the creation and growth of new companies to exploit university technology enhances economic development. For example, research by the Association of University Technology Managers (AUTM), the trade association of university technology licensing offices, estimates that, from 1980 to 1999, the direct economic impact of university spin-off companies was $33.5bn, or roughly $10m per company founded (Pressman, 1999).

University spin-offs also appear to have valuable job-creating capabilities. From 1980 to 1999, American university spin-offs were estimated to have generated 280 000 jobs, a rate of job creation per company that greatly exceeds the rate of the average new company in the US economy during the same period (Cohen, 2000). Perhaps more importantly, the job creation rate of spin-off companies exceeds the rate of job creation by established company licensees of university inventions, making them more valuable mechanisms for job creation than the alternative methods of technology transfer and commercialization by existing firms. Focusing solely on one university's technology licenses, those of the Massachusetts Institute of Technology (MIT), Pressman *et al.* (1995) showed that spin-off companies accounted for 70 per cent of all new jobs created from Institute-licensed technology, even though the spin-offs only composed 35 per cent of the licensees. Charles and Conway (2001) report similarly strong job creation properties of university spin-offs in the United Kingdom, suggesting that the job creation properties of university spin-offs is not restricted to the United States.

University spin-offs also enhance economic development because they commercialize academic inventions that would otherwise go undeveloped.

Surveys of potential licensees for university technologies reveal that spin-offs tend to commercialize different inventions from those commercialized by established companies. In particular, spin-offs focus on inventions that are too uncertain or at too early a stage for established companies to pursue (Thursby and Thursby, 2000; Thursby *et al.*, 2001). Spin-offs also permit the development of inventions that require substantial inventor involvement by overcoming incentive problems in ensuring further inventor involvement (Lowe, 2002; Jensen and Thursby, 2001). In fact, several researchers have noted that many university spin-offs have been founded precisely because established firms were unwilling to license specific technologies, and the inventors of those technologies founded companies to make sure that their inventions would be further developed (Matkin, 1990; Lowe, 2002; Hsu and Bernstein, 1997).

Several empirical studies also document the greater likelihood of university spin-offs to invest in the further commercial development of academic technologies once they are licensed than is the case for established firm licensees. For instance, Pressman *et al.* (1995) found that spin-offs accounted for three-quarters of the induced investment in the development of MIT technologies even through they made up only one third of licensees. Similarly Mustar (1997) and Blair and Hitchens (1998) found that French and British university spin-offs invest more heavily in research and development than typical startup companies, respectively.

The indirect economic impact of university spin-offs may be even larger than their direct effects. As spin-offs undertake business activity, they tend to exert multiplier effects on the economy through their hiring of employees and their sourcing of supply and production. These multiplier effects stimulate economic development. Because university spin-offs tend to be founded near the universities that spawned them, whether those spin-offs are located in the United States, Canada, Sweden or the United Kingdom (Pressman, 2002; Tornatsky *et al.*, 1995; Wright *et al.*, 2002; Wallmark, 1997), their multiplier effects on economic development tend to be localized.

As a result of these multiplier effects, university spin-offs can have a dramatic effect on the economy of a region. University spin-offs can make economies less dependent on older industries by diversifying a region's economic base (McQueen and Wallmark, 1991). They can create new industrial clusters, as occurred with biotechnology in Northern California. Perhaps more importantly, these clusters, once created, facilitate the development of a financing infrastructure that supports the creation and development of other types of new technology companies. For example, Audretsch and Stephan (1996) found that venture capitalists opened offices in areas near universities where leading biotechnology researchers worked as a way to facilitate the financing of their firms, thus providing a financing infrastructure for other companies.

The magnitude of the effect of university spin-offs on transforming a regional economy can be quite large. Goldman (1984) estimated that almost three-quarters of the high-technology companies founded in the Route 128 corridor in the early 1980s were initially based on MIT-created technologies. Mustar (1997) calculated that 40 per cent of new French high-technology start-ups from 1987 to 1997 were based on university technologies. Wickstead (1985) estimated that almost one-fifth of the Cambridge, England technology start-ups were university spin-offs. Therefore, even though we lack systematic evidence for the impact of university spin-off companies on economic development, fragmentary evidence does suggest that these companies have an important impact on economic development.

THE EFFECT OF GOVERNMENT POLICIES

The evidence presented above raises the central question of this chapter: what policies have been best practices for encouraging economic development through the creation of university spin-off companies? A review of available evidence suggests that federal and state governments have had a significant effect on the formation and growth of university spin-off companies, thus both directly and indirectly enhancing economic development through academic entrepreneurship, through six categories of policies: (1) funding of academic research; (2) the provision of property rights for academic inventions with universities not the inventors themselves; (3) the Bayh–Dole Act and related laws to encourage university technology licensing, particularly to small firms; (4) the use of direct mechanisms to support the development of spin-off companies; (5) programs to reduce the financing gap in early stage technological development; and (6) policies to encourage movement of technically trained academics between the academic and private sectors.

Federal Funding of Academic Research

Although frequently overlooked, perhaps the most important government policy that has encouraged the use of universities to promote economic development through university spin-offs is the federal government's policy of providing academics at American universities with large amounts of funding to conduct research, particularly in the biomedical area. Beginning during World War II, when the federal government began providing large amounts of money to engineering schools for academic research to help the war effort (Mowery and Sampat, 2001), the federal government has been the primary source of research and development dollars in American universities. In fact, currently, the federal government pays for approximately 60 per cent of all research conducted at American research universities (Geiger, 1993), an amount equal to approximately $30 billion per year.

The vast amount of federal funding has allowed universities to increase dramatically their research and development expenditures over the past five decades. As Figure 2.1 shows, since the 1950s, the real (1996 dollars) value of university research and development expenditures has gone up over 25 times. The result of this intense effort to support academic research has made universities far more important to technology creation in the United States than they once were. Whereas, in 1960, American universities undertook only 7.4 per cent of the R&D expenditure in the USA; in 1997, they undertook 14.5 per cent (Mowery *et al.*, 2001).

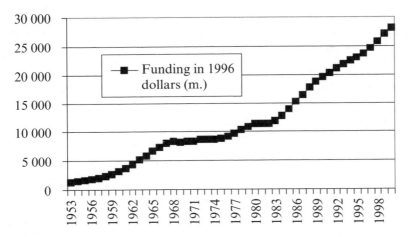

Source: National Science Foundation (2002), *Science and Engineering Indicators*, Washington, DC: US Government Printing Office.

Figure 2.1   Real university research and development expenditure, 1953–2000

The level of government funding of research in American universities is important in explaining the role of university spin-off companies in promoting economic development; research on university technology transfer shows a direct empirical relationship between the amount of research and development expenditure at universities and the number of licenses and spin-off companies that they create (Adams and Griliches,

1996; Siegel *et al.*, 1999). Each additional $4.62m. of R&D leads to approximately one additional patent and each $4.51m. in R&D leads to approximately one additional license (Siegel *et al.*, 1999; Payne and Siow, 2003). Moreover, controlling for other factors, the level of research funding has a significant positive effect on spin-off company creation (DiGregorio and Shane, 2003). Data from AUTM suggests that the R&D cost of each spin-off is approximately $9.2m.

The value of federal funding of university research as a way to turn universities into engines of economic development through entrepreneurship is most clearly seen in the biomedical area. Federal funding of biomedical research at American universities has grown dramatically since the 1970s, when the war on cancer was first initiated (Mowery and Sampat, 2001). This remarkable investment in biomedical research at universities has led to a dramatic increase in biomedical inventions at universities, which have grown from 11 per cent of all university patenting in 1971 to 48 per cent in 1997 (Mowery, 2001). Moreover, perhaps because of intensive government funding, the growth in the university share of inventions in the biomedical area has exceeded that in other fields (see Figure 2.2).

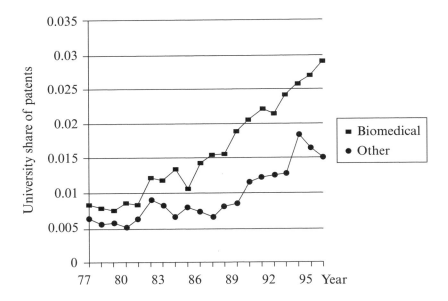

Source: National Science Foundation, *Science and Engineering Indicators*, various years.

Figure 2.2   Growth in the university share of patents

More importantly, the substantial National Institutes of Health (NIH) funding of biomedical research at American universities and hospitals, particularly of molecular biology research, has led to many of the scientific discoveries underlying the formation of biotechnology companies by university researchers (Mowery and Sampat, 2001; Etzkowitz, 1989). Biotechnology, as an industry, remains very closely tied to academic research, with American universities producing many of the technological discoveries that have led to the formation and growth of these firms. Stephan (2001), for example, reports that the 52 newly public biotechnology companies she studied had 420 university scientists affiliated with them.

Provision of Property Rights with Institutions

Another important aspect of policy that encourages economic development through university spin-offs is US federal government policy of placing property rights for federally funded inventions developed in universities in the hands of academic institutions rather than with the inventors themselves. This approach makes the United States different from most European nations, which place property rights to inventions developed on university campuses with individual inventors (Schmiemann and Durvy, 2003).

The assignment of property rights to universities rather than inventors provides three benefits that encourage university spin-offs and their subsequent effect on economic development. First, such a policy provides institutional support for entrepreneurship, and permits an entrepreneurial attitude to develop among faculty and university administrators (Goldfarb and Henrekson, 2003). Second, such a policy leads academic institutions to develop offices of technology transfer, which develop expertise in developing new companies (Golub, 2003). Third, such a policy makes it easier to pool the risks and costs of developing and licensing inventions over a large number of technologies, making decision makers more willing to bear the risks and costs of starting companies (Goldfarb and Henrekson, 2003; Collins and Wakoh, 2002).

Comparisons of the United States to other countries, such as Japan and Sweden, which produce a large amount of new technology in universities, but generate few spin-off companies, show the advantages of assigning property rights to universities in generating university spin-offs. For example, in Sweden, where patents are assigned to university researchers, not their institutions, the rate of patenting per inventor is half that of comparable US universities. Similarly Japan, second in the world after the United States in the creation of genetic sequencing discoveries, has very few biotechnology spin-offs in this area (Zucker and Darby, 2001).

Perhaps the best evidence for the value of the assignment of intellectual property rights to universities lies in an examination of Japan before and after a change in intellectual property laws. In 1998, Japan shifted to a policy of assigning intellectual property rights for inventions developed by faculty and staff of universities from the inventors themselves to the institutions in which they worked (Walsh and Cohen, 2004). Since the passage of this law, Japan has seen a dramatic increase in the number of spin-off companies created, from 17 in 1997 to 100 in 2000 (Kneller, 2003).

The Bayh–Dole Act

The Bayh–Dole Act of 1980, which gave universities the right to own federally funded inventions developed on their campuses and ended the requirement that universities use institutional patent agreements negotiated bilaterally with government agencies (Mowery, 2001), was another important policy that enhanced the rate of formation of university spin-off companies. The Act's stated goal is 'to encourage maximum participation of small business firms in federally supported research and development efforts'. Perhaps the most important contribution of the Bayh–Dole Act to economic development through spin-off company creation has been to make spin-off companies something that is considered acceptable, and even desirable, at universities. The typical American university administrator was once a staunch opponent of involvement in the creation of new companies based on research on campus (Mowery *et al.*, 2001). However, the Act led to a transformation of thinking among administrators at US universities to view spin-off companies as something for universities to create (Bok, 2003).

The Bayh–Dole Act also enhanced the use of university technology as a vehicle for economic development through entrepreneurship by making exclusive licensing of university inventions easier to undertake. Prior to the passage of the Act in 1980, federal government funding agencies required special justification to grant exclusive licenses. By establishing the federal government's support of exclusive licensing of the inventions that resulted from research that it funded (Mowery *et al.*, 2001), the Act made it easier for universities to engage in exclusive licensing than had been the case under the previous institutional regime (Pressman *et al.*, 1995).

Exclusive licensing is important to enhancing the creation of spin-off companies, for two reasons. Because start-up companies rarely have other competitive advantages at the time they are founded, they are often unwilling to develop new technology unless they have exclusive rights to use that technology once it is developed. In addition, spin-off companies often require additional external funding to support their development of technology, which is often at a pre-commercialization stage prior to licensing.

Investors are more likely to finance new ventures that have exclusive licenses to technology because such licenses minimize competition.

The existing evidence suggests that exclusive licensing enhances spin-off company formation. Pressman (2002) reports that 90 per cent of start-up company licenses issued in 1992 by American universities were exclusive, as compared to only 37 per cent of licenses to established companies. Moreover Roberts and Malone (1996), contrasting several research universities, found that Stanford University's opposition to exclusive licenses hindered its rate of spin-off company formation, while Hsu and Bernstein (1997) used interviews with spin-off company founders to show that many of the founders of MIT and Harvard University spin-offs would not have founded companies if they could not obtain exclusive licenses.

In addition to the US evidence, patterns of spin-off company activity in Japan following its 1998 policy change suggest the importance of exclusive licensing to the creation of spin-off companies. Kneller (2003) reports a dramatic increase in spin-off activity in Japan after Japanese universities were given the right to license their inventions exclusively. Prior to these policy changes, spin-offs were difficult to undertake in Japan because they lacked clear title to inventions. Thus exclusive licensing was difficult and fund raising was nearly impossible (Walsh and Cohen, 2004).

Direct Mechanisms to Support Spin-off Company Creation

Federal and state governments have also encouraged economic development through spin-off company creation by undertaking direct mechanisms. In case studies of university spin-offs, Feldman and Kelley (2002) report that state funding which subsidizes the development of new technologies through incubator facilities and applied research grants enhances the development of technologies by university spin-off companies. Other case study evidence suggests that state programs to create buffer institutions that translate academic research into a more commercial form enhance spin-off company creation by reducing the cost of development of technology and by reducing the need for academics to translate their work into commercial form (Brooks and Randazzese, 1998).

Research also has shown that states which allow their public institutions to provide university spin-offs with access to university research laboratories and facilities facilitate spin-off company creation by reducing the cost to the firms of using resources, such as wet labs (Tornatsky *et al.*, 1995). These policies also encourage the creation of spin-offs by facilitating a continuing relationship between the university laboratory that generated the spin-off's technology and the spin-off company which is important to the development of a spin-off's technology (Mustar, 1997; Steffensen *et al.*, 1999; Lowe, 2002).

Governments also facilitate the development of spin-off companies through procurement. Federal procurement contracts for the use of computers by the US military for air defense facilitated the development of spin-off companies in the computer industry (Etzkowitz, 1989). Moreover many university spin-offs benefit indirectly from procurement policies because these firms have contracts and strategic alliances with aerospace and defense related companies that are themselves heavy recipients of federal government contracts (Feldman, 1994; Saxenian, 1994; Leslie, 1993).

A particularly important direct mechanism by which state governments enhance the development of spin-off companies lies in the willingness to permit the investment of state government funds in spin-off companies in return for equity. These policies help spin-off companies by allowing them to conserve cash as well as by providing them with the legitimacy of association with a government agency or university (Feldman, 2001).

Feldman and Kelley (2002) report variation in state policies toward allowing state universities and government agencies to make equity investments in technology spin-offs in lieu of license fees; and Tornatzky *et al.* (2002) find that legislation that allows equity participation in start-ups at public institutions encourages new firm formation. DiGregorio and Shane (2003) showed that universities permitted to make equity investments in spin-off companies had a 69 per cent higher level of spin-off company creation than universities not permitted to make them. Lockett *et al.* (2002) found similar results in a study of spin-offs out of universities in the United Kingdom.

Policies to Reduce the Financing Gap

A fifth governmental approach to enhancing economic development through the formation of spin-off companies lies in policies to reduce the financing gap for early-stage technology development. Because the technologies that spin-off companies exploit are typically very early in their development, the costs of technical and market development are often quite high, and spin-offs need to obtain external capital to finance their development. However the long and uncertain time horizon of this development makes it difficult for spin-offs to raise capital from the private sector. Public sector funding fills this funding gap, allowing companies to develop technology to a point at which it is of interest to private sector investors, by providing a subsidy which reduces the cost to private sector investors of financing the development of the technology, and by reducing the level of risk borne by private investors.

Several researchers have pointed to variation across countries or states in pre-stage funding and its effects on spin-off company formation. For instance, Tornatsky *et al*. (1995) found that states with technology development financing programs have more university spin-offs than other states. Collins and Wakoh (2002) attribute the US advantage over Japan in creating new technology companies out of universities to the presence of organizations that provide pre-seed stage capital.

Several studies have looked at the effect of specific funding programs on the development of small, high-technology companies, many of which are university spin-offs. One set of studies has looked at the Small Business Innovation Research (SBIR) program, a program that requires federal government agencies funding innovation research to set aside 2.5 per cent of their budgets for contracts with small businesses. Audretsch (2003) explains that the SBIR program is important to financing the development of technology by small firms because it creates an early-stage capital pool approximately two-thirds the size of the entire venture capital industry.

Receipt of SBIR grants encourages the formation of spin-off companies. Lerner (1999) showed that receiving SBIR grants increased the likelihood that firms would receive venture capital funding. Audretsch *et al*. (2000) showed that the SBIR grants increased the formation of biotechnology companies, by motivating academic researchers to undertake more commercial activity, by providing a demonstration effect to other scientists and engineers, and by making more capital available to spin-off companies.

Similarly several studies have shown the effect of the Advanced Technology Program (ATP) of the National Institute of Standards and Technology on university spin-off development. Lowe (2002) provides case study evidence that ATP grants bridged a funding gap that allowed University of California spin-offs to develop prototype products from proof of concept technology and then raise private sector capital. Feldman and Kelley (2003) found that winning an ATP award helps companies to obtain venture capital financing because of the beneficial signal provided by the award.

Policies to Enhance Labor Market Mobility

A final area of government involvement that enhances economic development through the creation of spin-off companies lies in policies that affect academic labor market mobility. In general, policies that enhance the willingness of academics to participate in the formation of spin-off companies encourage the formation of these companies, and their subsequent effects on economic development. For instance, Gittleman (2000) explains that spin-off company formation is much lower in France than in the USA because French academics are barred by law from taking an equity stake in start-up companies, which reduces their incentive to form companies.

Moreover university spin-offs are more common in the USA than in most European countries because faculty of European universities cannot easily take leave of absence to found companies to exploit their technological discoveries. Research shows that leaves of absence are important to facilitating spin-off companies because faculty members do not want to bear the downside risk of giving up secure positions to start companies (Kenney, 1986).

Even within the USA, the data suggest a relationship between leave of absence policies and the formation of spin-off companies. For instance, those institutions which restrict the leave of absence of their faculty members have fewer spin-off companies than those institutions that do not restrict leave of absence (Shane, 2004). Kenney and Goe (2004) show that the state of California policy on leave of absence hinders spin-off company formation out of the computer science department at the University of California at Berkeley and makes it much lower than the rate of spin-off company creation at the comparable department at Stanford University.

POLICY IMPLICATIONS

This chapter reviewed the effects of university spin-offs on economic development, as well as the policies that federal and state governments have used effectively to enhance the formation and growth of spin-off companies. The chapter demonstrates that university spin-offs are important contributors to economic development.

While we do not have many large-sample statistical studies to support this proposition, we do have significant amounts of fragmentary data that, when amassed, provide convincing support for the contribution of university spin-offs to economic development. First, even a casual glance at the origins of major high-technology firms reveals that many of them originated with university inventions. Second, university spin-offs tend to commercialize technologies that otherwise would have gone untapped by the private sector, making them an important part of an effective innovation system. Third, studies have documented that spin-off companies induce relatively large amounts of investment (when compared to established firm licensees of university inventions) and have a job creation rate that exceeds that of the average start-up firm. Moreover the high localization of spin-off companies around the universities that spawn them allows localities with those universities to benefit from economic diversification, and the development of a venture financing infrastructure for new companies.

Federal and state governments have had a significant effect on the formation and growth of university spin-off companies, both directly and indirectly enhancing economic development through academic entrepreneurship. Again we lack systematic large-sample evidence for the effects of many government policies, but a review of the literature that does exist (fragmentary as it may be) suggests several 'best practices' in which government policies enhance economic development through enhancements to spin-off company creation. First, policies of intensive federal funding of academic research, particularly in the biomedical areas, enhance spin-off company creation because investment in research and development is an important precursor to the development of high-technology companies.

Second, the provision of property rights for federally funded academic inventions with universities, not the inventors themselves, is beneficial. Such a policy generates an institutional support system for entrepreneurship and permits an entrepreneurial attitude to develop among faculty and university administrators, creates an incentive for universities to market technologies and search out entrepreneur licensees who would commercialize their inventions by starting companies, and makes it easier to pool the risks and costs of developing and licensing inventions over a large number of technologies.

Third, the passage of laws like the Bayh–Dole Act, which gives universities the rights to federally funded inventions, enhances economic development through academic entrepreneurship by making exclusive licensing of university inventions – something of great importance to spin-offs – easier to undertake. These laws also enhance academic entrepreneurship by changing attitudes of faculty and administrators on university campuses to make them more supportive of spin-offs.

Fourth, federal and state governments have also encouraged economic development through spin-off company creation through direct mechanisms. Policies that subsidize the development of new technologies through incubator facilities, procurement, buffer institutions and applied research grants enhance the development of technologies by university spin-off companies. In particular, policies that permit government entities, such as state universities, to take equity in return for making cash payments to help develop spin-off companies are important mechanisms of economic development through entrepreneurship.

Fifth, state and federal government programs to reduce the financing gap in early-stage technological development enhance the growth of university spin-offs and facilitate economic development. Such funding allows companies to develop technology to a point at which it is of interest to private sector investors, provides a subsidy which reduces the cost to private sector investors of financing the development of the technology, and reduces the level of risk borne by private investors.

Sixth, government policies that enhance the willingness of academics to participate in the formation of spin-off companies encourage the formation of these companies and their subsequent effects on economic development. In particular, policies that facilitate leave of absence from academic institutions and permit academics to hold equity in spin-offs based on their own inventions enhance spin-off company creation and the economic development that comes along with it.

In short, while we do not have conclusive evidence of the economic development value of university spin-offs or the government policies that facilitate their development and growth, we do have enough partial evidence to suggest that university spin-offs are important contributors to economic development. Moreover we can identify best practices for policy makers in several areas that can be used to enhance economic development through the creation and development of spin-off companies.

COMMENTARY

Casey Porto

More than 20 years after the passage of the Bayh–Dole Act, the practice of transferring academic research results into the private sector in order to create new products and/or new companies is today recognized as having significant impact not only on the universities engaged in the practice, but also on the US economy. Universities typically engage in technology transfer as a 'service' to faculty researchers who desire to see their research outcomes put to use by society. A viable technology transfer program has also become a significant tool for a university's ability to recruit and retain top faculty in an increasingly competitive landscape. The billions of dollars generated by academic technology transfer activities in the USA have had a profound impact on academic institutions and their local economies, but most universities take the official position that they do not engage in technology transfer for the primary purpose of generating income.

Nevertheless the billions of dollars generated by academic technology transfer, especially through the creation of spin-off companies, have understandably gained the attention of state and federal policy makers. Scott Shane's chapter provides a framework for understanding and assessing policies which have enhanced university spin-off activity. His review provides a well-grounded perspective, and should be required reading for policy makers who are charged with enhancing economic development through the encouragement and support of spin-offs and commercialization of technology.

I would like to expand on two of the central points made by Shane in his review of government policies and their effect on the formation of university spin-off companies. The first of the policies reviewed by Shane is the intensive funding of academic research by federal agencies. The funding of academic basic research occurs so early in the chain of events which leads to spin-off companies that most people outside the technology transfer profession do not even grasp the connection, let alone the importance. In difficult economic times, federal, state and local governments look for the 'quick fix', and often the funding of academic basic research seems to be an unaffordable 'luxury' compared to other mechanisms which are perceived as having a more direct impact on economic health and the creation of jobs. Yet the areas of the country where spin-off creation and the birth of new industry clusters has been most prevalent are those areas which have the longest history of the deepest government funding of basic research. Academic technology transfer professionals operate at the narrow end of the funnel; the wide end of the funnel is basic research funding, which results in some number of inventions, a subset of which can be commercialized, and an even smaller subset of which can be the basis of a new company. The wider the funnel of research funding, the more possibilities for new spin-off companies.

The second policy reviewed by Shane is the provision of property rights for federally funded academic inventions to universities – not to the inventors themselves or some third party. Although seemingly simplistic in approach, this provision is quite profound, and in fact is often overlooked and undervalued by those outside the technology transfer profession. The investment by US universities in their technology transfer operations has been enormous.

The practice of technology transfer is often viewed by outsiders as an administrative function, requiring the simple patenting of inventions which result from funded projects. In fact the most successful technology transfer offices are complex and expensive operations, providing a wide variety of services by highly educated and experienced professionals. For instance, in order to interact effectively with a wide variety of scientists in a wide range of disciplines, technology transfer offices must be staffed by professionals who have at least a master's level education in a science/technology field, and the ability to understand new concepts and ideas across a number of fields. The same technology transfer professional must also have experience in sales and marketing, in order to be able to identify appropriate markets and best candidates for licensing new discoveries, and to approach these companies with an appropriate amount of technical and business information in order to garner their interest. The technology transfer professional must also have sound business sense and a deep understanding of contract law in order to conduct a businesslike negotiation with the candidate licensee while complying with all legal restrictions imposed by non-profit law and federal/state regulations. In addition to having in-depth scientific education, sales/marketing experience, a deep understanding of contract law, non-profit law and federal/state regulations, the technology transfer professional must also be knowledgeable in patent law in order to deal with many patent lawyers on many different patent matters, and, of course, be very good with people.

In support of the licensing professionals, the technology transfer office must also provide financial services for invoicing licensees and distributing royalties to inventors, paralegal services for corresponding with dozens of patent attorneys and tracking all patent matters, communications services for interacting with community groups, venture capitalists, faculty researchers and potential licensees, and of course a support infrastructure of administrative and database services.

In short, universities make quite significant investments in technology transfer infrastructure, with widely varying results. A few US universities generate hundreds of millions of dollars in revenue thanks to successful spin-offs or successful pharmaceutical products. The vast majority of US universities do not even come close to covering costs for technology transfer. If the property rights for inventions resulting from federally funded projects were put into the hands of individual inventors or third party interests, would hundreds of millions of dollars be invested in the technology transfer process?

3. Creating innovation networks among manufacturing firms: how effective extension programs work

Susan Helper and Marcus Stanley

INTRODUCTION

Between its most recent peak employment level in 2000 and 2004, the US manufacturing sector lost over 2.5 million jobs. This represents almost one fifth of its pre-recession total. The question of how to stop this catastrophic employment loss is clearly a critical one, but there are no easy answers.

Manufacturers are eligible for a variety of general business subsidies; the vast majority of these are tax abatements for locating or expanding an operation in a particular area (Lynch, 2004). These tax incentives, however, do not increase manufacturing efficiency. The main federal program for increasing the efficiency of manufacturing is the Manufacturing Extension Partnership (MEP). Despite its very low level of funding ($106 million in 2003, or $7 per manufacturing worker), it has been hit hard by budget cuts. Its 2004 appropriation was only $39.6 million.[1] There is a lack of consensus on how government could assist manufacturing, or whether such assistance is even really possible.

In this chapter, we examine data on a subsector of manufacturing, small and medium-sized (fewer than 500 employees) component manufacturing firms. Component manufacturers typically sell to other firms (rather than to consumers) and thus form a key part of the manufacturing supply chain. We are able to characterize these firms' strategies in some detail using national data gathered by the Michigan Manufacturing Technology Center's Performance Benchmarking Service. In the first section of this chapter, we describe the sector and some of the data we used to perform our analysis. In the second section, we summarize some of our previous research on factors that seem to be correlated with high value-added per worker and high sales growth. Our research has focused strongly on urban manufacturing firms, and we argue that these firms should be a special focus for economic development assistance. The third section discusses arguments for various economic development approaches, and examines how the MEP program has worked in practice. The fourth section concludes.

SECTOR DESCRIPTION AND DATA

The US Component Manufacturing Sector

The component manufacturing sector has long been important to the economies of the US Midwest. Firms in this sector fabricate and/or assemble molded, forged, formed and machined goods made of metal and plastic, principally for sale to other manufacturers. The sector stands at the base of such industries as automobiles and other transportation equipment; industrial, farm, and construction machinery; electrical appliances; and medical instruments. It accounts for more than 10 percent of US manufacturing employment. The sector is heavily concentrated geographically, with 45 per cent of total employment in the Great Lakes states of Wisconsin, Illinois, Indiana, Michigan and Ohio (as against these states' 36 per cent of US manufacturing generally). The customers and suppliers of these firms are also heavily concentrated in those states.

In contrast to the Original Equipment Manufacturers (OEMs) and large first-tier suppliers they serve, most of these firms have fewer than 500 employees. In part because of their small size, they are often deeply anchored in their regions, and dependent on surrounding regional institutions in obtaining new knowledge. However this cluster is dispersing, spreading out both within the USA and around the world. For example, in 1975, 50 per cent of US employment in the auto industry (assembly and parts) was concentrated in just 16 of the more than 3000 US counties. By 1990, these counties accounted for only 30 per cent of automotive employment, a dramatic decline.

Like the rest of the US manufacturing sector, the component manufacturing industry has lost a substantial number of jobs to foreign competition during the recent recession. US Department of Labor data for the three most relevant industry classifications show a loss of almost 20 per cent of the 3.8 million jobs that existed in these industries in June 2003 (Figure 3.1).[2] Interviews with plant managers and some of the data in our survey indicate that many of these job losses can be ascribed to competition from cheaper foreign imports. Component manufacturing is thus a good case study in the effects of globalization on manufacturing in the USA.

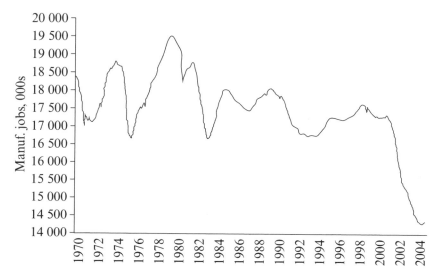

Source: US Bureau of Labor Statistics, seasonally adjusted.

Figure 3.1   US manufacturing jobs, January 1970–June 2004

As our data source in examining this sector, we draw on two surveys conducted as part of the Michigan Manufacturing Technology Center's (MMTC) ongoing Performance Benchmarking Service (http://www.mmtc. org/services/PBS). The project enlists a panel of about 600 plants to submit benchmarking data on a continuing basis to the MMTC. Each year, firms in the panel are also mailed a more detailed survey that asks additional questions about their business practices. The panel is not a random sample (firms must volunteer to participate), but it is broadly representative of the component manufacturing industry.

During the winter of 2003, we submitted a survey to all 600 firms that included detailed questions about the nature of their ties to other firms, including customers and competitors. Firms also submitted basic accounting data on their revenues, costs, employment and wages. In total 250 surveys were returned by US firms.

We then linked the survey data to data from the US Census Bureau's Zip Code Business Patterns file released in the year 2002. This file contains information on the number of establishments by detailed industry in every zip code in the United States as of 2000. We use this information to create measures of the urban density of the firm's location, and whether or not the firm is located in a cluster of firms in similar industries.

SOME RESEARCH FINDINGS

There are, of course, numerous determinants of productivity and success in this sector, as in all of manufacturing. In our research, we have focused on the issue of agglomeration economies (Stanley and Helper, 2003). These are the productivity benefits that emerge from locating in areas of concentrated economic activity, either in the same industry or in an urban location more generally (Rosenthal and Strange, 2003). Agglomeration economies offer an important potential 'lever' in economic development strategies, since it may be possible to manipulate either the location of firms or the interconnections among nearby firms so as to generate a productive cluster. Economic development theorists and practitioners have eagerly adopted the language of agglomeration, or 'cluster economies', as part of their efforts (Porter, 1990). Our findings are thus quite relevant to economic development policy. That said, we do not pretend to fully analyze sources of productivity and success in this sector. Our key findings are listed below.

This manufacturing sector is characterized by urban economies, but not by cluster economies. We differentiate between two types of agglomeration economies. One is associated with location in dense concentrations of other establishments (urban economies), while the second (cluster economies) results from location close to similar firms in the same industry. We find that firms located in urban areas have considerably higher levels of value-added per worker than non-urban firms with similar levels of capital investment, even after controlling for industry.[3] Location in clusters of other manufacturing firms in the same or similar industry, however, is associated with no additional productivity benefit beyond the effects of the urban location.

Urban economies can have a considerable impact on firm productivity. An increase in our urbanization measure from the 25th to the 75th percentile leads to a 10 per cent increase in value-added per worker, with capital held fixed.

Many of the benefits of location in urban areas are captured by workers, not firms. Increases in our urbanization measure seem to be associated with firm payroll premiums roughly proportional to the extra value-added. This is true even after controlling for industry and the (limited) measures of worker skill that we have.

Certain types of urban firms in our sample appear to earn higher profits. Because we do not have perfect measures of the value of capital, we are hesitant to make definitive statements about profits. But, at least in our sample, firms in more urbanized areas appeared to earn higher profits than other firms. This naturally raises the question of why all firms do not move to urbanized areas. Preliminary findings indicate that only smaller firms are able to earn a profit advantage due to urban location; larger firms do not seem to receive the same kinds of profit benefit. We are continuing to investigate this finding. A rationale for this finding is that small firms are particularly dependent on their environment to provide inputs such as skilled workers, specialized inputs and new ideas. (The economist Alfred Marshall called these resources provided by a firm's environment 'external economies'.) In contrast, large firms have enough scale to provide many services in-house profitably. For example, they can set up a program to train their own workers, rather than rely on a pool of skilled workers that already reside near the plant.

Self-reported social capital and networking measures do not seem to account for the agglomeration economies we found. On the smaller supplemental survey, there are a series of questions that ask firms to self-report both the extent of their networking contacts with other firms in the same industry and the perceived value of those contacts. We found that both the extent and the perceived value of inter-firm networking was completely uncorrelated to location in urban areas, and also to location in clusters of firms in the same industry. Firms appeared able to network with their peers independently of their geographic location.

However, information transfer through networking does have an effect on productivity for single-plant firms. In general, we found no clear effect of either the extent or value of inter-firm networking for our full sample of firms. But we did find that single-plant firms, firms that had only a single plant and no branch plants, showed a strong correlation between the perceived value of inter-firm networks and value-added. A move from the 25th to the 75th percentile on our measure of the value of firm networking was associated with a jump of over 10 per cent in value-added at these firms. In contrast, firms with multiple plants showed a negative relationship between information transfer through networking and value-added.

Firms that do extensive amounts of engineering to order and design work appear to get stronger productivity impacts from urban location. Firms that had a relatively large fraction of sales from engineered-to-order products (engineering a customized prototype, as opposed to working with a pre-determined product) or that performed significant design work, appear to get a larger benefit from urban location than other firms. Depending on the model specification, the urban impact on productivity could be up to 50 per cent higher for firms in the top quartile on our measures of design intensity. However, urban location still has a significant productivity impact for other firms as well.

Trends in manufacturing are running against the kind of firms that are most successful in urban agglomerations. Over the 2001–3 period, we found that high-wage firms were particularly likely to lose sales and employment. Among firms that paid less than the median level of annual earnings in our sample (about $37 000), employment dropped by about 4 per cent and sales by less than 1 per cent over the 2001–3 period. In contrast, sales dropped by 13 per cent and employment by over 14 per cent among firms paying more than the median annual earnings level. These trends can be seen using skill measures as well. Sales dropped by only 5 per cent for firms that did high levels of repetitive mass production, a relatively low-skill production style that requires little customized design. But sales dropped by 15 per cent for firms below the median on our measure of repetitive mass production.

Urban location may still provide some protection from the general trend against high-wage, high-skill firms. High-skill urban firms apparently have been able to weather the storm better than similar firms located further away from urban concentrations. To take one striking example, firms that are above the median on our measure of the percentage of sales from engineered-to-order products, and are also located in urban areas, lost 4 per cent of sales and 12 per cent of employment over the 2001–3 period. Firms that did similar percentages of engineer to order work but were located in areas that showed less urban concentration lost 20 per cent of both their sales and employment over the same period.

WHAT CAN (AND SHOULD) ECONOMIC DEVELOPMENT POLICY DO?

Our analysis suggests several ways in which markets may fail to maximize social welfare, leading to potential improvements from public policy. Below, we describe five types of market failures: wage externalities, information externalities, training externalities, coordination problems and liquidity constraints. These failures lead to the possibility that government intervention could increase social welfare. That is, a dollar of public spending might lead to more than a dollar's worth of benefits. Our research suggests that at least the first two forms of market failure may be operating, and that coordination problems may be present as well. It is also possible that government intervention could reduce social welfare. In this section, we examine these potential effects of government policy.

We will also examine other research on how the MEP program has performed in these areas, and present some new information from our survey on the extent of MEP use among these smaller firms. First, our findings on urban wages suggest a potential 'wage externality' for highly productive urban firms. Firms that pay a higher wage are advantageous to workers. However, profit-maximizing owners will not take into account the benefits of higher wages that accrue solely to workers. Luria (1996b) has found that certain production practices, such as capital intensity and distinctive products, are associated with higher wages.

We also found that firms in urban areas are more productive than are other firms, and that most of these productivity benefits are captured by wage earners. Assuming the correlation between urban location and productivity can be interpreted causally, since firm owners do not benefit much from the increased productivity of urban locations, they are likely to undervalue the urban productivity advantage, leading to inefficiently low urban employment. In economics language, the urban productivity advantage is largely an 'externality', a benefit not taken into account by those who make firm location decisions. Policies that benefit urban firms can remedy some of this inefficiency. That is, a dollar of tax money spent in some way on an urban firm has the potential to return more than a dollar of benefits to society, in the form of a rise in productivity that is shared among firm owners, workers and consumers.

Second, our finding that single-plant firms benefit from networking with other firms implies potential market failure. Information exchange is subject to many market failures. A key issue is that knowledge is 'expensive to produce, but cheap to reproduce' (Varian and Shapiro, 1998). That is, if one firm knows something, it is inefficient for another firm to discover that same thing for itself. Yet it is usually not profitable for a firm to give away its knowledge for nothing.[4] Therefore spending a dollar of tax money on knowledge diffusion may yield more than a dollar of benefits by avoiding duplication of discovery.

The discovery process is particularly expensive and difficult if changes are complementary (for example, if two modifications made together yield greater performance gains than the sum of the two modifications made separately). For example, adopting Toyota-inspired 'lean production techniques' leads to higher quality and lower inventory, but only if inventory reduction and quality control are coupled (MacDuffie, 1995). Each of these initiatives is complex, but firms that do inventory reduction without quality control are likely to be plagued by supply shortages.

A third problem is training externalities. In our data, we find that employees work for several firms during their careers. As Becker (1975) has pointed out, if workers are mobile, profit-maximizing firms will provide less than the socially optimal amount of general training, because they fear that they will not get the full benefit of their training expenditure because the trained employees will be hired away by other firms.

A fourth problem is liquidity constraints. Adopting the production processes that lead to high wages and high value-added requires capital and product development capability. These upgrading activities require fairly large upfront expenditures. Since many of these expenditures do not result in a tangible asset, banks are usually not willing to lend money to help finance them.

A final problem is coordination. Most component manufacturers serve a number of customers. We found that the typical firm gets only 30 per cent of its sales from its largest customer. If customers can rely on suppliers to provide timely delivery and high-quality products, they can adopt more efficient production processes. For example, they can eliminate receiving inspection and expediters. But if suppliers do not all invest in these activities, customers cannot risk running low-inventory production processes.

Our findings on urban agglomeration economies may also imply the potential for coordination failure, although this is unclear without further investigation of the causes of the agglomeration economies. If these economies depend on the simultaneous presence of many different types of firms and institutions, firms may create significant externalities by locating in urban areas. However our finding that cluster economies do not appear to be important for this manufacturing sector does lower the chance that these externalities are taking place within manufacturing; they are likely present in other supporting institutions or in urban infrastructure. Further research is necessary here.

The above processes suggest ways that government intervention could improve welfare, but there also are a variety of ways in which it could reduce welfare. It is possible that programs such as MEP might be welfare-reducing: by promoting capabilities that the market does not want, by subsidizing firms to do things they would otherwise pay for themselves, and by allowing low-wage firms to obtain skills they would otherwise have to pay higher wages to get.

As we have seen, the trend in component manufacturing appears to go against the types of firms that do relatively better in urban areas, and those that pay high wages. Above we considered the possibility that market failures are leading firms to underinvest (from a social point of view) in training, wages and capital. But it is also possible that public money spent on capability improvement does not have an acceptable rate of return even when these externalities are considered.

A second possibility is that subsidized assistance merely substitutes for expenditures on training and consulting services that firms (rather than taxpayers) would otherwise make themselves. Even worse is the possibility that subsidized assistance helps drive out more responsible competitors who develop capabilities on their own. In this scenario, the subsidy would be a negative externality to 'good' firms (Luria, 1996b).

To summarize briefly, we suggest that policy would be likely to be welfare-improving if it (a) promotes the growth of firms that are urban and high-wage, (b) provides firms with information about techniques that may be useful to them, and (c) helps suppliers and customers coordinate on adopting complementary modern manufacturing methods. It would be welfare-reducing if (a) firms were not able find a use for capabilities gained through MEP training, (b) it duplicated services already available on the private market, or (c) it primarily benefited low-wage firms (and did not lead to higher wages).

To move from theory to more specific policy options, there are three kinds of policies typically recommended for improving manufacturing. The first set is essentially transfers, such as tax reduction, from some other group toward manufacturers. Despite their strong backing by groups such as the National Association of Manufacturers, these policies typically do not influence plant location, let alone increase national welfare. The reason is that (a) taxes are a small part of manufacturers' costs and (b) when taxes fall, so do public services that manufacturers depend on, such as roads, police protection, education and so on (see the review by Lynch, 2004). The second set of policies tries to improve the supply of high-quality inputs, by subsidizing such activities as training, R&D and capital. Many of these policies have positive effects. The third set attempts to improve the way that the inputs are mixed together. That is, these policies attempt to change firms' production functions.

The Manufacturing Extension Partnership has tried to implement the second and third types of policies. The MEP program was loosely modeled on the agricultural extension program, although the rate of subsidy was much lower (Shapira, 1995). The MEP was set up in 1989 and is administered by the National Institute of Standards and Technology (NIST). Federal support for manufacturing extension activities grew from $6.1 million in 1988 to $138.4 million in 1995, before dropping to $106.6 million in recent years. Federal support to individual centers must be at least matched by state and local sources. Jarmin (1999) describes the activities of the centers:

> Manufacturing extension centers provide technical and business assistance to small and medium-sized manufacturers, much as agricultural extension agents do for farmers. This assistance often consists of providing 'off-the-shelf' solutions to technical problems. Examples might include helping a plant install a CAD/CAM system or switching to newer, lower cost, higher performance materials. Manufacturing extension centers can also channel more recent innovations generated in government and university laboratories to SMEs that lack access to such information. Besides helping plants adopt modern manufacturing technologies, most centers also offer business, marketing, and other 'softer' types of assistance.

How well have MEPs done in improving firm productivity? Jarmin (1999) conducted a careful study of the early years of the MEP program that is superior to what is possible with our data. Using the Census Bureau's Longitudinal Research Database, he estimated that productivity at MEP client firms rose 3.4–16 per cent more between 1987 and 1992, compared to productivity at non-client firms (depending on the method of estimation).

Jarmin's study takes a novel approach to the problem that participation in the program is not random. Firms who are either more productive than average (and therefore more aggressive) may be more likely to seek out the program, or firms who are less productive than average (and therefore more desperate for help) may be more likely to use the program. In either case, the estimates of the effect of the MEP 'treatment' will be biased. Jarmin corrected for this bias by observing that firms that are closer to an MEP are more likely to use it. His statistical method thus implicitly compares the productivity of two firms that are identical except that one is close to an MEP center and one is not.

Jarmin does not attempt to compare these benefits to the costs of the program. However a rough estimate is possible using data contained in Jarmin (1999) and in Shapira (2003). Project costs charged to the client average $67 787; Shapira says that these are typically one-third of total costs (one-third of the total comes from the federal government and one third from the state match), so total costs would be $191 361. If the increase in value-added is conservatively estimated at 3.4 per cent (Jarmin's lowest estimate), the average firm had $306 340 more value-added as a result of the program than it would have had otherwise. If we assume that the gain compared to non-clients dissipates over time, so that after five years value-added is the same as at non-clients, the payback period is 1.6 years – not a bad investment. If the productivity advantage continues, the investment is even more productive.

This result suggests that total benefits to society outweigh the costs. This finding, plus overwhelming reports by participants that the services provided were useful (Shapira, 2003), suggests that MEP is developing capabilities that have market applicability. However, the case for MEP intervention in the previous section relied heavily on the existence of externalities – benefits that flow to people other than those who make decisions for the firm. Benefits that flow to workers could relatively easily be measured by comparing wages in treatment and control groups. Using a different methodology, Luria (1997) did this comparison, and found no difference. The benefits to customers would be hard to measure. To the extent that the MEP program increases the supply of qualified suppliers, component prices will fall. This effect would cause measured productivity (dollar value of output/ labor hour) to fall, suggesting that Jarmin's estimate of total productivity increase is conservative.

Jarmin also provides data on who participates in MEP programs. Firms are much more likely to participate if an MEP center is geographically close to them. Since centers are more likely to be in urban areas, this benefits urban firms.

Small firms benefit more from MEP programs, but participate less. We found that most of the small firms we surveyed did not appear to take advantage of MEP assistance. Only 6 per cent of these small manufacturing firms reported receiving external assistance from a publicly supported manufacturing extension center at any time in the previous three years. Since these centers are especially aimed at small manufacturing firms, this is somewhat surprising (Shapira, 2003). There may be some recall error here, but use of the centers does not appear to be widespread in our sample.

Why do small firms make so little use of this resource? MEPs often teach courses piecemeal, without offering an overall improvement plan to the firm. Even if such a plan is offered, liquidity constraints and lack of organizational slack make it difficult for small firms to undertake a sustained program of improvement (Helper and Kiehl, 2004). Cutbacks in federal funding since the time of Jarmin's study have caused several MEPs, such as CAMP, the MEP in Northeast Ohio, to focus efforts even more on large firms which often require less subsidy (interview with CAMP president Stephen J. Gage, January 2004). On the other hand, the Pennsylvania MEPs are serving disproportionately small firms (Deloitte and Touche, 2004).

Most MEPs focus their work on either remedying information problems or coordination failures. They offer a wide variety of activities, and the programs emphasized by centers vary even within states. (For example, in Pennsylvania, some centers focus almost exclusively on teaching lean production, while others do very little on lean production and much more on introducing new technology.) However MEPs could do much more to remedy coordination failures by organizing their work around value chains rather than focusing on individual firms.

An exception is the consortial model of supply chain modernization used by the Wisconsin MEP. It set up the Wisconsin Manufacturers' Development Consortium (WMDC), which provides a single venue for training providers and trains suppliers in general (rather than OEM-specific) competencies, and promotes mutual learning by harmonizing supplier certification and encouraging cross-supplier communication. This framework meets diverse supplier needs through multiple institutional supports. For example, major improvements at formerly struggling suppliers resulted from a mix of WMDC supplier training, OEM-led (project-based) development and internal initiatives at suppliers (Whitford and Zeitlin, 2004).

There is limited evidence that MEPs are keeping alive 'bad' competitors. Deloitte and Touche (2004) found that the credit scores of Pennsylvania MEP clients are worse than those of non-clients. Deloitte and Touche argue that this is a positive finding, since it means that the MEPs are not cream skimming. On the other hand, low credit scores in the absence of some market failure may be an indication that MEPs are aiding inefficient firms. Jarmin

(1999) finds that the typical MEP user is a fast-growing, low-productivity firm. These firms could either be firms that have a distinctive product but are inefficient producers, or are low-cost, 'commodity' firms (Luria and Wiarda, 1996). If they are inefficient producers, Luria and Wiarda found that MEP customers improve faster than non-MEP customers in adopting most technologies, except information technologies. In his review of this literature, Shapira (2003) concludes that the studies 'suggest that not all desired policy outcomes can be achieved simultaneously'.

CONCLUSION

This chapter has argued that the Manufacturing Extension Partnership has been a modest success in its current form. A careful study by Jarmin finds significant productivity increases for MEP clients. A variety of studies suggest that the benefits to the public outweigh the costs (Shapira, 2003). Changes to the program could increase these spillover benefits, by renewing the focus on urban firms and coordinating more directly with firms' customers. It would be useful to restore MEP's ability to provide subsidized training, allowing the program to reach out with an integrated program to small firms that lack the capability to plan a coherent change effort, giving priority to firms that plan to increase wages as a result of the services.

However the MEP program is not universally popular. According to the Detroit Free Press (2004),

> Critics call the program corporate welfare and say it gives an unfair advantage to small companies. The Bush administration agrees, and has repeatedly tried to cut federal funding despite protests from Republicans in key election states like Michigan and Ohio. Michael LaFaive of the Mackinac Center for Public Policy, a Midland, Mich., think tank that promotes free markets, said the program uses tax revenue from companies that might otherwise have spent the money to train their own workers. 'Robbing Peter to pay Paul is no way to improve the overall economy,' he said.

These comments seem to misunderstand the nature of the program. In contrast to tax abatements, the MEP is not just a transfer from taxpayers to companies. As discussed above, MEP assistance improves efficiency, providing the potential to make companies' workers and taxpayers all better off. However, government intervention should not be the only response to market failures. The benefits of supplier upgrading accrue most strongly to manufacturers. Associations of these firms could capture the general interest that manufacturers share in an improved supply chain, and could internalize the training externality. Firms could maximize their collective self-interest by changing existing institutions (for example, by requiring measurable progress at suppliers in order for an OEM to renew its ISO quality certification). Private consultants can and do help with knowledge diffusion, but they tend to emphasize short-term cash generation rather than long-term capability development (Helper and Kiehl, 2004).

As Honeck (1998) points out, the USA has lacked an effective 'regional productivity coalition' that can lobby for broad-based industrial upgrading. Countries such as Germany, Italy and Japan have a more integrated, 'redundant' approach to industrial upgrading that the USA could learn from. However even an excellent program may not be enough to restore the health of a sector. There are frequent reports of Chinese firms that offer finished product for less than US makers' cost of raw material, because of cheap labor, subsidized capital and a subsidized exchange rate.

Thus the Manufacturing Extension Partnership is not a cure-all. A variety of policies are necessary to deal with a problem as multifaceted as manufacturing job loss. Such policies may include retraining for laid-off workers, and revised trade policies as a complement to an expanded MEP program.

NOTES

1. In fall 2004, the House of Representatives approved a FY2005 budget of $106 million for the program while the Senate Appropriations Committee approved $112 million (Taylor, 2004).
2. Based on data for the Fabricated Metal Products, Machinery, and Electrical Equipment manufacturing sectors, from the Bureau of Labor Statistics B series of establishment payroll data between June 2000 and June 2003 (http://www.bls.gov/webapps/legacy/cesbtab1. htm).
3. Our measure of urban location is the number of non-manufacturing firms located within 10 miles of the plant. Our measure of same-industry clustering is the number of firms in the plant's same two-digit industry located within ten miles of the plant. We derive these from the Zip Codes Business Pattern database.
4. Firms can benefit from 'know-how trading' with other firms that reciprocate (von Hippel, 1988) or by gaining a reputation as a cooperator (Rege, 2003). However, unless firms gain all of the benefit of the knowledge they share, there will be a partial externality.

COMMENTARY

Daniel Luria

In this interesting, ambitious paper, Helper and Stanley define and report on the performance of 250 component-sector firms surveyed in 2003. They find that plants located in dense concentrations of other plants have higher productivity, but that the higher pay levels at these more urban plants generally absorb most of the productivity premium. The urban productivity effect is stronger for design-intensive firms, but such firms, along with other high-pay companies, are actually growing more slowly than their lower-wage counterparts. Helper and Stanley surmise that these firms' inability to capture the gains from higher productivity for owners and managers may lead them to undervalue the 'urban productivity externality'.

In evaluating the largest federal program aimed at helping such manufacturers, the Commerce Department's Manufacturing Extension Partnership (MEP), they point out that a high priority should be placed on helping urban firms increase productivity yet more. However, they offer a sober assessment of some ways in which the MEP program might actually make things worse, undercutting high-pay urban firms by helping lower-wage firms 'to obtain skills they would otherwise have to pay higher wages to get'.

The authors' findings – that high productivity is not a predictor of sales or employment growth, and that untargeted productivity assistance could advantage lower-productivity vis-à-vis higher-productivity firms – are consistent with analyses of the Performance Benchmarking dataset from which their 2003 study population was drawn. My colleagues and I at the Michigan Manufacturing Technology Center (MMTC), who built and maintain this dataset, have noted these seeming anomalies as early as 1989 (see list of references). Helper and Stanley's main contribution may be to have ruled out a key hypothesized source of urban productivity advantage: the presumed formal and informal cooperation among firms in dense agglomerations of manufacturing activity.

POLICIES FOR PRODUCTIVITY

Since Helper and Stanley have carefully controlled for many other logical predictors of higher labor productivity, including capital stock per employee, one is left to conclude that the urban effect they uncover is primarily the result of higher labor quality, or 'skill'. Certainly this interpretation would be satisfyingly neoclassical, since this is precisely what the higher wage, in equilibrium with a higher marginal physical product, should reflect.

From a policy standpoint, it is also consistent with the thrust of many northern states' approach to economic attraction: rather than merely 'chase smokestacks', they seek to create 'cool cities' to which educated, presumably skilled, workers would wish to migrate.

WHERE CAN POLICY DO THE MOST?

I would like to finish this brief comment by trying to join Helper and Stanley in drawing out some implications for MEP and programs like it. Quite obviously, such programs should not be untargeted entitlements, but rather are better reserved for companies whose success will secure well-paid employment. This means a bias toward higher-wage urban firms.

Such programs need to be efficient with scarce resources, however, and there are a large number of urban firms. MEP should therefore focus on industry sectors that sell most of their output to industries that export or that compete significantly with imports. Because MEP is supported by state, as well as federal, public investment, sectors that also buy a high proportion of their input value within the state in which they are located should be favored. A set of 'screens' used in Wiarda and Luria (1989) and Luria *et al.* (1994) suggest that 14 Bureau of Economic Analysis two-digit final-goods and 12 two-digit intermediate-goods sectors qualify in 22 major metropolitan areas in the United States: Los Angeles–Long Beach, Anaheim–Santa Ana and San Jose–Santa Cruz (all in California); Hartford–New Britain and Bridgeport, Connecticut; Chicago, Illinois; Cincinnati, Cleveland and Dayton (all in Ohio); Philadelphia and Allentown–Bethlehem, Pennsylvania; St Louis, Missouri; Detroit, Michigan; Greensboro–Winston–Salem–High Point and Charlotte–Gastonia, North Carolina; Greenville–Spartanburg, South Carolina; Dallas–Fort Worth, Texas; Indianapolis, Indiana; Milwaukee, Wisconsin; Minneapolis–St Paul, Minnesota; and New York City and Nassau–Suffolk, New York. Some large industrial cities (Pittsburgh, Seattle, Atlanta, Houston, Boston and San Francisco–Oakland, among others) fail the screens, typically because they are no longer sufficiently manufacturing-intensive (Pittsburgh, Boston) or because their large final-goods companies show no particular preference for in-state, or even in-region, purchasing (Seattle, San Francisco–Oakland).

How does the siting of MEP centers match up against this logic of favoring urban firms in tight commercial linkage with other in-region firms? The 22 metropolitan areas just listed host 43 per cent of US manufacturing jobs. Fully 58 per cent of US factory jobs in industries in which imported goods satisfy at least one-third of apparent consumption are located there. Twenty, or one in three, MEP centers are in the states that are home to these 22 urban areas, but 14 of those 20 are located elsewhere in their states. Thus, for example, it is a good thing that Pennsylvania and New York have, between them, 13 of the 60 MEP centers to go with their four of 22 core metropolitan agglomerations. It is less clear that the center-in-every-state political logic that makes MEP service a small-manufacturer entitlement is as wise.

WHICH POLICY CONTENT?

At least as important as which sectors, in which urban places, can do the most with productivity-enhancing services, there are two critical remaining questions: which companies are the best candidates for intervention and which services would such companies benefit most from receiving?

The first of these issues should be: increasing the productivity of high-pay US urban firms facing threats to their survival and growth from low-wage firms in the US and elsewhere is job one. The second issue requires some further analysis. My and my colleagues' analysis of the same dataset used by Helper and Stanley concludes that, while there is a strong correlation between high worker pay and high productivity, there is a great deal of 'leakage' in the linkage between high productivity and high profits. As has already been noted, high-productivity component manufacturers are not just making the same output with fewer inputs, but different output (for example, more engineering-intensive products, which typically also take more office labor to define and sell) with more capital and lower, but better, labor inputs.

Our analysis finds that the key leakages are in the higher-productivity firms' excessive office labor associated with marketing, sales and distribution and with the low utilization of their larger capital stock. The clear implication is that the emphasis on factory-level 'lean manufacturing' services that accounts for at least half of MEP centers' service portfolio is better suited to low-wage than to high-wage, high-productivity manufacturers. Recall that this is an example of precisely the worst possibility raised by Helper and Stanley: that MEP centers could be subsidizing the better firms' lower-wage competitors. Instead, I argue, a service mix focused more on office function streamlining and higher asset utilization in high-wage metropolitan firms would be more likely to make a real contribution to the US economy.

4. Investing in the MEMS regional innovation networks and the commercialization infrastructure of older industrial states

Michael Fogarty

INTRODUCTION

Virtually every state seeks to identify and support early-stage technologies that are believed to offer significant economic development opportunities (Coburn, 1995). Ohio has identified and supported microelectrical mechanical systems (MEMS) as one such technology. (MEMS combines computation, sensing and actuation with miniaturization to make mechanical and electrical components.)[1]

This chapter uses the case of MEMS to illustrate the importance for a state or region of taking a 'systems' approach to guide investments in university research. By system, we mean 'regional innovation system', which includes the various components of a region's innovation infrastructure that interact to transform university research, industry and federal lab R&D into new technology. It also includes the region's commercialization infrastructure. Together the two components of a regional innovation system produce the specific innovations that create new companies and industries, generate a higher rate of productivity growth, and support a region's rising standard of living.

The analysis of the MEMS network (system) is dated. A surge in MEMS patenting began in about 1987 and has continued to the present. The patents we use to identify and examine the MEMS network cover the period 1985–95. However the underlying pattern identified in the chapter is not likely to have changed in any significant way; places like Ohio that were far behind in the mid-1990s will still be far behind when 2005 data are available. Nevertheless, given the pace of change, it is possible that prospects for a niche within Ohio may have improved significantly since 1995. Without new data and analysis, we simply do not know. However it is almost certainly the case that Ohio's overall MEMS position has not changed sufficiently to have overcome the disadvantaged status.

CAPTURING ECONOMIC BENEFITS FROM STATE S&T INVESTMENTS

A high *national* social rate of return to investment in a new technology is not sufficient to justify a state or region's investment in university research.[2] The reason is straightforward: knowledge spillovers are available to everyone, so benefits get widely dispersed. States and local areas face a dilemma, namely that top research programs are essential for producing globally competitive technology, but the most valuable research with the greatest commercial potential will quickly become known throughout the world. At best, geographic proximity of research confers only a temporary advantage on a region and its industries.

It is not enough to do the research, obtain patents, license the technology, or even create start-ups. To produce significant local economic benefits, new technology must be commercialized and take the form of investment in local facilities. This can occur either directly, through various university–industry mechanisms or paths, such as start-ups, further development of the technology by local industry R&D labs, attraction of new industry labs, or inducement of additional R&D by existing labs, or indirectly, by raising the area's education level and specific skills in support of important regional industries. One implication is that the ultimate destination of graduates from local institutions will substantially affect the calculation of pay-off from state and regional investments in research.

This chapter asks two basic questions: what can states do if they are not already a major player in the development of a new technology, and what mechanisms can be employed to increase the capture of technology?

The next section briefly describes Ohio's MEMS initiatives as of 2000. The third section explains why MEMS may be a good choice for Ohio, briefly discusses a new methodology for identifying a region's technology strengths and applies the methodology to MEMS, and asks: is BioMEMS a good niche for Ohio? The fourth section describes the components of a region's innovation system. Interactions characterizing the innovation system are then used to establish a framework for assessing Ohio's MEMS innovation system, which includes university research, MEMS infrastructure disciplines, university technology transfer and commercialization, and connections with Ohio industry. The final section presents conclusions and discusses implications.

OHIO'S MEMS INITIATIVES

Only about 200 firms worldwide were actively engaged in MEMS R&D in 2000. Roughly 80 of them were US firms; Japan was the second major player. According to the Department of Defense, the MEMS market was $1 billion in 1994. Projections made several years ago for 2000 range from $8 billion to $14 billion.

In keeping with technology's emerging character, the development of MEMS is strongly connected to research in university and government laboratories. About 30 university and government labs are actively pursuing MEMS technologies. Between 1989 and 2000, the National Science Foundation (NSF) sponsored 124 MEMS-related projects at 61 organizations (mainly universities), with funding of about $25 million. Approximately $1.4 million consists of SBIR grants.[3] Until recently, US industry investment in MEMS research was fairly modest (about $120 million in 1995). In contrast, federal R&D support of MEMS was a large component (about $35 million in the same year, of which $30 million came from the Department of Defense, mainly Defense Advanced Research Projects Agency (DARPA)).[4]

Ohio's MEMS Programs: will the Whole Exceed the Sum of its Parts?

Ohio is pursuing an impressive array of MEMS initiatives, all of which involve various government–university–industry partnerships. The state's funding of MEMS is intended to jump-start MEMS in Ohio's universities; that is, provide the seed funding to create competitive MEMS research with commercialization potential for Ohio. The state contributed to all four initiatives, with total funding of about $15 million (Governor of Ohio, 2000). While not explicitly stated, the hope is that investing in MEMS infrastructure and linking capabilities located around the state will compensate for the absence of a critical mass of MEMS capabilities in one metropolitan region.

The first of the four initiatives was MEMSnet, founded in 1995. MEMSnet, which is funded by the Ohio Board of Regents' Hayes Investment Fund, was developed to provide a statewide design, fabrication and testing infrastructure for MEMS. The participating institutions are Case Western Reserve University (CWRU), Ohio State University, University of Cincinnati, University of Toledo, Wright State University, University of Dayton, the Air Force Institute and the Cleveland Clinic Foundation.

The following summarizes the primary capabilities located in several of Ohio's universities.

- The Microfabrication Lab is a state-of-the-art facility with $8 million worth of equipment, including a recent $3.75 million facilities update that was funded by the Ohio Board of Regents and Case Western Reserve University.[5] The lab's purpose is to provide faculty and students at each of the participating institutions with access to the infrastructure for research on MEMS devices. The 5500-square-foot lab contains the clean-room facilities necessary to perform many types of MEMS processes. Case Western also has a separate MEMS laboratory, whose hardware and software assist in the design, testing and characterization of MEMS devices.
- The University of Cincinnati has two labs suitable for MEMS work. The first is an older, 4000-square-foot clean room that is fully functional. In 2000 the University was constructing a second clean room, which was to be a state-of-the-art facility, capable of supporting bioMEMS research. Faculty and students had begun to conduct research.
- Both Ohio State University and the Cleveland Clinic have bioMEMS facilities. Those at Ohio State, although usable, are still in a state of construction and expansion. Furthermore various laboratories at education and research institutions throughout the state have the potential to be utilized in MEMS research. The Medical Imaging Devices, Detectors and Biosensors Laboratory at the University of Akron, for example, are used for work on biosensors, which are increasingly important in bioMEMS work.

With leadership from Cleveland Tomorrow and Battelle, the Glennan Microsystems Initiative was founded in 1998. Its purpose was to help make Ohio a leader in the field of microsystems for harsh environments.[6] This was to be accomplished by cultivating closer interactions among NASA–Glennan, Case Western Reserve University and industry. With NASA's contribution of $16 million, Glennan was responsible for the lion's share of funding; the state had contributed $4.5 million.

The Consortium for Novel Microfabrication Methods Using Nonsilicon Materials began in 1999 with a grant of $1.4 million from the state. Its purpose was to establish Ohio as a leader in the trend toward nonsilicon microfabrication methods. The consortium involves partners at Ohio State University, the University of Cincinnati and Case. Funds were being used to upgrade Ohio State's facilities. The program offers new bioMEMS classes and introduces PhD students to clean-room facilities.

The Ohio MicroMD is a network of six Ohio labs at Ohio State, CWRU, the Cleveland Clinic Foundation, the University of Cincinnati, the University of Akron and Battelle. Its purpose is to use multidisciplinary teams to conduct collaborative research that will help commercialize academic and clinical research in the form of medical products. Education in bioMEMS is a primary goal of the consortium.

Building from a Disadvantaged Position as a Source of New Technology

This subsection briefly discusses the regional economics of MEMS. Our analysis of MEMS patents shows that only a handful of places are influential sources of MEMS technology. Ohio is a minor influence. The state's challenge is, first, to invest sufficiently to develop the critical mass necessary to overcome its disadvantaged position within the technology and, second, to invest strategically in the infrastructure necessary to commercialize and capture the technology within the state.[7]

Why MEMS seems to be a Good Choice

Why should Ohio invest in MEMS if the state is so far behind the leaders? MEMS seems to be a good Ohio choice for several reasons. First, the technology is highly important worldwide. Second, the data indicate that MEMS has the characteristic features of an 'enabling' technology: universities and government labs play a disproportionate role, R&D spillovers are broad-based (their effects cut across a number of industries)[8] and the technology is highly geographically concentrated (Fogarty *et al.*, 2002). Third, the market for MEMS is big: in 1999 it was projected to be $30 billion by 2004 (Systems Planning Corporation, 1999). Its major components, by market size, are information technology and peripherals, medical and biochemical, automotive, industrial and automation, environmental monitoring and telecommunications. Fourth, Ohio has several excellent MEMS assets and has shown a willingness to commit substantial new funding for research and development of the technology.

THE METHODOLOGY FOR IDENTIFYING MEMS REGIONAL TECHNOLOGY CAPABILITIES

New technology develops from complex interactions among numerous R&D labs located in particular places. The interactions among labs form R&D networks, which influence the rate of invention, the geography of spillovers (that is, the location of social benefits associated with a university's research and patents), innovation and technology diffusion. This section provides a brief description of the methodology for identifying and analyzing R&D networks using patents and patent citations.

R&D networks are constructed from interactions between R&D labs of particular organizations (for example, IBM or MIT) located in a specific region, working on a specific technology (for example, 'Dynamic Information Storage and Retrieval'), in a particular time period. Interactions are identified using the references on the front page of a patent, which serve the legal function of identifying 'prior art' upon which the current invention builds. These citations have been shown to capture knowledge flows among citing/cited organizations (Jaffe *et al.*, 2000). Patent citations are interpreted as reflecting communication. Communication takes many forms, which include reading papers, attendance at conferences, hiring consultants, word-of-mouth, analyses of patent data, hiring university graduates and personal communication.

R&D Networks: the Influence of a Region

Once nodes have been organized into networks, we measure the 'system influence' of each node. The estimate of each node's system influence is based on the strength of its communication with other nodes, weighted or compounded by the strength of communication of the interacting nodes with the rest of the system. Once network node strengths are mapped, it is possible to accumulate the 'system influence' of each node (that is, a measure of the influence of a particular lab, technology or metropolitan region within the innovation system). A region's influence within a specific technology, such as MEMS, reflects interactions within the region's R&D network as well as among MEMS R&D networks worldwide.

MEMS Patents

The data are drawn from the universe of patents granted by the US Patent Office from 1963 to 1995. Information on patent citations begins in 1977. Electronic data on assignee are available, beginning in 1969. We locate patents geographically, using the inventor's address, which means that location in our analysis is the R&D lab's location, not the headquarter (assignee) location. In addition to country and state, inventors have been sorted first into counties and then into metropolitan areas.

We developed a core database of about 1200 MEMS patents, starting with a short list of key inventors and federally funded MEMS projects. Citations of these initial patents were used to identify additional MEMS candidate patents. Each candidate patent abstract and exemplary claim was read to ensure that the patent was a MEMS technology.[9]

MEMS is Highly Geographically Concentrated

Our analysis of US regions shows that the development of MEMS is highly concentrated in a handful of places. The San Francisco Bay Area, Boston, Los Angeles, New York, Chicago and Dallas account for the bulk of the technology; Ohio is a minor player (Fogarty *et al.*, 2002).

Figure 4.1 graphs the relative MEMS influence of US metropolitan regions. (Regional influence is calculated in two ways: as a source and as a destination for knowledge flows, both of which are communicated in patent citations. The top metropolitan regions are distinguished by being influential as sources of as well as learners from R&D networks.)

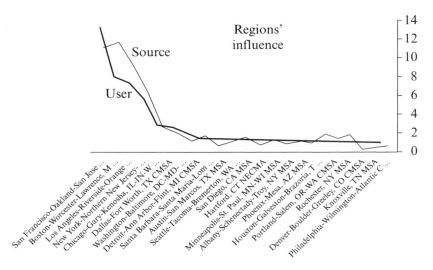

Figure 4.1   Regional distribution of MEMS technology, 1985–95

Following this figure are two additional charts: Figure 4.2 identifies the top 25 most influential MEMS technologies (patent classes); Figure 4.3 lists the top 25 most influential organizations producing MEMS technologies. Each was derived using the methodology described above. IBM was identified as the most influential organization. One university (MIT) and one federal R&D lab (the DOE) rank within the top 25 as a source of MEMS technologies.

An important characteristic of enabling networks is location in a successful regional agglomeration supportive of new technology development. In a pre-competitive, incubation phase, geography plays a critical function: the accumulation of a critical mass of strong network connections

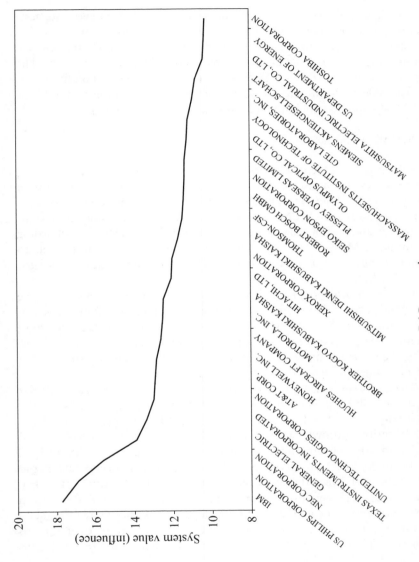

Figure 4.2   Fuzzy MEMS organization R&D networks

that speed growth of the enabling technology. Because R&D labs have a specific location, an agglomeration of strong R&D networks serves a dual function; good regional sources of a technology are also good learners worldwide.

A high degree of geographic concentration of MEMS technology suggests the necessity for a region to invest sufficiently to develop 'critical mass' to compete. As Figure 4.1 showed, not one of the top 20 MEMS regions is in Ohio. Only a handful of regions are real players (the top five or six). The implication is that Ohio's MEMS R&D network is weak, a condition that largely reflects the absence of a large number of well-connected industry R&D labs specializing in the technologies critical to MEMS.

A BioMEMS Niche?

The high geographic concentration of MEMS technology suggests that, to be successful, states like Ohio would have to identify a niche within a range of technologies represented by MEMS. Ohio cannot be competitive for all categories of MEMS, certainly not without impossibly large sums of money and a whole new cast of industry R&D labs. Therefore, choosing to invest in MEMS does not make sense unless Ohio commits itself to building sufficient scale to be competitive. One niche that has emerged is bioMEMS.

Figure 4.4 below depicts a hypothetical, stylized pattern reflecting one possible outcome that keeps advantaged regions in the lead for many years. The pattern indicated by MEMS as a whole, as well as other important technologies, suggests that markets tend to split regions into two groups: advantaged (a net inflow of ideas, talent, venture capital, investment) and disadvantaged (a net outflow of these key resources).

The figure shows a region's share of a specific technology in a particular year (say 2000) as depending on its share of the technology in an earlier year (say 1995). The technology results from the interactions of R&D organizations (knowledge flows) in our regional innovation system and technology transfer mechanisms linked to the region's university, Federal and industry R&D labs. Its shape and position reflect both capabilities and connections. To the left (places with sparse local MEMS R&D networks), the market works against the region; to the right (places with dense local R&D networks), the market works for the region. Without intervention by the state, a region with a share of the technology equal to A will tend to lose share (from A to B, C, D); a region with a share equal to E will tend to gain share (from E to F, G, H).

If this condition characterizes MEMS, then to overcome the disadvantage associated with a position below critical mass, public investment must raise

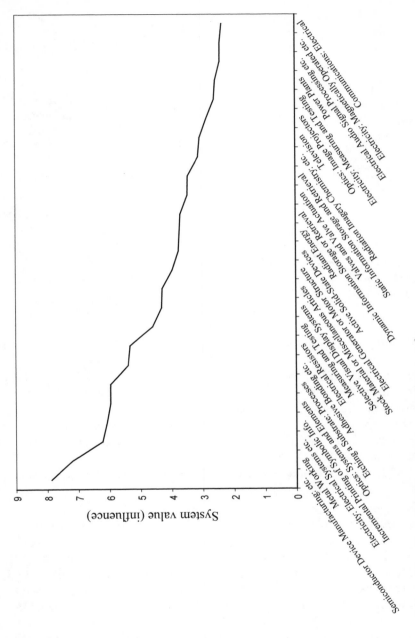

Figure 4.3   Fuzzy MEMs technology R&D networks

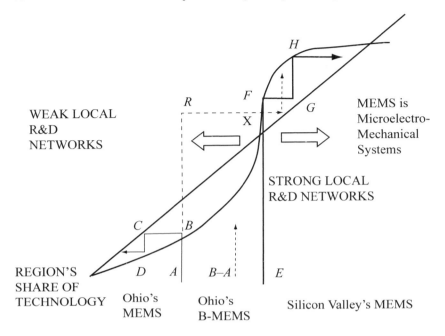

Figure 4.4   Geographic concentration reflects 'critical mass'

the state's MEMS' capabilities from *B* to *R* (above critical mass) to produce permanent effects. Above the critical mass share, the market would tend to work to the region's advantage, causing the flows to be reversed.

Developing a more informed policy requires learning more about the necessary scale for critical mass. The scale of investment necessary to achieve critical mass for bioMEMS is clearly less than what is necessary for all of MEMS. Because it represents a slice of MEMS, bioMEMS' scale would lie closer to the 'tipping point' *X*.

One Approach to Identifying a Region's Potential BioMEMS Influence

One indication of Ohio's prospects for bioMEMS comes from a comparison of metro regions' ranks in two technologies: biomedical devices and MEMS. These ranks include a separate analysis of R&D networks associated with biomedical devices using the same methodology as applied to MEMS (Fogarty *et al.*, 2000). Remarkably all of the country's top R&D centers are top-ranked in both technologies (the San Francisco Bay area, Los Angeles, Boston and New York–New Jersey). However, below these leaders, not one metropolitan region appears to play an influential role in both technologies. Within the Midwest, Minneapolis is clearly the next-best region. It ranks third as a source of biomedical device technologies and fourteenth in MEMS. Detroit is the Great Lakes top MEMS region, ranking eighth nationally. However, because Detroit is absent from the list of influential sources of biomedical device technologies, and because of its poor performance creating and building new companies, it is unlikely to become competitive in bioMEMS.

How do Ohio's metropolitan areas stack up? In MEMS, Cleveland ranked 25th in influence, while Columbus was well below, in 36th place. No other Ohio metropolitan area was ranked for the period we have analyzed (1985–95). For biomedical devices, Cincinnati (13th) and Cleveland (14th) were essentially tied. Columbus was ranked 17th.

SELECTING TECHNOLOGIES WITH 'BROAD-BASED' ECONOMIC BENEFITS

The economic benefits associated with investments in a specific technology will vary significantly to the extent that R&D (knowledge) spillovers are widely distributed across industry sectors. Of course the goal must be to invest in technologies that create significant spillovers for industries located in the state. This section illustrates the application of the methodology to the analysis of technology spillovers that cut across five broad industries: Automotive, Aerospace, IT, Advanced Materials and Bio-Medical Devices (Fogarty *et al.*, 2002).

Imagine an Ohio-funded MEMS R&D joint venture involving MIT, Honeywell and Xerox. Honeywell is ranked eighth and Xerox is ranked 13th in our full (worldwide) MEMS network. Suppose that the collaboration supports MEMS research that advances technology in one MEMS patent class, 'Dynamic Information Storage and Retrieval'. This patent class is highly ranked in both MEMS and the auto industry. Consequently it is reasonable to anticipate that, with diffusion, the auto industry would be a significant beneficiary of MEMS spillovers from the project.[10] Because organizations will vary in the extent to which their networks overlap the R&D networks underlying different industries, a state's choice of projects can significantly influence the distribution of spillovers across industries. One implication is that a state should seek to invest in technologies that produce spillovers for existing local industries, or industries with the potential to be local.

For example, MEMS' top patent class (Semiconductor Device Manufacturing) was ranked 16th in importance (influence) within the IT network.

Because of the defense and aerospace origins of the technology, MEMS has disproportionately created spillovers for the Aerospace industry (roughly 60 per cent of its total estimated spillovers). The second most important recipient of MEMS spillovers was Biomedical Devices (about one-fifth of the total). The remaining 20 per cent of spillovers were somewhat evenly distributed among the other three industries. The implication is that MEMS spillovers have influenced many of the core technologies of four of the five industries. This is shown by the relatively large number of top 25 technologies for each industry that were influenced by MEMS R&D spillovers from 1985 to 1995.[11]

The Crucial Importance of University–Industry Interactions

Universities play a central role in determining a region's capability for cultivating enabling technology. Evidence from previous research indicates how interactions between universities and industry reinforce the concentrated new technology pattern. For example, investments in projects with strong connections to San Francisco's MEMS network create more spillovers and faster development of the technology, reinforcing the Bay Area's advantaged status. This permits leading regions to capture a larger share of spillovers, both locally and worldwide (Fogarty and Sinha, 1999).

To gain insight into the way university–industry interactions shape knowledge flows among regions, previous research focused attention on universities' patents in nine US metropolitan regions (Consolidated Metropolitan Statistical Areas, or CMSAs) (ibid.). Our objective was to select places where universities are producing influential patents (university patents receiving at least 20 citations). The nine metropolitan regions are New York, San Francisco, LA, Boston, Chicago, Detroit, Philadelphia, Washington–Baltimore and Cleveland. The question we ask is, what are the geographic R&D spillover implications of influential university technology? The analysis incorporates all technologies for which university–industry interactions were important over the 1985–95 period. However we would anticipate a similar pattern for MEMS R&D networks.

The evidence indicates that strong regions (regions with a high 'system' value; that is, the most influential sources of new technology) learn disproportionately from universities, both locally and externally. Boston stands out as having an R&D network with exceptionally high local university–industry interactions. Among the nine regions, Cleveland has the least influential R&D center and learns the least from universities (both locally and from universities located elsewhere). This means that Cleveland's industry R&D labs interact very little with universities, indicating dominance by the region's mature technologies. Cleveland's scale of university–industry interaction is roughly one-eighth that of the San Francisco region. Further, like the other older industrial regions, Cleveland draws a low percentage of R&D spillovers from local university–industry interactions. Much of the difference between the two types of regions reflects two factors: the scale of research and the maturity of the technologies. One example is the increasing importance of electronics and computer technology relative to other technologies in automobiles. As a result, Cleveland's R&D is becoming less important to its own auto industry, while Silicon Valley's role is expanding.

Although this illustration covers all technologies, the finding is certainly important to MEMS. It is no accident that the top four MEMS regions are among the metropolitan regions exhibiting the strongest degree of interactions with universities. One implication is that R&D spillovers associated with interactions between universities and industry favor the 'advantaged' MEMS regions (the existing, dominant sources of MEMS). Without intervention, most knowledge flows would be absorbed by the dominant MEMS regions.

CAPTURING MEMS: THE REGIONAL INNOVATION SYSTEM MUST 'FIRE ON ALL CYLINDERS'

Building a critical mass of influential BioMEMS technology is necessary for producing significant economic benefits for the state, but it is certainly not sufficient. This section examines the second half of the regional innovation system – that is, the infrastructure essential to commercialize and capture the technology. Ohio's innovation system must 'fire on all cylinders' to have a reasonable chance of success (Barker, 1999).

Policy makers must invest in both capabilities and connections. Moreover the 'devil is in the details'. States such as Ohio must take the responsibility for understanding the details and fully utilizing all available mechanisms for capturing the economic benefits associated with its investments in research and technology.

This section uses the regional innovation system framework to illustrate some of the intricacies of the region's commercialization infrastructure by providing an initial assessment of Ohio's MEMS system. What stands out is that successful commercialization hinges on numerous mechanisms. The evidence presented makes it clear that we cannot take for granted the important connections that transform capabilities into a successful regional innovation system. Ohio would accomplish little by investing in a top-ranked MEMS research program if, for example, it had no companies capable of further developing the technology and then using it. Ohio will reap the benefits of its investments in MEMS only if there is a strong path between university and government lab research and Ohio's industries, and if the state organizes to capture the benefits (Fogarty and Sigha, 1999).

Seeing the innovation system as an interactive process with distinct quadrants helps to identify the major players in developing and commercializing a new technology. Figure 4.5 depicts the major components and connections that define the regional innovation system (research, industry R&D, technology and industry). Of course, these operate within a more complex system, including government policies, science and technology intermediaries, financial institutions and the entrepreneurial culture. Fundamental research is sometimes the starting point, and applied academic research sometimes yields more directly to production than to industry R&D.

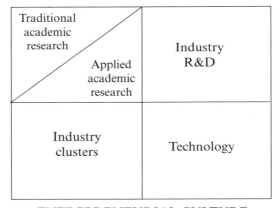

GOVERNMENT POLICIES
S&T INTERMEDIARIES
FINANCIAL INSTITUTIONS

ENTREPRENEURIAL CULTURE

Figure 4.5   The regional innovation system

The following are three common examples of system failure.

- Top-ranked fundamental research is coupled with ineffective technology-transfer/commercialization mechanisms. Very little technology moves out of the university. These are lost opportunities.[12]
- Top-ranked fundamental research is coupled with highly effective commercialization mechanisms but no connection to local industry R&D. The technology gets exported through faculty consulting, licensing, published papers, informal mechanisms involving university–industry

research centers, and graduates moving to other states or countries. One possible avenue for commercialization is start-ups.

- Top-ranked fundamental research and highly effective commercialization mechanisms are well matched to local industry R&D, but all production is located elsewhere. The technology gets exported to other states and countries.

OHIO'S MEMS INNOVATION SYSTEM

Ohio's MEMS innovation system consists of capabilities specific to MEMS and the mechanisms that connect them. These include (a) MEMS research (university, federal labs, research hospitals), (b) university MEMS infrastructure disciplines, (c) technology transfer infrastructure mechanisms (patents, licensing, start-ups, graduates, faculty consulting, local industry R&D lab connections, university–industry research centers), and (d) MEMS connections to local industry.

This section uses data on various components of Ohio's MEMS innovation system to characterize its strengths and weaknesses. The primary purpose of this exercise is to illustrate the importance of a systems approach to investments in university research and graduate programs as well as the commercialization infrastructure. One conclusion is that disadvantaged states must take a systems approach to supporting commercialization infrastructure (that is, utilize all mechanisms for capturing the technology).

MEMS and University Research

We can characterize Ohio's university MEMS basic research capabilities with two types of data: (1) receipt of MEMS grants from DARPA, and NIH from 1990 to 2000; and (2) the relative federal research funding for each institution's MEMS infrastructure disciplines. Because federal grants are awarded competitively, their receipt is a reasonable measure of a university's research capabilities.

A small handful of universities receive the lion's share of federal MEMS grants.[13] For example, California's receipt of MEMS NSF grants exceeds Ohio's by a factor of ten. The implication is that, in the aggregate, Ohio's universities are not competitive on a scale sufficient to make it a major player, despite specific Ohio professors' status as individual players.

MEMS Infrastructure Disciplines

Assessments of a university-based technology typically focus on the technology, neglecting the status of various core academic disciplines that serve as infrastructure for the technology. Building an excellent infrastructure for MEMS would help assure higher-quality MEMS research and increase the odds that Ohio will trigger a flow of new technology – not just a one-shot episode.

We asked some of Ohio's leading university MEMS researchers the following questions. What do you consider to be the 'infrastructure disciplines' for bioMEMS? Which university departments must be strong in order to support a strong MEMS research program? Each field was scored from one to five (five being highly significant).

To illustrate, one researcher rated infrastructure disciplines supporting bioMEMS as follows: FAR AND AWAY MOST IMPORTANT (5): Biomedical/Medical Science; VERY IMPORTANT (4): Chemistry; IMPORTANT (3): Materials Science and Engineering, Physics, Informatics, Electrical Engineering, Chemical Engineering. (All other fields are 1s and 2s, but mostly 1s.) We then analyzed each university's receipt of federal research support in 1998 by discipline, ranked as either 'highly important' (ranked 5) or 'very important' (ranked 4). To indicate the 'competitiveness' of the institution's discipline, we arbitrarily ranked infrastructure disciplines relative to the top quintile (that is, institutions among the top fifth among all universities in receipt of federal research funds, by discipline in 1998). To adjust for scale differences among universities (some places are simply larger), we made parallel calculations for research expenditures per degree awarded in the discipline.

Our analysis of Ohio's MEMS infrastructure disciplines identifies several very important university strengths (which we define as disciplines ranked in the top quintile nationally in receipt of federal research funds); it also shows several major gaps. What we find is that no one institution hosts all top-ranked infrastructure disciplines, even though Ohio as a whole does. (A more complete assessment would incorporate strengths residing in the state's research hospitals and government labs.) Given Ohio's fragmented MEMS capabilities, the effort to create a network of connections among the various capabilities is no surprise.

University Technology Transfer and Commercialization: Different Places use Different Mechanisms

To produce local economic benefits, various mechanisms must move knowledge between its academic settings to the marketplace. The mechanisms affecting the development and commercialization of university-based technology are more numerous and often more subtle than generally recognized. States tend to focus on the more visible 'technology transfer' aspects, such as licensing of university patents and start-ups.

The knowledge associated with university research and technology moves in many other ways, including graduates taking jobs with companies, faculty consulting, students and faculty doing industry research projects, interactions through university–industry research centers, and companies learning from academic papers and presentations. The narrower perspective substantially misses potentially valuable opportunities for localizing economic benefits. For disadvantaged region cases, such as Ohio's, the state must utilize all available mechanisms to increase the odds that economic benefits will land in the state.

This section initially analyzes university patents, licenses and start-up companies for each of Ohio's universities and a set of comparison institutions. (The index values are based on the full set of universities providing data to the Association for University Technology Managers [AUTM].)[14] In some cases, to adjust for scale of research, each calculation is measured relative to the sum of federal plus industry research dollars. Although the findings are not specific to MEMS, it is reasonable to assume that the general observations apply.

Patents and their importance
Figure 4.6 compares patents awarded to Ohio's universities over the past 30 years, ending in 2000. Altogether, the state's universities were granted 1275 patents. Patents provide only a crude indicator of the technology created from university research. One reason is that their value varies dramatically; most have little or no value. Figure 4.7 shows that, on a per-research-dollar basis, Ohio's institutions as a group compare favorably with leading research institutions, although the scale (quantity of research and patents) differs sharply.

One important indication of a patent's value is the number of citations (references) made to it in subsequent patents (patents that build on earlier patents). The number of references on subsequent patents has been shown to be correlated to the market value of the 'cited' patent (Lanjouw and Shankerman, 1997). Therefore we can improve our measures of university patenting by focusing on the number of patents receiving a large number of citations. Because of evidence indicating an important threshold, here we identify university patents from 1980 to 1995 that received more than ten citations.

If we use this measure, Ohio universities do not perform nearly as well as raw patent counts would indicate (see Figure 4.8). For example, a recent assessment of the 'technology strength' of the nation's universities shows that only Ohio State and CWRU are among the top 50, and both are ranked relatively low (Ohio State was 34 and Case Western was 47). Rankings are based on an assessment of patents awarded between 1994 and 1998.

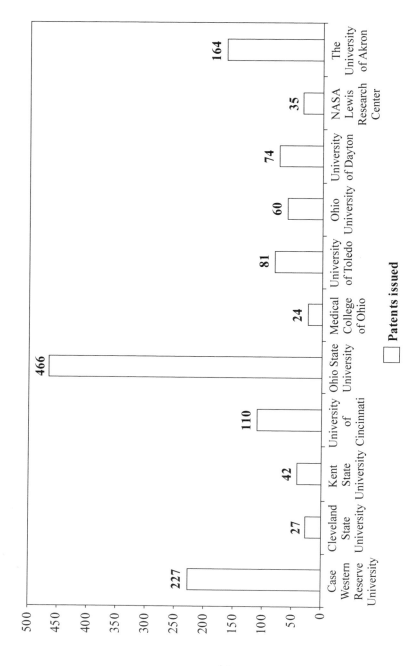

Figure 4.6 Ohio's university patenting activity in the last 30 years

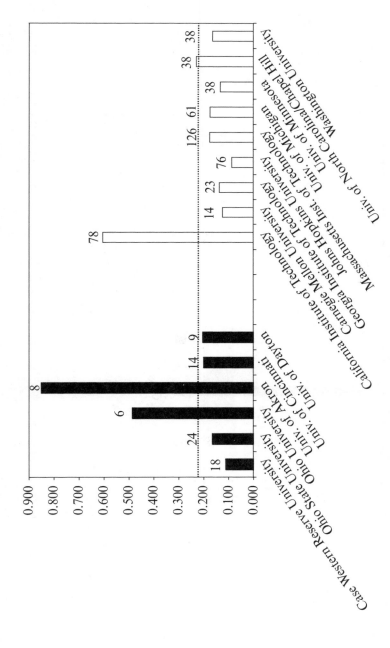

Figure 4.7 FY 1998 US patents per million $, federal plus industrial research expenditures

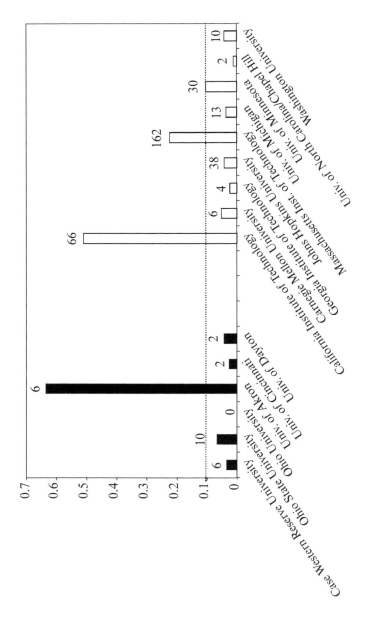

Figure 4.8   Patents cited 11+ times, 1980–95, per FY 1998 million $, federal plus industrial research expenditures

'Technological strength' is simply the number of US patents multiplied by an index that adjusts for the average number of patent citations received per patent (Zacks, 2000).

A relatively small number of universities contribute 'important' patents. For example, during the study period, MIT produced 162 highly cited patents, more than six times the number of important patents contributed by all of Ohio's universities. The difference reflects both the scale of research and the significance of the research for producing influential new technology.

To gauge a region's possibilities, it is useful to compare highly-cited university patents by metropolitan region. We summed university patents that have more than ten patent citations for all universities located in each metropolitan area from 1980 to 1995. Universities in Boston, for instance, produced nearly five times as many important patents as all Ohio universities combined. As with other key measures, influential university patents are disproportionately concentrated in a few dominant regions. Below Boston and the San Francisco Bay Area, there are few contenders.

Patent analysis can give states a powerful tool for developing a more strategic approach to investments in university research (Rivette and Klein, 2000). For example, university patents that receive a large number of citations are the best candidates for significant commercialization. The rich detail available on patents can help guide investments in a university's research infrastructure, strategically focus commercialization initiatives to maximize economic benefits for the state, and market university technology. Citations can also be analyzed to identify a state's potential industry partners in order to strengthen university–industry connections. Although an Ohio company may cite local university patents, it may be necessary to recruit the company to support a specific research program. More detailed analyses of citations to university patents can identify networks of R&D labs that can help build critical mass within Ohio for specific technologies, speeding up the commercialization process and increasing the capture of economic benefits for Ohio (Fogarty and Sinha, 1999).

Licensing of university technology
Ohio's universities do well in terms of licenses per research dollar in comparison with other universities (see Figure 4.9). Four of Ohio's six institutions rank within the top quintile on a licenses per-research-dollar basis. Ohio State's licensing rate in 1998 (licenses per research dollar) was roughly equivalent to that of the University of Michigan, which is probably a reasonable benchmark for a large research institution like Ohio State. OSU's total number of licenses differs largely due to the scale of research. In contrast, CWRU's licensing rate was about one-third that of Washington

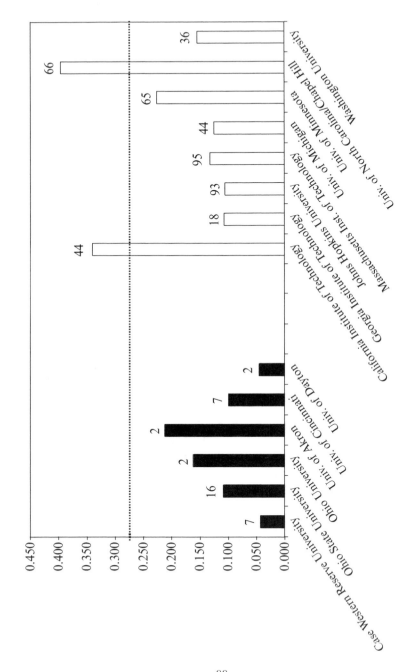

Figure 4.9   FY 1998 licenses per million $, federal plus industrial research expenditures

University, also indicating that scale matters a lot. Washington University licensed about five times as many patents as Case Western.

University start-ups
Start-ups reveal even more stark differences among institutions (see figure 4.10). One important observation is that places use different mechanisms to commercialize. For instance, on a per-research-dollar basis, Cal Tech dominates in starting companies; in contrast, they fall below MIT in the propensity to license. Without additional information we cannot judge the relative success of their respective start-ups or, certainly, the implications for localizing economic benefits. How good were the newly created companies? Have the start-ups been the genesis of a new local industry? Although the data do not exist, we would expect that these institutions also vary considerably with respect to less visible mechanisms, such as graduates taking jobs, faculty consulting and knowledge flows through published papers and presentations.

University–Industry Research Centers
State and local economic development personnel frequently assume that virtually any university–industry interaction creates economic development. University–Industry Research Centers (UIRCs) illustrate the importance of paying attention to the details embedded in specific mechanisms. UIRCs provide an important mechanism for influencing the mix and character of university research as well as increasing the speed of commercialization. But the composition of a UIRC's company sponsors can profoundly influence the likelihood of localization. The devil is in the details. For example, it would be foolish to represent a UIRC's commercialization potential by simply counting the number of company sponsors, perhaps weighting the count by the company's size (as measured by sales, for example), or by adding up industry funding or patents or licenses associated with the UIRC.

The mix of companies matters a lot. A good place to start in examining a UIRC's likely effectiveness in commercializing a university technology and capturing economic benefits is its membership list. Perhaps Ohio's best-known UIRC disappointment is the Center for Advanced Liquid Crystalline Optical Materials (ALCOM). ALCOM's 1998 membership list is impressive; it contains some of the country's leading companies (3M, Corning, Dow Chemical, Eastman Kodak, Hughes Research Laboratories, Lucent, National Semiconductor, Motorola, Polaroid, Raychem and Rockwell). The list truly is a testament to the importance of the liquid crystals technology originating in northeast Ohio. But only five of the 30 companies (one-sixth) have any Ohio presence. Another telling indication that knowledge associated with the technology was being exported is that

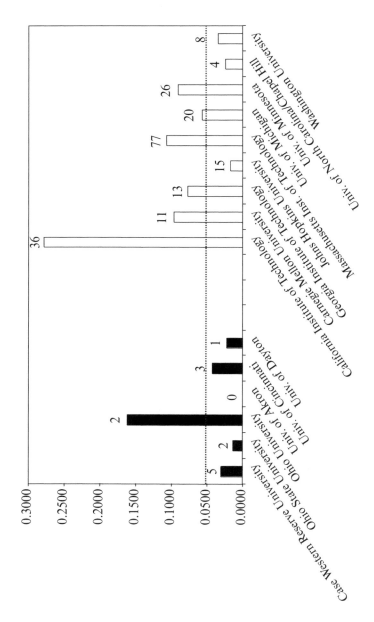

Figure 4.10 FY 1994–98 start-ups formed per million $, FY 1998, federal plus industrial research expenditures

not one of the roughly 500 citations of Kent State's liquid crystal patents by 2000 came from an Ohio company.

The membership list is a vital signal that the technology is important and known worldwide, which should be one goal for a state's S&T investments. In this case, however, the geographic and stature balance is too uneven. As pointed out earlier, states and local areas face a dilemma, namely, that top research programs are essential for producing globally competitive technology, but the most valuable research with the greatest commercial potential will quickly become known throughout the world. The best offense is to build from the temporary advantage conferred by geography, first, by investing in a technology that has significant local potential and, second, by creating a commercialization infrastructure that can capture a significant share of economic benefits.

Graduates

Graduates from programs affected by a MEMS research program can provide another critical connection to local industry – if they choose to stay in the state. Although our evidence is fragmented, it is clear that, while some MEMS graduates have taken local jobs, a disproportionately large number take jobs in the handful of states that are the dominant sources of MEMS technology and MEMS industry demand. California ranks first among these.

Information on MEMS graduate students was gathered from three sources: industry and academic interviews, the Internet, and a survey of MEMS graduates.[15] Of the 627 students to whom the survey was sent, only 52 returned their questionnaires, for a return rate of only 12 per cent. Consequently the findings should be interpreted as merely suggestive rather than definitive.

The most complete Ohio data were obtained from Case Western. Of its 36 MEMS graduates, seven took jobs in Ohio, representing 29 per cent of all known destinations. Three of these were employed by AMMI, which was a MEMS start-up company created by Professor Mehran Mehregany at CWRU. The same number took positions in California. Less formal data from the University of Cincinnati's MEMS program also suggest that graduates are employed in a variety of locations with companies such as Lucent, TI, Intel, GM and Nova Sensor. One student took a position with Delphi, an Akron firm. In 2000 Ohio State's program was too new to have developed a track record for MEMS graduates.

University of California–Berkeley's MEMS graduates illustrate the market imbalance. Of the 33 Berkeley graduates, two-thirds stayed in California. One took an assistant professor's position in electrical engineering at Case Western. Of the combined number of Case and Berkeley MEMS graduates, nearly one-half took positions in California. Given the school's location, California's MEMS graduates are more likely to take jobs locally (two-thirds) than Ohio's MEMS graduates (one-fourth). The location of demand for MEMS graduates (and the most influential MEMS university research) is clearly a major factor determining graduates' destination.

Although not comprehensive, data on MEMS employment opportunities by state give a pretty good reason for the imbalance illustrated by Ohio versus California: in 2000, 40 per cent of all posted MEMS jobs were located in California; three states (California, Massachusetts and Texas) account for two-thirds of all posted MEMS jobs; none were in Ohio. Ohio listed zero MEMS jobs. Even if the true number is not zero, clearly Ohio cannot hope to raise the percentage of graduates staying in Ohio by much without a significant increase in MEMS employment opportunities.

The survey evidence also suggests the potential for graduate students to contribute to local industry through UIRCs. For example, according to web site information, 34 of 52 respondents to the survey have a connection with a university–industry research center (UIRC) that is MEMS-affiliated. The high percentage of graduate student UIRC involvement highlights the significance of company sponsorship composition, especially the need to recruit the right Ohio companies as members.

Although based on only five cases, the data also show the potential significance of graduates as a means of accelerating technology transfer. One piece of corroborating evidence can be gleaned from patents at a company with an MEMS graduate as an inventor and references to the advisor's patents and/or published papers. (Patents can include references to both academic papers and prior patents.) Dissertation abstracts were used to identify thesis advisors. These data were coupled with patent records to trace graduates' patenting to companies. After applying various criteria to ascertain the link between the graduate and his/her institution, including analysis of non-patent references listed on a patent (possible ties to the graduate's faculty advisor), only five graduates could be analyzed.

The sparse evidence suggests the significance of working with an important faculty inventor during graduate school. One especially important MEMS advisor had been patenting since the 1970s and had 16 patents. Citations of these patents ranged from zero for a recent patent to 56. (More than ten citations is considered a large number, indicating potential commercial value and a higher likelihood of licensing.) The inference is that the former graduate student is building from his/her MEMS research while a student. Comparison with the graduate students of another faculty member, an influential inventor who had advised many students, found no patent links with those students.

Although the five examples represent few cases, they suggest the important possibility that programs and policy can increase commercialization and improve the local capture of technology embodied in the specific research experiences of students through company contacts with graduate students during graduate school.

Faculty connections with industry: a mid-1980s perspective

Faculty consulting is another critical, normally invisible mechanism that affects localization of benefits. Although there are no current data, given the significance of this mechanism, this section summarizes several important findings from a mid-1980s study that surveyed science and engineering (S&E) faculty at Case Western and Cleveland State regarding their consulting activity (Bania *et al.*, 1987). We conducted two surveys. The first investigated connections between industry and S&E faculty at Case and Cleveland State. (Because universities have become increasingly involved in commercialization, analogous data today would very likely reveal substantially greater involvement of S&E faculty with industry. We could only speculate concerning the extent to which current connections are local versus non-local.)

Roughly one-quarter of respondents from CWRU's S&E faculty had some regional connections; two-thirds had national connections. More than half of Case Western's faculty was actively consulting with industry. About half of the respondents helped industry recruit from their departments, participated in industry-funded projects, or used lab equipment jointly with industry. About 10 per cent were partners in a business venture; 4 per cent were members of a university–industry research consortia. Also one-quarter of Case's respondents obtained one or more patents during this period.

Most of the respondents from Cleveland State's S&E faculty responding to the survey had national and international affiliations. Like Case's faculty, their local and regional links were much weaker than their national connections. Slightly over half of respondents reported working on industry-funded projects and consulting, which are the most frequent connections (14 per cent and 17 per cent, respectively, did projects and consulting on a regular basis). About one-third helped industry recruit from their departments. Only 3 per cent of Cleveland State's S&E faculty reported being partners in a business venture; only 1 per cent were members of a university–industry research consortium. About 20 per cent of S&E faculty collaborated with researchers from another university or from industrial labs.

Northeast Ohio's R&D lab connections with local universities

We also surveyed 57 northeast Ohio R&D labs regarding their connections with local universities (via research, staff training and recruitment). Labs identified use of faculty consultants as their most 'intense' research tie. Thirty-six labs used faculty consultants; 25 of these were at a medium to high level. Next in importance was the use of university equipment, contracted projects and joint projects.

The results showed that most labs had some local activity. Proximity was reported to be the prime criterion for training. Department and faculty quality and availability of special equipment were the keys to research and recruitment decisions. Of the three primary activities, the lab's research connections reach farthest. These were being done in 22 other states and six countries (training and recruiting were much more limited geographically). However 34 of the 57 labs had some northeast Ohio research connection; 21 had connections elsewhere in Ohio (17 with Ohio State); 24 pursued research connections with neighboring states (PA, WV, IN, MI and KY); and 22 had research connections in other states.

These data, though 15 years old, deserve a new look. University links to Ohio's industry R&D are essential as a path for commercializing university technology. Evidence shows that local R&D labs are connected to the region's best-performing high-tech industries (Fogarty, 1998). But over the past decade Ohio's industry R&D labs have been shifting projects to other locations (ibid.).

Is MEMS Connecting with Ohio Industry?

Is MEMS connecting with Ohio industry? Unless companies build from the state's MEMS research and graduate programs, incorporating the resulting new technology in Ohio production facilities, investments in university research programs will have little effect on the state's economic performance.

A good start for examining Ohio's MEMS innovation system is to look at the companies involved in the state's MEMS initiatives. We identified companies that had become partners or affiliates of Ohio's MEMS research programs, including those of the Glennan Microsystems Initiative (GMI). Using data on patents by inventor location and company, we then determined whether each company had R&D or production facilities within Ohio.

Because many of these relationships are confidential, the picture is not comprehensive. Nevertheless it yields a sufficiently accurate portrait of industry connections within Ohio to draw several broad conclusions. First, by 2000, Ohio's MEMS initiatives had caused the growing involvement of some very interesting companies. Second, and most important, nearly half of these companies operate both R&D and production facilities in Ohio. The local connection between R&D and production raises the odds that benefits can be localized. (Only 20 per cent of affiliated companies clearly had neither Ohio R&D nor production facilities. We could not get the information for 24 per cent of the companies.)

One implication is that Ohio should examine these relationships very carefully to be better informed about the potential for capturing economic benefits linked to its science and technology investments. The state should also seek ways to strengthen connections strategically. For example, the likely pay-off from public investments in MEMS will be greater if there are incentives for developing university connections with companies that have both R&D and production facilities in Ohio.

CONCLUSIONS AND IMPLICATIONS

To have a chance of rebuilding their industries and communities, disadvantaged states must commit themselves to a new approach to economic development. First, as a prerequisite for making smart investments that support a successful strategy, these states must develop the analytical infrastructure necessary for accurately assessing the technology and economic strengths of their urban regions. Otherwise, almost certainly, they will continue to decline as sources of new, enabling technology.

Second, the disadvantaged states should use this information to guide investment in several niches, reflecting the science and technology capabilities of each of the state's metropolitan regions. Moreover the level of investment must be sufficient to create critical mass within a technology. A statewide network, constructed by the state to link geographically and institutionally fragmented S&T capabilities, cannot be a permanent solution to gaps in a state's regional capabilities.

Third, disadvantaged states must take a systems approach to supporting commercialization infrastructure (that is, utilize all mechanisms for capturing the technology). The broadest conclusion is that, to increase the likelihood of success, these states must take a much higher level of responsibility for understanding their economies and technology and connecting investments in science and technology to regional economic performance. The rest of this section discusses each of these conclusions.

Currently states make enormous investments in higher education and state S&T programs with the intent of creating new sources of economic development in highly disadvantaged regions. But typically they do this with very poor information. What is needed is a dramatic new commitment to what we might call 'Community R&D'. Community R&D should become a permanent policy research capability, much in the same way that high-tech corporations support their R&D labs in the pursuit of new technology. Such a capability requires comparable information on all states and metropolitan regions and a level of sophistication typically not associated with states, or with most of the consultants hired to do various studies. One challenge is to identify a state's technology strengths.

One possibility would be to develop the analytical capability as a partnership between states and one or two federal agencies with related responsibilities, such as the Advanced Technology Program or the Economic Development Administration. In other words, it makes more sense for states to share the capability. One could easily imagine collaborations formed among several states to pursue common issues.

Although universities must play a central role in the partnership, alternative institutional forms should be carefully considered. For example, one possibility would be a non-profit structure that would support a mission of sustained work ranging from fundamental research to implementation and evaluation of policies and programs. For a variety of reasons (for example, gaps in knowledge, insufficient funding and politics), quite a few states have tended to fragment S&T investments, that is, spread them among the various universities and communities. One implication has been separation of decisions about research from decisions about commercialization and connections to Ohio's industries.

The older industrial states cannot expect to turn around their mature economies unless they take a dramatically different approach. For example, the bioMEMS case suggests that a successful strategy may require choosing to invest primarily in one of Ohio's metropolitan regions. One partial solution to the politics of S&T investments would be to view MEMS as only one component of a portfolio of comparable science and technology investments, each tailored to a particular metro region's research capabilities and industries.

Ohio's Electromedical Industry

How might attention to regional capabilities affect Ohio's investments in MEMS? A rough approximation can be gleaned from data on the electromedical (EM) industry for the three largest metropolitan regions over the period 1990–96. Each region's national share of the EM industry, the degree of local EM concentration and the industry's total regional employment was calculated. Cleveland hosts the largest EM concentration; Cincinnati's concentration is lower, although its national industry share is growing whereas Cleveland's is not; Columbus has no concentration of the industry. A separate study ranked Cleveland–Akron, with employment of 16 000, 18th among biomedical regions nationally; Cincinnati ranked 28th. Columbus was not ranked in the top 30 metro regions. Both

Cleveland–Akron and Cincinnati rankings were based on employment in medical devices and instruments.

Can Ohio Substitute a Statewide Network for Localized Capabilities?

The analysis of MEMS infrastructure disciplines and related research strengths presents Ohio with a difficult challenge. Aware of its fragmented MEMS capabilities, Ohio has encouraged its research institutions to form stronger connections involving MEMS. This approach raises a fundamental question: can capabilities scattered around a state be networked, in effect compensating for a geographically fragmented MEMS strategy? The statewide network attempts to create connections where either none existed or where they are weak. This strategy offers the hope that, through various forms of communication and interaction, a substitute statewide network can be formed sufficient to compensate for the absence of strong localized MEMS capabilities (that is, the R&D networks, commercialization infrastructure and industry).

But the network supported by the state cannot be a substitute for an investment strategy that builds localized capabilities based on advantages in research, graduate programs and industry. In fact it could hinder strengthening of a state's regional innovation networks if the network redirects investments away from metropolitan regions and technologies with the greatest potential. The influence of Ohio's MEMS technology might increase with time, but not to the same extent as it would with equivalent investments in a single metropolitan location.

To utilize higher education investments to cultivate better-performing industries, the state must also form strong connections all the way from research to industry. Policy makers must be able to trace the benefits associated with each university's MEMS research to the state or specific local areas. This requires a new commitment by the state to understanding and utilizing all commercialization mechanisms effectively.

Measures frequently used to describe commercialization, such as patents, licenses and start-ups, are typically not very useful in evaluating the local economic significance of these investments. For example, citations of university patents must come from R&D labs located in the state for anyone to expect that Ohio's companies will build on Ohio's university research; a significant number of graduates must take jobs with Ohio companies; licenses must be developed with local companies that invest in the technology within Ohio; and start-ups have to originate locally – and stay local.

Our analysis shows that universities commercialize in many different forms, with varying degrees of success. To expect success, Ohio must become exceptional at utilizing every means at its disposal. For example, the data we presented on the destination of MEMS graduates demonstrate the potential for capturing economic benefits when graduates take jobs within the state. But they also show Ohio's difficulty in employing these graduates when it starts from a position of insufficient industry demand for them. It will take special patience, funding and hard work to create the necessary connections between MEMS graduate programs and existing companies.

Some connections are even less visible. The papers stemming from university research provide one example. Academic papers cited on corporate patents have recently been shown to represent the growing importance of university research in patenting, especially in biotechnology. Company patents increasingly identify academic papers as an important source of knowledge underpinning specific patents. The connections between universities and companies found in university patents, published papers and graduates underscore the significance of universities in the development of emerging, enabling technologies. The often invisible character of these connections should not stop the state from making investments based on knowledge of these connections.

NOTES

1. Applications are mainly in pressure sensors, optical switching, inertial sensors, fluid regulation and control, and mass data storage. These cut across a number of manufacturing industries, including sensors, industrial and residential controls, electronic components, computer peripherals, automotive and aerospace electronics, analytical instruments and office equipment. See US Department of Defense, 'Microelectromechanical Systems: A DoD Dual-Use Technology Industrial Assessment' (Final Report, December 1995).
2. Federal policy could explicitly choose to leverage its R&D funding by favoring projects and institutions in regions, such as Silicon Valley, where returns to R&D are clearly strong and increasing.
3. Universities are playing a critical role in the development of MEMS. Ranked in 1997 by total NSF support of MEMS projects, the top ten institutions included Stanford, University of California–Berkeley, University of Michigan, Cornell, University of Utah, University of Pennsylvania, University of Illinois–Chicago, Case Western Reserve University, University of Minnesota and University of Hawaii. Most of the MEMS university projects are associated with fairly extensive patenting. Our 1997 assessment indicated that the country's 61 MEMS universities accounted for 312 MEMS patents.
4. Our research showed that DARPA had funded 62 projects at 48 organizations (17 universities, 5 government labs, 18 large companies, and 8 small firms). DARPA funded five SBIR projects at four companies; they previously funded an additional five SBIR projects. The Army funded 17 MEMS-related projects at 14 firms through its SBIR program. The projects amount to nearly $2 million. NASA has sponsored 20 MEMS-related SBIR projects. (No dollar amount was available for these; however the MEMS

    working group at NASA–Lewis in Cleveland supported \$2.5 million of MEMS R&D by 17 S&Es.) Ohio MEMSnet funded \$2.4 million for capital investments in 1995 and 1996.

5.   See http://mems.cwru.edu/Pages/MFL/facilities.html.

6.   See http://www.glennan.org/.

7.   How would we know when Ohio's universities have achieved critical mass in research? One approach would be to examine the characteristics of the top university programs, including several that trail the top five or so but are moving up. We should expect several early indicators, including these: faculty members' papers are read and cited by leaders in the field (including industry researchers); programs find it easier to recruit top-notch faculty; a growing share of support for MEMS research comes from federal sources; universities receive applications from substantial numbers of outstanding MEMS graduate students; graduates are vigorously recruited by industry; leading companies seek to sponsor MEMS research programs; universities produce strong growth in MEMS invention disclosures and generate a growing number of frequently cited MEMS patents; ideas stemming from the state's MEMS research programs result in expanded seed- and venture-capital funding; research nurtures an expanding pool of MEMS start-ups; and the state's regions are beginning to create an increasingly visible group of companies that either produce or use MEMS devices.

8.   Our analysis suggests that R&D networks generating pre-competitive, enabling technologies may have certain characteristics, such as the following: (1) universities and government labs play significant roles as sources of the technology; (2) the R&D network is sparse and evolving; (3) the technology is new (for example, cited patents are relatively current); (4) total spillovers within the MEMS innovation system worldwide increase significantly and technology gets diffused rapidly; (5) influential companies perform significant basic research; and (6) technologies become geographically concentrated in important regions serving as incubators for the technology.

9.   The analysis of MEMS patents was done by David Hochfelder, a research assistant on the ATP project. Hochfelder has a Masters degree in electrical engineering.

10. Importantly, even though this patent class grew significantly in importance within the auto industry, its average rank over the period 1985–95 was not high. One implication is that it may be possible (and desirable) to analyze emerging technologies that trigger the evolution or change in the mix of influential technologies within particular industry sectors, such as autos.

11. The MEMS totals and percentages by industry are Auto: 1700 (8.4 per cent); Aerospace: 12 185 (60.0 per cent); Advanced Materials: 1422 (7.0 per cent); IT: 1117 (5.5 per cent); and Biomedical Devices: 3878 (19.1 per cent).

12. Ohio's liquid crystals case provides the best local example of how a missing component can cause loss of a highly important technology to other countries and regions. Because related R&D was being performed by well-established companies, and none of Ohio's R&D labs chose to build on Kent State University's research and patents, the technology was, for the most part, exported. The sharpest indication of this was that not one of the roughly 500 patent citations of Kent State University's liquid-crystals patents came from Ohio R&D labs (Jim Hoshiko, 'Polymer Displaced Liquid Crystals: A Case Study', unpublished paper, 1994).

13. Data from each source were obtained from the funding agency's website. We have included only those grants specifically categorized as MEMS as of about 2000. Consequently our calculations miss grants that support MEMS research but are not identified as MEMS; however it is likely that the two sources are highly correlated.

14. The data on university patents, licenses and start-ups are derived through various annual surveys by the Association of University Technology Managers (AUTM). The latest data are for 1998.

15. Melinda Miller conducted the survey as part of a Case economics honors thesis. See 'An Exploratory Examination of Ohio's Funding of MEMS Graduates Students',

Department of Economics, Case Western Reserve University, Spring 2000. The survey was posted on a web site and e-mail messages were sent to a sample of 627 MEMS students nationally. The return rate was only 12 per cent, excluding messages returned due to incorrect address. The highest return rate came from Berkeley, with 33/47 or 70 per cent; Cal Tech students provided the next highest return (30 per cent with 3/10).

COMMENTARY

William Seelbach

I would like to offer a few comments on 'Investing in the MEMs regional innovation networks and the commercialization infrastructure of older industrial states'. While I do not have any independent statistical analysis, my personal experience would support a number of Michael Fogarty's assertions about elements critical to gaining economic development (spin-off) benefits from R&D investments.

I would like to make four points. First, we need scale/critical mass in size and quality of R&D. In the case of Ohio, this means focusing on a niche, as Professor Fogarty suggests. Second, we need geographic proximity of industry R&D and especially industry product development and production. Third, we need robust commercialization mechanisms and multiple interaction points between universities and industry. This includes technology transfer and commercialization activities, as well as faculty consulting, student internships and other channels as Professor Fogarty points out. Fourth, we need supportive entrepreneurial and capital environments.

Given the above, I also agree with Professor Fogarty's assertion that a state or region trying to create economic development from research and development investment must take a systems approach. A region needs all of the previously mentioned elements if it is to succeed. Moreover it is highly likely that a disadvantaged state or region will have several gaps. Therefore creating some public capacity to analyze all elements of the system (and benchmarking against required scale) is important for states and regions to make smart investment decisions. Speaking from personal experience, I do not think that many of the analytic techniques and research approaches cited by Professor Fogarty are used by many state and local policy makers.

While I agree with the above assertions, I am not sure that Professor Fogarty has made a compelling case for the assertion that MEMS or bioMEMS is a good choice for Ohio to focus on. Looking at his analysis, Ohio did not historically have sufficient scale or critical mass. Moreover the state does not have a lot of industry overlap/interaction, and, at the time of Professor Fogarty's investigation, Ohio did not have supportive commercialization processes, although the situation is better today.

Finally, I think that Professor Fogarty's paper offers some interesting areas for follow-up research. One issue is this: how do we define critical mass and an adequate scale? Another is: how can fragmented university efforts in a state such as Ohio be networked to reach sufficient scale? Or are interorganizational barriers typically too great for there to be any chance of success?

5. Buying Ohioans' loyalty? How state financial aid affects brain drain

Eric Bettinger and Erin Riley

INTRODUCTION

Brain drain is a perennial issue concerning cities and markets of all sizes both here in the United States and abroad. Brain drain, or the loss of skilled human capital, often deprives cities of many of its most talented students – students in whom a state may have invested tens of thousands of dollars. Ambitious and educated young students often form 'a striving class of young Americans for whom race, ethnicity and geographic origin tend to be less meaningful than professional achievement, business connections and income' (Harden, 2003). And since job and schooling opportunities often draw these students and their incomes (and tax revenues) away from their home states, states have become increasingly attuned to competitive strategies that might stem this loss.

In Ohio, concern over brain drain has filtered down from policy makers to the general public, as the popular press often cites the brain drain struggle. For example, the *Cleveland Plain Dealer* labels brain drain from Cleveland a 'Quiet Crisis' (Livingston, 2003). In addition a recent Census Bureau report found that the Cleveland region was one of three of the USA's 20 largest metropolitan areas to lose young, single college graduates to other cities in the late 1990s (Census Report, 2003).

Policy makers, like the popular press, often concentrate on job development. However there are other policy options that may also affect brain drain. For example, policy makers have long recognized that academic institutions are one of the central battlegrounds in the fight to retain talented students. Academic institutions are often responsible for both importing and exporting talented students. They play a part in the major 'exit' points at which brain drain occurs: undergraduate college attendance, transitions from college to employment and graduate school attendance. And, often, an academic institution's goal to maximize its prestige by sending students to top jobs or universities conflicts with policy makers' desire to stem the outflow of top students.

State governments are one of the largest contributors to higher educational expenditures. In 2000–2001, state governments spent almost 150 billion dollars on higher educational institutions (Census, 2004) and, in recent years, states have become increasingly active in attempting to direct these expenditures in ways that may combat brain drain. For example, one of the central purposes of Georgia's Hope Scholarships, one of the largest state-run, merit-based scholarships in the nation, was to arrest the outflow of top students to neighboring states. Georgia's Hope Scholarships did just this. By 2002, Georgia had retained 76 per cent of students with SAT scores over 1500 as opposed to retaining only 23 per cent of them prior to Hope (Cornwell *et al.*, 2002).

While Georgia's Hope Scholarships potentially provide a model for other states, they are not without problems. Georgia has spent over 1.4 billion dollars giving scholarships to over 625 000 students, and, while top students have increasingly stayed in Georgia during their undergraduate education, it is not clear that Georgia has been able to retain these students after this point. Moreover it is unclear whether, why and how Georgia's Hope Scholarships or any other state-run scholarship program can influence students' location decisions after their college education.

This chapter seeks to identify and outline some of the mechanisms by which state-administered financial aid, particularly in the case of Ohio, may affect students' long-term mobility decisions. Financial aid may reduce the cost of education and provide short-run incentives for students to remain in a state. However it generally does not affect long-run decisions. This chapter argues that, if state-run financial aid programs affect long-run mobility, they do it by 'buying time' for 'life events' to occur.

By 'buying time', we mean that financial aid increases the amount of time an individual remains in a state. By 'life events', we mean significant events that may affect an individual's attachment to a specific region: marriage, child bearing and, in the case of entrepreneurs, business formation. Life events tend to increase the cost of moving from a given geographic location. While policy makers cannot legislate life events, the longer they can keep students in their state, the more likely these life events are to occur.

Additionally these life events play a significant role in the 'return migration' of students. The academic literature on brain drain often focuses squarely on students' decisions before and immediately after their education. However many individuals who initially leave a state for employment or schooling often return later in life. Academic analysis of brain drain often neglects these 'round-trippers' and, as we show in the chapter, this group is potentially large.

The first section of the chapter reviews previous academic work on brain drain and defines brain drain more exactly. In the second section we present a model to demonstrate the effects of both financial aid on students' short-term decision-making abilities and life events on students' mobility decisions. We outline descriptive evidence on the way life events influence mobility in the third section. The fourth section presents examples of state financial aid policies that affect brain drain and the fifth section concludes.

DEFINING BRAIN DRAIN

Brain drain is a longstanding, widespread problem both in the USA and throughout the world. The problem affects developing as well as highly industrialized economies, with the term 'brain drain' being coined in the 1950s by the Royal Society of London to describe the loss of scientists to the USA and Canada (Chu, 2004).

Nearly every American state, including states whose net student migration is much higher than Ohio's, complains about the affects of 'brain drain'. For example, Boston, a city renowned for its educational offerings, complains that over half if its recent college graduates have left for Atlanta, Georgia, Austin, Texas, California and other hubs for high-technology industries (Greater Boston Chamber of Commerce, 2003). These complaints illustrate the difficulty in defining brain drain. In 1998, Massachusetts lost 12 474 students to four-year colleges in other states. However they imported 21 302 students, realizing a net gain of 8828 students, the highest net gain of any state (US Department of Education, 1998). Boston likely absorbs much of this gain so the significance of their problem is questionable given that they start with a net inflow.

In addition to US states, both industrialized and developing foreign countries worry about brain drain, particularly the loss of educated young people to the USA. Developing countries, such as India, primarily worry about brain drain as students leave undergraduate institutions for careers in the United States. Students educated in India's top colleges and universities, especially those in technical fields, migrate to the USA in search of higher paying jobs. India Institute of Technology (IIT) professors have estimated that 25 to 30 per cent of graduates leave India immediately after graduation for more lucrative opportunities in the USA (Hariharan, 2004). An important implication of this brain drain is that investments in education will not lead to faster economic growth for India if the highly educated workforce continues to leave the country.

The loss of return on investment is an issue for developed countries to contend with as well. Amongst industrialized countries, Canada is especially concerned with this growing problem. De Voretz and Laryea (1998) estimated that 4.8 billion dollars were invested in managers and professionals who migrated to the USA between 1982 and 1996. This investment included 2.71 billion dollars of publicly funded post-secondary education.

While countries around the world are addressing brain drain as undergraduates leave for the higher paying jobs abroad, brain drain in the USA is a re-sorting of individuals to different markets rather than an exodus abroad. State policy makers are competing for their top students in several areas, not just wages or job opportunities, as some students take climate and amenities into account. However students migrate for different reasons at different times in their education or career. Students and their families face different pressures at each of the four major 'exit points' at which brain drain occurs: entry into college, entry into graduate school, entry into the workforce, and return migration later in life.

Undergraduate Attendance

The first point at which brain drain may occur is when students decide where to attend college between ages 17 and 20. Ohio has nearly 200 colleges and universities, including 52 public institutions, where students can receive undergraduate training. Many of these options, particularly the publicly funded institutions, are affordable. Thanks to aggressive building in the late 1960s, every student in the state lives within 30 miles of a public higher educational institution (OBR, 2001).

Yet, despite the large number of offerings in the state of Ohio in 1998, 10 424 students left Ohio and initially enrolled in colleges outside the state (US Department of Education, 1998). While this may appear small relative to the 57 843 Ohio residents who remain in the state for higher education, there are potential problems. First, most of the students who leave Ohio attend four-year colleges. Looking only at students initially enrolling in four-year colleges, Ohio loses almost 19 per cent. Second, many of these exiting students have high test scores and grade point averages (GPAs). Secondary schools and parents often encourage these students to attend the most prestigious institutions available. Shaker Heights School District, for example, was recently recognized as a top feeder school for the nation's elite colleges (Shaker 2004). Unfortunately Ohio lacks top-tier public higher educational institutions. The state's most prestigious public institutions, Ohio State University and Miami University, rank 60th and 64th in the US News and World Report rankings. Oberlin College, one of Ohio's top private undergraduate institutions, is small, enrolling only 750 first-year students, of which 92 per cent come from outside the state of Ohio (US News & World Report, 2004).

Ohio, however, may not experience significant brain drain in this period. Certainly Ohio loses a significant number of residents to other states, but, Oberlin and other colleges attract students from other states as well. In 1998, Ohio attracted slightly more students than left the state (U.S. Department of Education, 1998). The correct means of comparison should be to evaluate whether the net influx of students lowered the average college entrance exam scores of college freshmen in Ohio relative to Ohio's graduating high school seniors. Unfortunately we were unsuccessful in acquiring data to facilitate such a comparison.

Despite the fact that Ohio imports more students than it exports, there are still concerns about brain drain. Students who attend high school and college in the same state are more likely to remain in that state (Sumell *et al.*, 2003). It is likely that those students who migrate to Ohio for college will be harder to retain after graduation as they might not have the same ties to the region or state that in-state students have after graduation.

Over time, and barring changes in policy, the trend of students attending college outside Ohio will likely continue to rise. Since the late 1960s, transportation and communication costs have steadily dropped, increasing the likelihood that students, particularly top students, can easily attend colleges further from their home (Hoxby, 1997). As these costs continue to fall, Ohio students may continue to move elsewhere.

Graduate School Attendance

The next exit point for students to migrate out of their home state is graduate school. The pressures at this time are similar to those involved in choosing an undergraduate institution. A student may feel pressures for personal reasons as a result of life experiences (that is, relationships or family responsibilities) to remain close to home. However, while the student may have formed an attachment to the area, graduate school decisions may be largely affected by the cost of attendance and the prestige of the program.

The US News and World Report does not disaggregate the rankings for undergraduate, masters and doctoral degrees. Therefore the rankings reported above also reflect the quality of Ohio's postgraduate offerings. However a recent ranking of America's most successful 'feeder' colleges (Bernstein, 2003) suggests that Ohio may be exporting top students again. The rankings are based on a sample of 5000 students at the nation's top ranked business, law and medical schools and demonstrate which undergraduate institutions are most successful in placing students in top graduate schools. In Ohio, Case ranked 49th on the list of top 50 feeder schools in the country, while Miami University was ranked 22nd out of the top 30 feeder state schools. While it is not clear if this is due to institutional pressures or individual choice, it is clear that Ohio's best students may be exiting at the point of graduate school attendance.

Transition from School to Work

The next major group of exiting students includes those leaving their undergraduate and graduate programs to gain employment. There is a large literature focusing on how brain drain may be the result of shifting industries and the demand for workers. For example, Gottlieb (2001) argues that workers leave after either undergraduate or graduate education because they cannot find employment. Other factors, such as amenities or scholarship programs designed to attract or retain educated students, are only marginally effective, if at all. There are also suggestions that amenities such as transportation, entertainment and schools may also play an important role (Greenwood, 1985).

The academic literature also looks at brain drain as a response to educational milestones rather than a response to shifts in labor demand. Sumell *et al.* (2003) describe factors affecting students' migration after postgraduate degree studies. In general, students move to the state or region in which they will maximize their income, but other factors influence the decision. For example, marriage, children and work experience tend to increase the likelihood that students will remain in a given area. Students who are 'home grown', having received their PhD in the same state as their undergraduate degree and high school diploma, are more likely to stay as well. By contrast, younger students and those with higher debt burdens are more willing to leave the geographic area where they attended college.

Sumell *et al.* (2003) also describe how college quality interacts with brain drain. A graduate from a top ten program in a private school is far more likely to leave their immediate surroundings than a graduate from a lower-ranked public school.

Return Migration

The final group affected by brain drain includes people who may return to their home state later in life: 'round-trippers', as we refer to them in this chapter. Round-trippers are a group often ignored in the debate over brain drain, but are an important component for policy makers to consider. For instance, policy makers need to consider whether they are facing a loss if a student leaves the state to be educated at a top institution but later returns to their home market with additional human capital. Furthermore round trippers may return home with work experience, connections or venture capital that would only enhance their contribution to the local economy.

ECONOMIC MODEL OF MIGRATION

In this section we will model the choices that people make when deciding to move, examining what affects those choices and the role personal characteristics play.

Wage Considerations

People will seek to maximize their utility by maximizing their earnings potential. Therefore people will migrate, given a greater earnings potential. Wage considerations include not only the salary but the probability that a worker will find work at a higher rate. Simply put, individuals will migrate if there exists a city where $p_i w_i > p_o w_o$ where p_i is the probability of finding work at wage w_i in city i. Ignoring other factors, people will move from place to place to resolve this inequality. Since probability of employment is a factor in the decision to move, the availability of information will affect migration. As the distance from employment increases, that uncertainty may also increase, hence individuals will be less likely to move if the prospective job is further away.

Wage considerations also include the cost of living because it will affect the realized wage. Thus the wage w_o should be read as the relative wage. Hence one would expect that, if $(CPI^{-1}) \times (salary) \times (employment\ rate)$ is greater for city a than for city b, then people would flock from city to city as conditions changed. Consider the example in Table 5.1. This table shows price deflators, salaries and the average employment rate for Cleveland and San Francisco. Although the nominal wage is higher in San Francisco, the real wage difference is much smaller. It seems clear that people would still migrate from Cleveland to San Francisco. However wages and associated wage characteristics are not the only considerations when moving from city to city or state to state.

Table 5.1   City employment comparisons

	Consumer Price Index^{-1} (weighted)	Mean annual salary for management occupations	Employment rate	Total
Cleveland	0.005974	$80 140	0.938	449.07
San Francisco	0.005092	$103 240	0.956	502.57

Source: Bureau of Labor Statistics.

Non-wage Considerations

There are equally important non-wage factors, namely the amenities and characteristics of the city, as well as a person's individual characteristics. Different cities possess different amenities, as well as drawbacks which contribute to the overall quality of life. Cities that boast a strong economic outlook along with a vibrant culture (an active nightlife, sports teams, varied dining options, parks) will increase their ability both to attract new labor and to retain current residents. However a city is unable to alter all of the amenities that may attract or keep its residents. These unalterable attributes include natural amenities, namely location and climate. Proximity to the coast or mountains, average rainfall and temperature are all factors in an individual's migration decision. Cities which offer amenities similar to the ones described above will be highly attractive and, consistent with this view, quality of life variables may prove to be more important than economic variables in the long run for migration (Greenwood, 1985).

Cost of Moving

Economic theory predicts that migration will occur when $PV' - PV_0 - C > 0$, where PV' is the present discounted rate of future earnings in the new city, PV_0 is the present discounted rate of future earnings in the current city, and C is the cost of relocation. As the cost of moving increases or the wage differential decreases, the likelihood of migration decreases as well (Borjas, 1996). The cost of moving, like wage considerations, is determined in part by what a city offers its residents in terms both of economic opportunities and of quality of life. In addition, the longer an individual is a resident of a given metropolitan area, or state, the more likely they are to stay in the region (Sumell *et al.*, 2003). Our model characterizes this phenomenon as a change in costs. While the actual nominal amount to move is generally static, the non-dollar amount is dynamic and generally increasing over time. For example, an individual born, raised and educated in Columbus, Ohio will have ties to that area. They will have friends and most likely family. They will have business and social connections that have taken years to build. Additionally they will have accumulated information about their city and its potential offerings. If they move, they will lose this stock of information and will have to begin accumulating connections and information all over again. The stronger ones' connections are to a specific area, the higher the cost of moving.

Round-trippers and Uncertainty

If a decision to move is made, it is likely that there is some degree of uncertainty about the destination city and job opportunities. In other words, a great place on paper may not seem as attractive once an individual relocates. With any move there is a degree of uncertainty, and as the distance increases the uncertainty will also increase. People who relocate under uncertain conditions may migrate again, often to their place of residence before the move (DaVanzo, 1983). This may be because the information about economic considerations was faulty (difficult job market, lower than expected salary). On the other hand, amenities which are difficult to gauge may be lacking when compared to home. Finally a round-tripper may return home because the cost of being away from family, friends or business connections may prove too high. Individuals may return if they misjudged these costs or if the costs from being away from these connections continue to rise over time. Furthermore, as people start families and buy homes, costs of living and quality of education in the area may present new variables for consideration.

Public Policy and Decision to Migrate

Public policy can influence the model in a number of ways. For example, economic development may improve both the probability of getting jobs and individuals' earnings. These policies may discourage outward mobility.

There are additional policy options in the model. The longer a student can be enticed to stay in a region, the more likely their cost of moving will increase. Retaining students at the two exit points around education, attending undergraduate as well as graduate school, will lead to increased costs of migration. Scholarships and grants offer one way to keep a student in-state. Georgia's Hope Scholarships, for example, increased the likelihood of students attending college in the state of Georgia (Dynarski, 2000). The longer students remain in a state, the more likely life events may occur. Life events such as marriage, childbearing and entrepreneurial activity may permanently link an individual to a given region.

BRAIN DRAIN AND LIFE EVENTS

There are few data sources that reliably track individual mobility. While not ideal, the decennial census provides some information on individual mobility. The Census Bureau makes an anonymous 5 per cent sample available to researchers. The census includes information on where individuals lived five years earlier. It also includes individuals' state of birth and self-reported information about employment and education. We use these data to provide descriptive information about brain drain in Ohio.

Undergraduate Attendance

To isolate recent high school graduates, we limit our sample to students aged 18–21 who have finished high school. We restrict our sample further by looking at only those people who are currently enrolled in school and attending college. The 5 per cent public use sample of the census includes 289 565 such individuals, including 11 966 students living in Ohio as of 2000. We also focus on a subsample of 278 638 who lived in the United States five years earlier, presumably during their high-school years.

We track mobility patterns within this group. For example, nationwide, about 84 per cent of individuals lived in the same location in 2000 as they did in 1995. Ohioans, in this age group, are less likely to leave the state. About 90 per cent of college-bound Ohioans were still in the state of Ohio after five years. Georgia, which had been successful throughout the 1990s in retaining top students through its Hope Scholarships only retained about 85 per cent of college students from 1995 to 2000. Ohioans, like those in other states, are more successful at retaining students who attended high school and were born in the state. Ohio retains 90 per cent of such students, while the nationwide average is 86 per cent.

Table 5.2 includes some regressions of the likelihood that students do not migrate on student characteristics. Column 1 focuses on the national sample, while columns 2 and 3 focus on the subsamples of students from Ohio and Georgia, respectively. We include Georgia because of their unique and generous public scholarship program, mentioned above.

Nationally women and Caucasians are slightly less likely to stay in the same state. However, in Georgia, race and gender have no significant relationship. If an individual is married within their first year or so of college, it reduces their probability of staying in the same state in the national and Ohio samples.

Two key variables in this model are whether the students live in the same state as they were born and whether students were born in the same state where they lived five years ago. Students born in the same state are much more likely in every case to remain in the state. Nationwide the average is a 66 percentage point increase in the likelihood that students stay in the state where they were born. When looking at the students who lived in Ohio and Georgia five years ago, students were 14 percentage points and 13 percentage points, respectively, more likely to remain in the state if they were born there. The constant in this model can be interpreted as the proportion of students who are male, non-white, single and living in the same state as five years ago. These base probabilities of staying in state are similar across the national, Ohio and Georgia samples.

Table 5.2   Probabilities of staying in-state after high school

	National sample	Ohio sample	Georgia sample
Female	-0.005^{**}	-0.010^{*}	0.006
	(0.001)	(0.006)	(0.009)
White	-0.043^{**}	0.006	0.0001
	(0.001)	(0.009)	(0.010)
Ever married	-0.090^{**}	-0.098^{**}	0.017^{**}
	(0.002)	(0.010)	(0.013)
Born in same state	0.655^{**}	0.144^{**}	0.130^{**}
as now	(0.002)	(0.008)	(0.009)
Born in same state	-0.406^{**}		
as 5 years ago	(0.002)		
No years of college	-0.026^{**}	-0.004	0.016
completed	(0.006)	(0.046)	(0.049)
Currently attending college	-0.044	-0.036	-0.027
	(0.006)	(0.045)	(0.048)
Constant	0.794^{**}	0.793^{**}	0.723^{**}
	(0.006)	(0.046)	(0.049)
R-squared	0.34	0.04	0.03
N	278 638	11 864	6 619

Notes: Standard errors appear in parentheses; ** denotes significance over a 95 per cent confidence interval; * denotes significance over a 90 per cent confidence interval. The Ohio and Georgia samples are restricted to students living in the respective state five years earlier (dependent variable).

There are a few of key observations from these results. First, the relationship between marriage and location decisions appears negative, although it varies by state. Marriage at an early age does not seem to be positively related to location decisions. In the sample of college degree earners, this will be very different. Second, the probability of retaining someone who lived in the state five years ago increases if the student is native to that state, but decreases if that student is native of another state. This suggests that even by the end of high school, students have developed state-specific relationships which influence the likelihood that they will stay there. Students who graduated from high school in the same state where they were born are much less mobile than other students. Finally, despite Georgia's Hope Scholarship program, Georgia does not appear more successful than Ohio in retaining students who attended high school in the same state. Ohioans are as likely to stay in Ohio if they were born there as Georgians born in Georgia. This does not mean that the Georgia Hope program does not affect geographic location. There may be other explanations. For example, Georgia may have improved its student retention dramatically over this period relative to Ohio.

Transition to the Labor Market after Undergraduate Studies

A second major point where brain drain occurs is the transition from undergraduate studies to the labor market. To understand how life events affect mobility decisions at this point in time, we limit our sample to students aged 21–25 who have completed at least a four-year degree in college. The 5 per cent public-use sample of the census includes 118 522 such individuals, including 4500 students living in Ohio as of 2000. We also focus on a subsample of 111 721 of these individuals for whom we can verify where they lived five years earlier, presumably during their undergraduate education.

Table 5.3 examines the probability that these students have not moved over the last five years. Like Table 5.2, the table focuses on students in a nationwide sample and in subsamples from Georgia and Ohio. Women are slightly less likely to move in the national and Ohio samples. Whites are less likely to be in the same state, although in Ohio they appear more likely to do so. As before, being born in the respective state dramatically increases the probability that one stays in the state.

In Table 5.2, marriage negatively affected the likelihood of staying in the same state in the nationwide sample and in Ohio. In Table 5.3, there is no significant relationship between the likelihood of staying and marriage. In the Georgia sample, there is even a positive correlation. Additionally having children has a positive relationship with the probability that one stays in the same state. These life events become more important in individual's location decisions. Labor market activity is not a significant predictor, although entrepreneurial activity, particularly in Ohio, is a marginally significant predictor of students staying in the same state.

Overall Ohio has a slightly higher retention rate than the national average. Nationally about 73 per cent of recent college graduates stay in the state where they did their undergraduate work. In Ohio, the average is 75 per cent. Georgia's retention rate is even higher, as it is able to retain 77 per cent of its recent graduates. Ohio is particularly able to keep students who lived in Ohio five years ago and were born in Ohio, with 81 per cent of these students staying in the state after graduation.

Transition from Graduate Studies to Labor Force

Another point when brain drain occurs is the transition from graduate studies to the labor market. To understand how these students make decisions, we

Table 5.3   Probabilities of staying in-state after undergraduate studies

	National sample	Ohio sample	Georgia sample
Female	0.008**	0.042**	0.016
	(0.002)	(0.015)	(0.016)
White	–0.092**	0.032**	–0.037**
	(0.003)	(0.012)	(0.019)
Ever married	0.004	0.017	0.032*
	(0.003)	(0.015)	(0.019)
Number of children	0.024**	0.043**	0.033
	(0.003)	(0.019)	(0.023)
Born in same state	0.596**	0.250**	0.200**
as now	(0.003)	(0.014)	(0.016)
Born in same state as	–0.202**		
5 years ago	(0.003)		
Active in labor market	–0.001	0.013	0.008
	(0.003)	(0.021)	(0.024)
Self-employed	0.014*	0.093*	–0.017
	(0.008)	(0.051)	(0.057)
Currently attending college	0.008**	0.025*	–0.039**
	(0.003)	(0.014)	(0.019)
Constant	0.596**	0.461**	0.667**
	(0.005)	(0.031)	(0.031)
R-squared	0.29	0.07	0.06
N	111 721	4 703	2 643

Notes: Standard errors appear in parentheses; ** denotes significance over a 95 per cent confidence interval; * denotes significance over a 90 per cent confidence interval. The Ohio and Georgia samples are restricted to students living in the respective state five years earlier (dependent variable).

limit our sample to students aged 22 to 35 who have completed at least a Master's, Doctorate or Professional Degree. The 5 per cent public-use sample of the census includes 150 773 such individuals, including 5021 students living in Ohio as of 2000. We also focus on a subsample of 134 637 of these individuals for whom we can verify where they lived five years earlier, presumably at a time close to their graduate education.

Table 5.4 examines the probability that these students have not moved over the last five years. As in the other tables, Table 5.4 focuses on students in a nationwide sample and in subsamples from Georgia and Ohio. Similar to other tables, it shows women are less likely to move. Whites are slightly more likely to move in the national sample, but less so in Ohio. As before, being born in the respective state also increases the probability that one stays in the state.

Table 5.4 Probabilities of staying in-state after graduate school

	National sample	Ohio sample	Georgia sample
Female	0.0413**	0.0483**	0.0623**
	(0.0024)	(0.0125)	(0.0142)
White	−0.0415**	0.0358**	−0.0250
	(0.0030)	(0.0179)	(0.0167)
Ever married	0.0138**	0.0290**	0.0039
	(0.0027)	(0.0146)	(0.0165)
Number of children	0.0340**	0.0551**	0.0453**
	(0.0014)	(0.0069)	(0.0081)
Born in same state as now	0.3282**	0.2569**	0.2571**
	(0.0037)	(0.0130)	(0.0146)
Born in same state as 5 years ago	−0.0171**		
	(0.0036)		
Active in labor market	0.0077**	0.0232	0.0412*
	(0.0039)	(0.0229)	(0.0229)
Self-employed	0.0618**	0.0787**	0.0558**
	(0.0049)	(0.0272)	(0.0270)
Currently attending college	0.0186**	0.0107	−0.0343*
	(0.0033)	(0.0175)	(0.0196)
Has PhD	−0.1038**	−0.1339**	−0.1298**
	(0.0047)	(0.0252)	(0.0273)
Has professional degree	−0.0107**	−0.0259*	−0.0315*
	(0.0028)	(0.0148)	(0.0170)
Constant	0.5519	0.4296	0.5403
R-squared	0.1326	0.1197	0.1025
N	134 637	4 907	3 979

Notes: Standard errors appear in parentheses; ** denotes significance over a 95 per cent confidence interval; the Ohio and Georgia samples are restricted to students living in the respective state five years earlier (dependent variable).

In Table 5.4, unlike earlier tables, there is a significant positive impact of marriage. If one is married by the end of graduate school, one is more likely to stay in the state. Having children also increases the probability that one stays in the same state. These life events significantly influence the likelihood of students staying in the same state.

The labor market also positively affects location decisions. Being active in the labor market increases the probability that students remain in the state in which they attended their undergraduate institution. Self-employment also positively affects enrollment decisions. The relationship of self-employment and mobility is consistent with the existing literature on the individual decision to become an entrepreneur (see Shane, 2003, for review of literature). Entrepreneurs are more likely to be active in areas where they have significant social networks (Aldrich, 1999). These social networks are likely to be formed through experience in the state. Entrepreneurs are more successful if they know potential investors before starting their business (Shane and Stuart, 2002). Interestingly individuals who are married or who are married with a working spouse are also more likely to engage in entrepreneurial activity (Shane, 2003).

Table 5.4 also demonstrates other difficulties in Ohio and other states with brain drain. Students who have completed advanced degrees, particularly doctoral degrees, are much less likely to stay in the same state after five years. Considering that about 7 per cent of this sample has completed or is currently attempting doctoral degrees, this is a significant loss; however Ohio's loss is only slightly worse than the nationwide average. Census data are limited for tracking the mobility patterns for these students. It is unclear whether the mobility observed in this chapter is the result of new doctorate holders finding work in other states after attending undergraduate and graduate studies in their native states, or whether the mobility arises from native students who completed their degrees in other states and then returned home. Sumell *et al.* (2003) provides a more in-depth analysis of doctoral recipients' mobility decisions. A key finding in their paper is that doctoral students are less likely to leave their state of residence if they completed their undergraduate studies in the same state, and even more so if they have additional experience in the same state.

Return Trippers

The literature on brain drain frequently ignores individuals who return to their native state later in life. We are particularly interested in individuals with college degrees and whether they return. To identify these patterns, we limit our sample to individuals ages 35 to 55 who had at least a bachelor's degree. In the 5 per cent sample of the census, there were 2 279 742 individuals, including 84 049 from Ohio. One of the weaknesses in census data is that we only observe three locations: birthplace, location five years ago and current location. Many people may have been born in Ohio but quickly lost contact with the state. While ideally we would have more information about individuals' mobility patterns, we make the assumption that people born in Ohio have a permanent link to the state. While this clearly is an overstatement, it is a useful benchmark for describing retention of college graduates later in life.

Figure 5.1 plots the retention rate of Ohioans and of the nation by age. The Ohio retention rate shows what proportion of native Ohioans who have college degrees are currently living in Ohio. The national retention rates show the proportion of people currently living in their state of birth. Ohio's average is high relative to the national average. At age 35, about 58 per cent of native Ohioans are living in Ohio. This number slowly (and somewhat erratically) declines until it reaches 55 per cent around ages 45 to 48. Past age 48, as in the national average, the proportion of native Ohioans in Ohio declines until it reaches 50 per cent at age 55. The national average is fairly static from age 35 to 47, hovering near 50 per cent. After age 48, it too begins to decline reaching its low at 43 per cent at age 55. While college graduates continue to leave Ohio later in life, Ohio fares much better than the national average.

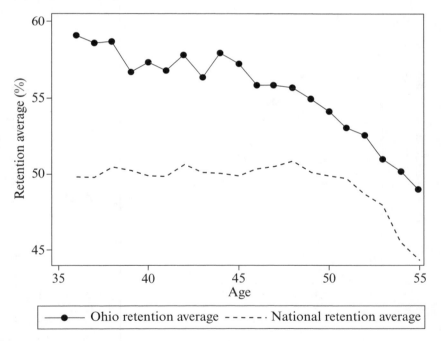

Figure 5.1   Retaining native born residents, by age

One of the goals of this chapter was to identify what proportion of native Ohioans return later in life. To do this, we restrict our sample to indi-

viduals who five years ago were not living in their state of birth. There are
1 127 007 such individuals in our sample. We call these people 'returners' if
they move back to the state of their birth after leaving that state. Nationwide
only 3 per cent of such individuals return between ages 35 and 55. Ohio's
average is 4 per cent.

 As Figure 5.2 illustrates, the rate of return of Ohioans is higher than that
of the rest of the nation until the late 40s. After about age 48, the trend in
Ohio is similar to the national trend. Of particular interest is the returning
rate of college graduates between the ages of 25 and 35. In this period, Ohio
is three to four percentage points above the national average. This boom of
return Ohioans is often forgotten. Many of the students who leave in their
early 20s return shortly thereafter. These ages are particularly common
ages for child rearing. One caveat, however, is that among the returning
native Ohioans few have doctoral degrees. Among returners aged 35 to

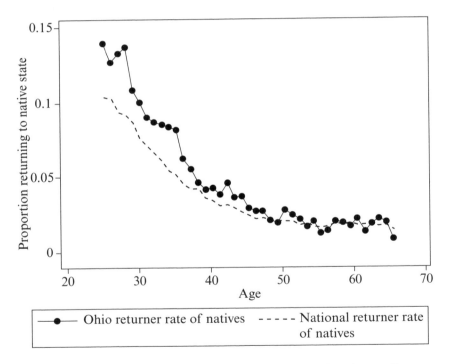

Note: Sample is restricted to individuals who were not living in their native state five years
earlier. The proportion returning to their native state is defined as the proportion of people
living in Ohio divided by the total number of individuals born in Ohio.

Figure 5.2   Probability of native born resident returning

55 in Ohio, 1.6 per cent of returners have doctoral degrees while 2.6 per cent of non-returners have doctoral degrees. This difference is statistically significant over a 95 per cent confidence interval.

STATE POLICIES TO COMBAT BRAIN DRAIN

Most policies looking to reduce the negative effects of brain drain focus on business development and economic improvement, such as the Third Frontier in Ohio. Though these solutions are popular tools for state policy makers to address brain drain through business formation, this chapter focuses on policies that use financial aid to affect migration decisions. As we have shown, the longer a student remains in-state the greater the likelihood he or she will stay in the future. Policies aimed at stemming the outflow at exit points during education or early in a career may be effective in fighting the brain drain.

Innovative Programs after High School

Encouraging students to attend Ohio's post-secondary schools is an important aspect of addressing the brain drain. While several institutions in the state offer both financial and merit aid, there is no comprehensive program in place to retain Ohio's best and brightest high school graduates. However many programs are in place throughout the USA that attempt to do just that. The first of these comprehensive programs was Georgia's Hope Scholarship, mentioned throughout this chapter.

In Georgia, the Hope Scholarship was implemented in 1992 to help retain the state's top high school graduates. The program, paid for in part by the state lottery, provides students with a B or better average with full tuition, a book allowance and money for mandatory fees if they attend a public college in the state. Students choosing to attend a private college in-state receive $3000 and an additional $1045 dollars from the Georgia Tuition Equalization Grant if they qualify. Ten years after implementing the program, the state retained 76 per cent of students with SAT scores over 1500 as opposed to retaining only 23 per cent of them prior to Hope (Cornwell *et al.* 2002).

Ohio does not offer scholarships statewide on the same scale as Hope or similar programs in other states. There are a handful of merit-based awards for the elite students, but there are few enough awards for the program probably not to affect brain drain of top students. There are also Ohio Choice Grants. However the goal of the Choice Grants is not to retain top students but to narrow the tuition gap between public and private universities. In 2002–3, the grant was worth only $1038 for any Ohio resident attending a private school in state (Ohio Board of Regents, 2004).

One caution, however, is in order. The Georgia Hope Scholarship program was extremely expensive. Georgia has spent over 1.4 billion dollars giving scholarships to over 625 000 students. While part of the purpose of Georgia's program was to increase college access, one of the other stated purposes was to decrease brain drain. Georgia likely would have retained half of these students regardless of the scholarship program. Moreover we are still awaiting evidence on whether Georgia was able to stem the long-run outflow of talented students. In any case, there may have been a much cheaper way to identify the top students and influence their long-run mobility decisions.

Innovative Programs after Undergraduate Years

Keeping students in state after graduation from college is the underlying goal of brain drain prevention. A study by the American Institutes for Research found that 161 programs exist in 43 states which cover college costs or repay loans for students agreeing to work in certain occupations or regions. About 75 per cent of these programs are loan-forgiveness programs, providing financial aid while in school in exchange for a future work commitment, while the rest of the programs repay existing debt (Schmidt, 2004). Most of these programs do not consider financial need, but many do require state residency or take academic merit into account. While the report found little evidence that the programs reduce workforce shortages or attract those who might not otherwise have entered the occupation, it is unclear whether they can be implemented to keep students in-state successfully. Also most of these programs focus on nurses or teachers, rather than students in high-tech fields or those with advanced degrees.

Recently Governor Bob Holden of Missouri announced a plan to forgive up to $10 000 in student loans for Missouri college students who pursue math or science degrees and work for life science-related companies in Missouri after graduation. The loan repayment incentive is part of the Jobs Now program to create new jobs in the state (Samuel, 2004). The program would repay up to $2500 a year for four years, and hopes are that it would send a message to companies that Missouri has a highly qualified life sciences workforce.

Not only are states developing programs to attract top students, but legislation has been introduced in the Federal government to help recruit the 'best and the brightest' into government service. The proposed legislation, the Generating Opportunity by Forgiving Educational Debt for Service (GOFEDS) Act would allow federal agencies to offer tax-free student loan forgiveness. Currently loan forgiveness offered to federal employees is taxed. Tom Davis, the Government Reform Committee Chairman feels that the cost of the program is minimal, whereas the benefits could be great. Davis said, 'For too long, the federal government has been bleeding highly trained and skilled workers to the private sector. This legislation will help the government acquire 21st-century skills for a 21st-century workforce.'

Within Ohio, most public initiatives focus on job formation. However the Third Frontier does have components that aim at student retention. For instance, money from the Third Frontier supports the Greater Cleveland Growth Association in Northeast Ohio which has formed iCleveland (formerly the Graduates Council). This organization has formed a network between high-achieving college students and area professionals to try to keep the 'best and brightest' minds in Northeast Ohio. Whether the formation of this network and the ties that students make to area business leaders prevent migration after graduation is unclear. Additionally there have been efforts to improve technology transfer between academic institutions and potential entrepreneurs. The findings in this chapter suggest that this type of program may effectively retain entrepreneurs.

Innovative Programs after Graduate School

Ohio is especially concerned with losing its students who earn advanced degrees. New legislation proposed in October 2003 may address this concern. The proposed legislation would offer loans to students with advanced degrees in engineering, computer science, chemistry, physics or biomedical technologies which would be forgiven if the student worked in Ohio or started a business in a high-tech field after graduation. If the recipient leaves the state, the loan must be repaid in five years (Sheban, 2003).

If passed, the new legislation may mark a change in the way Ohio lawmakers approach the problem of brain drain by encouraging and providing financial assistance to students who undertake to live and work in Ohio for a period of time. Keeping students in the state will also have the effect of strengthening individuals' familial and business relationships in Ohio and, thereby, improve Ohio's ability to retain students.

Round Trippers

Bringing people back to Ohio is another factor in the brain drain problem. In order to attract people back to the state, the quality of communities and schools is important and should be a top priority for improvement in order to reduce brain drain. States should keep track of those who leave and use recruitment techniques to let them know Ohio welcomes them back. Very few policies focus on this level and data are scarce.

CONCLUSION

This chapter attempts to describe brain drain in Ohio, focusing on the four key exit points at which students leave Ohio: undergraduate school attendance, transition after undergraduate studies, transition after graduate studies and migration later in life. The chapter provides a review of literature on brain drain. It also provides a brief model that characterizes how individuals make decisions, including the role of public policy in individual mobility decisions. The chapter also provides brief evidence from the 2000 US Census on the nature of brain drain at these key exit points, and discusses some innovative programs within and outside Ohio which attempt to influence individual decision making at each point.

The chapter contributes to the existing literature on brain drain in two key ways. First, it provides some discussion of the role of financial aid, together with some suggestive evidence that financial aid may influence students' decisions to stay in the state for an additional few years. In these extra years, students may start families or businesses. Having children and, to some extent, marriage reduces the likelihood that students will stay in the same state. Particularly strong, however, is the role of self-employment. Students who start their own business are much more likely to stay in the same state. To the extent that financial aid preserves students' relationships with a given state, entrepreneurial students are more likely to start their business in that location.

Another contribution of the chapter is to identify the patterns of mobility implied in the most recent US Census. According to US Census data, Ohio fares better than the national average in retaining its college graduates. Ohio, like other states, tends to lose students who receive doctoral degrees. The census data are also limited in showing whether individuals with high ability or earnings potential return to the state. Ohio, however, does experience a return of college graduates much higher than the national average between the ages of 25 and 35.

While most of the policy debate on brain drain in Ohio has focused on job creation, this chapter suggests that encouraging entrepreneurial activity among young college graduates may be an effective way of stemming brain drain. The chapter also provides some perspective on the role and the ways in which financial aid may affect long-run mobility decisions.

COMMENTARY

Robert Sheehan

The authors of this chapter present as their main thesis that state financial aid increases the likelihood that college students will remain in Ohio. This causal link between receipt of financial aid and staying in Ohio is suggested through a decrease in student mobility and an increase in the time students will spend in Ohio while concurrently participating in Ohio-based 'life events'.

The authors introduce a helpful 'cycle of mobility' for understanding the stages in a young person's education when they might leave or enter a metropolitan region: (a) students enter college, (b) students exit with undergraduate degrees, (c) students enter and exit graduate school, (d) students leave Ohio, with or without a college degree, then return as round trippers. One suggestion I make to the authors is that they enhance their model with a preliminary stage: students exit high school. This suggestion is made in recognition that Ohio has an above-average high school graduation rate and a significantly below-average high school to college matriculation rate. A component of brain drain is the state's persistent lack of success in developing its own college-educated workforce from its own high school graduate population.

The authors are to be commended for placing the focus of their analysis on a metropolitan area such as the Cleveland metropolitan area. The authors could just as easily have identified Greater Toledo, Greater Columbus or Greater Cincinnati. Metropolitan regions are certainly the geographic areas where brain drain issues become evident.

In contrast, there is no reason to believe that the entire state of Ohio is experiencing a disproportionate loss of high school graduates or indeed college graduates. Several sources of data indicate that, as a state, Ohio's out-migration of individuals pursuing a college degree, or of recent college graduates, is at or below national levels. One way to measure mobility is to examine young adults, the most mobile of college-educated individuals. Mortenson (2004) reports US Census data showing that Ohio has the lowest percentage (22 per cent), among all states in the nation, of young adults aged 25 to 39 who are single college graduates who lived in-state in 1995 and had moved out of state in 2000.

These data were reviewed (Sommers, 2003) at a briefing entitled 'Brain Drain or Weak Attraction?' to Ohio Governor's Taft's Governor's Commission on Higher Education and the Economy. As Sommers reports, migration is common, especially among young individuals. Ohio has a net loss of college graduates, not because too many individuals left Ohio, but because too few individuals with college degrees migrated into Ohio. The statewide pattern is too little brain gain, not too much brain drain. In addition to Sommers' presentation, available from the Ohio Board of Regents, see Paul Gottlieb's working paper entitled 'Brain Drain Policies in the US States: Treating the Symptom Instead of the Disease?' (April 2003)

The authors note that Ohio imports more out-of-state students to its colleges and universities than it exports. In 1998, 10 424 Ohio high school students left to study out-of-state but they were replaced by 11 960 students entering Ohio to pursue a college degree (Mortenson, 2002). The authors ask, 'Are we exporting our brightest?' The answer to this is probably yes, high school students who attend college out-of-state are quite possibly attracted by the abundance of complete scholarships for students with excellent high school performance.

The authors might pose a related question: 'Are we importing brighter students from out-of-state than we have in-state?' The answer to that question is definitely yes. I recently analyzed the college grade point averages (GPA) of all 4500 first-year Ohio university students, for Fall 2002, comparing the GPAs of the non-resident students to their Ohio counterparts'. The out-of-state students studying in Ohio had an average GPA of 2.7, significantly higher than their in-state peers (2.5). When looking at all 12 public universities serving undergraduates, this trend was evident at eight of them (HEI, 2004).

The authors suggest to state policy makers that public financial aid is one tool to retain Ohio students, much as Georgia's Hope Scholarships are intended to keep Georgia students in the state. Unlike Ohio, far more Georgia high school graduates were leaving Georgia for college study than were entering from out-of-state. I caution the authors that, in Ohio, financial aid policies are historically created to affect an entire state, not just metropolitan regions that might be experiencing true brain drain. Even though increased state financial aid might attract students to rural campuses (for example, Athens, Ohio, the home of Ohio University), it is unlikely that financial aid policies will cause students to remain in a region that does not have a workforce infrastructure to employ them after graduation.

The authors might wish to examine the Ohio statewide practice of charging a tuition surcharge to out-of-state undergraduate students. This concept has its origins in the state policy of providing no state support for undergraduate out-of-state students.

The surcharge was initially intended to replace missing state support for out-of-state students. In the 1970s, when many surcharge rates were being established, Ohio was providing state support equal to or greater than the tuition charged to students. Accordingly many universities set their out-of-state surcharge at equal to the cost of in-state tuition and this was added to in-state tuition rates. By 2004, state support for undergraduate education had dwindled to approximately 35 per cent of the total cost of educating a student – a dramatic decline. Put differently, state subsidy for freshmen and sophomore students might be as little as $1000 per full-time student whereas campus out-of-state surcharges might be as high as $7000. The net effect is that few out-of-state students can afford to study at public universities in Ohio. A change in surcharge pricing for metropolitan-located campuses might have even more impact on brain gain than any statewide financial aid program or policy.

In Ohio, the past two decades are noteworthy as an era of significant cost shifting from taxpayers to students, while keeping inflation-adjusted college expenses equal. The authors suggest that, over time and barring changes in state funding policies, the trend of students attending college outside of Ohio will likely continue to grow. In-migration and out-migration of college students in Ohio has varied over the years but the 1986–2000 time period reveals a net gain of 804 more students coming to Ohio for college study than leaving (Mortenson, 2002). The authors might wish to explore an alternative hypothesis: As state funding for public universities continues to decline, with corresponding rise in tuition to offset the loss, there is likely to be an increasing enrollment of students at independent institutions in Ohio where the net tuition paid by students is becoming much closer to public tuition.

To understand why state policies are driving public and independent universities' tuition to converge, one must go beyond the stated tuition prices of independent universities and consider the discounting that is common at most independent universities. Price discounting to entering students of 30 per cent to 40 per cent is common throughout Ohio.

Consider John Carroll University in University Heights, Ohio, whose stated tuition for 2003–4 was $20 906. Looking a bit further, US Department of Education data (COOL, 2004) reports that 94 per cent of entering undergraduate students received institution awards of $8663 (41 per cent discount) in addition to any additional financial aid that students receive. If a student had maximum financial need, the student might be eligible for federal Pell grants of approximately $3500 and their state-based need award, the Ohio Instructional Grant (OIG) is more than doubled, from $2190 to $5466, for students choosing to enroll at an independent university (Ohio Board of Regents, 2004). The state of Ohio provides another $1000 Choice Grant, unrelated to financial need for the same student. The net effect is that stated tuition of $20 906 could become as little as $2277. A public university charging $7000 would result in net tuition of $1310. The public university tuition is lower than the independent college tuition but the difference is not especially competitive.

Note that John Carroll University is mentioned as one example of many that would make the same points. Case Western Reserve University reported that 62 per cent of its entering undergraduates received institution-funded aid (functional price discounts) of $13 462 from its stated tuition price of $24 342.

The financial aid programs receiving greatest statewide interest today are need-based aid for students who are quite limited in their mobility. It may be unrealistic to believe that absence of financial aid will decrease the chances of a student leaving Ohio; however it is completely realistic to assume that absence of financial aid will cause fewer students to enter college at all – thus resulting in a statewide failure to develop the workforce with college-educated workers.

In closing, I offer the following comments. The authors are conducting their research in an area of critical statewide importance. They are encouraged to be sensitive to the difficulty of solving regional problems with statewide solutions. The authors might wish to consider how state financial aid policies can be applied regionally for maximum impact. As noted, while state funding may result in a decline in an in-state college-educated population, the causal factor may be that too few Ohio students can afford to enter higher education. Addressing the accessibility of higher education to financial needy students may have greater statewide benefit than financial aid programs to all students.

6. On SBA-guaranteed lending and economic growth

Ben Craig, William Jackson and James Thomson[1]

INTRODUCTION

The promotion of small businesses is a cornerstone of economic policy for a large number of industrialized countries. Right or wrong, there appears to be a widely held perception that the small business sector is the incubator of growth, the place where innovation takes place and new ideas become economically viable business enterprises. Moreover, despite the research findings of Davis *et al.* (2000) that the small business sector is not a net creator of jobs in the United States, policy makers routinely point to small businesses as important sources of employment growth. Therefore it is not surprising that there is widespread political support for government interventions aimed at promoting small business in the United States and increasingly around the world.

A widely held view among economists is that, while markets are the best way to allocate scarce resources, sometimes government interventions can improve upon market outcomes. Credit market imperfections, particularly in the market for small enterprise credit, are among the usual suspects cited as rationale for government intervention. After all, there is reason to believe that the information-related problems that drive the credit rationing equilibrium of Stiglitz and Weiss (1981) may be particularly severe in the market for small-firm finance. To the extent that small firms are credit-rationed, government interventions in the form of direct credit or Small Business Administration (SBA) loan guarantees may be justified because of the deadweight losses associated with not funding all the projects in the economy that have positive net-present value.

We are interested in the efficacy of SBA guarantees of small enterprise loans. After all, the level of SBA activity in the small business loan market is not trivial. The SBA's current business loan portfolio of roughly

219 000 loans worth more than $45 billion makes it the largest single financial backer of US businesses in the nation. Over the ten-year period (fiscal year) 1991–2000, the SBA assisted almost 435 000 small businesses in obtaining more than $94.6 billion in loans, more than in the entire history of the agency before 1991 (SBA, 2004). Hence the redistributive effects of the SBA's loan guarantee programs may be economically important and raise the question as to whether the net benefits of these programs are positive.

To the extent that SBA loan guarantees mitigate credit market frictions these guarantees will result in improved capital allocation in the economy. This in turn should have an impact on economic growth and development. On the other hand, if SBA guarantees do not serve to reduce credit rationing in lending markets, we should not observe a significantly positive correlation between the level of SBA guarantees and economic performance. In the latter case, SBA activities might be detrimental to economic growth as they would misallocate credit. To examine this question we construct a data set containing all loans guaranteed by the SBA under its two main lending programs from 1990 to the end of 2000, measures of economic conditions, and market structure variables. Using observations at the local market level we examine whether SBA-guaranteed lending significantly affects economic performance and economic growth, as measured by per capita income and log change in per capita income, respectively. We find evidence consistent with SBA loan guarantees providing a positive impact on future economic growth.

The remainder of the chapter is organized as follows. In the next section we provide a brief history of the SBA and an overview of its major lending programs. Understanding the role Congress intended this agency to perform is essential in evaluating the social welfare implications of the SBA's activities. The historical record clearly shows that Congress created the SBA to mitigate perceived market imperfections that were reducing credit availability for small businesses. In the third section we provide a brief review of the academic literature on credit rationing and relationship lending. This literature is consistent with the hypothesis that information problems in lending markets are particularly severe in the small enterprise credit market and hence provide a rationale for SBA loan guarantees. The fourth section outlines the data, our hypotheses and empirical strategy, with the results appearing in the fifth section. Overall, our empirical results are consistent with a positive, albeit small impact of SBA guaranteed lending on personal income growth. Our conclusions and future research questions are outlined in a final section.

A BRIEF HISTORY OF THE SBA AND ITS MAJOR CREDIT-EXTENDING PROGRAMS

The SBA was created on 30 July 1953 by the enactment of Public Law 163. However the SBA's legislative purpose and mission had begun to take shape years earlier in a number of predecessor agencies. These predecessor agencies included the Smaller War Plants Corporation (SWPC), the Small Defense Plants Administration (SDPA) and the Reconstruction Finance Corporation (RFC). All of these agencies were created mainly as a response to the pressures of the Great Depression or World War II.

The primary predecessor agency of the SBA was the Reconstruction Finance Corporation (RFC), created in 1932 during the Hoover Administration. Its mission was to help mitigate the financial crisis of the Great Depression by providing emergency capital generally to firms. With the passage of the Emergency Banking Act of 1933 the RFC's mission was extended to include the rehabilitation of troubled commercial banks (Todd, 1992). The RFC continued to be a full fledged federal lending program for all firms hurt by the Depression, both large and small businesses and both financial and non-financial firms. The authority of the RFC to lend directly to businesses is often considered the beginning of the present SBA 7(a) loan guarantee program (Rhyne, 1988). The RFC was also given the authority and responsibility to provide relief loans to individuals and organizations severely affected by natural disasters. When the RFC was closed, the SBA was created to assume both the disaster and general business lending functions of the RFC.[2] However the SBA's business lending function was directed exclusively toward small business. Some suggest that this limitation was the direct result of the banking industry's successful lobbying to reduce the competition of government-provided business lending programs, especially those that aided large businesses (ibid.). The enabling legislation empowers the SBA to make loans to small business concerns either directly or in cooperation with banks or other lending institutions.[3]

It is clear from the legislation that created the SBA that Congress perceived both that small businesses face special problems in obtaining financing and that small business is a very important part of the American economy. Congressional intent is stated distinctly in the act.[4]

> The essence of the American economic system of private enterprise is free competition. Only through full and free competition can free markets, free entry into business, and opportunities for the expression and growth of personal initiative and individual judgment be assured. The preservation and expansion of such competition is not only to the economic well-being but to the security of this Nation. *Such security and well-being cannot be realized unless the actual and potential capacity of small business is encouraged and developed. It is the*

declared policy of the Congress that the Government should aid, counsel, assist, and protect insofar as is possible the interests of small-business concerns in order to preserve free competitive enterprise, to insure that a fair proportion of the total purchases and contracts for supplies and services for the Government be placed with small-business enterprises, and to maintain and strengthen the overall economy of the Nation. (Public Law 163, s. 202)[5]

Developments in Loan Programs

By 1954, the SBA was already making direct business loans and guaranteeing bank loans to small businesses, as well as making loans to victims of natural disasters, working to get government procurement contracts for small businesses and helping business owners with management and technical assistance and business training. Then, in 1958, the Investment Company Act established the Small Business Investment Company (SBIC) Program. This program added directly to the credit-granting authority of the SBA. Under the program the SBA licensed, regulated and helped provide funds for privately owned and operated venture capital investment firms. These firms specialized in providing long-term debt and equity investments to high-risk small businesses. Although the program was established as a temporary remedy to a specific problem, the program is still alive and fully operational today (Rhyne, 1988).

Over the years, the statutory authority and administrative structure of SBA's business lending programs have been remarkably stable. However, within this legal framework, the SBA has made at least one major concession to the fact that private financial institutions are typically better at deciding which small business loans to underwrite than are government agencies. This recognition led the SBA, in the mid-1980s, to move away from making direct loans and toward making relatively more guaranteed loans. Currently the SBA makes direct loans only under very special circumstances, and guaranteed lending is the main form of SBA lending. The SBA's main business lending programs are the 7(a) guaranteed loan program and the 504 loan program.

The 7(a) Guaranteed Loan Program

The 7(a) loan program is the most basic and most significant among the SBA's business loan programs. Its name comes from Section 7(a) of the Small Business Act, which authorizes the agency to provide business loans to American small businesses. Loans from the 7(a) program are only available on a guaranty basis. This means that they are provided by lenders who choose to structure their own loans according to the SBA's requirements and who apply and receive a guaranty from the SBA on a portion of these loans. The SBA does not fully guarantee 7(a) loans. The SBA guaranty is usually in the range of 50 per cent to 85 per cent of the loan amount, and the maximum guaranty is $1 000 000. The guaranty is a guaranty against payment default; the lender and the SBA share the risk that a borrower will not be able to repay the loan in full. The guaranty does not cover imprudent decisions by the lender or misrepresentation by the borrower (SBA, 2004).

Under the guaranty concept, commercial lenders make and administer the loans, and small businesses apply to lenders for their financing. The lender decides whether it will make a loan internally or if the application has some weaknesses which, in the lender's opinion, mean the loan will require an SBA guaranty before it will be underwritten. The guaranty that the SBA provides is available only to the lender. It assures the lender that, in the event of a payment default, the government will reimburse the lender for its loss, up to the percentage of SBA's guaranty. Under the 7(a) program, the borrower remains obligated for the full amount due.

The 504 Loan Program

The 504 loan program is a long-term financing tool for economic development within a community. It provides growing businesses with long-term, fixed-rate financing for purchasing major fixed assets (such as land or improvements, including new or existing buildings, grading, street improvements, utilities, parking lots, landscaping, the modernization, renovation or conversion of existing facilities, and long-term machinery and equipment). SBA financing is provided through a certified development company (CDC), a non-profit corporation set up to contribute to the economic development of its community. CDCs work with the SBA and private sector lenders to provide financing to small businesses. There are about 270 CDCs nationwide, and each covers a specific geographic area (SBA, 2004).

Typically a 504 project includes a loan secured by several entities: a senior lien from a private sector lender covers up to 50 per cent of the project cost. A loan secured with a junior lien from the CDC covers up to 40 per cent of the cost (this loan is backed by a 100 per cent SBA-guaranteed debenture). A contribution of at least 10 per cent equity from the small business being helped is also required.

The maximum SBA debenture is $1 000 000 per project, where the project is defined in terms of a given set of job creation criteria or a community development goal. Generally a business must create or retain one job for every $50 000 provided by the SBA. The maximum SBA debenture is $1.3 million for projects that meet specific public policy goals recognized by the SBA.[6]

SBA LENDING AND THE ECONOMICS OF CREDIT MARKETS

Over the last ten years the SBA has been responsible for well over $100 billion in small business credit extensions, more than any single private lender. Of course this is what the SBA was created to do. The agency's primary mission as set forth by Congress, after all, is to assist small businesses in their quest for credit on reasonable terms. But is the SBA program well-conceived public policy in the sense that it has been designed to improve the efficiency and equity of lending markets?

The answer to this question would appear to be 'yes' if Congress made at least three assumptions when it created the agency. First, lawmakers had to assume that small business lending differs from large business lending, in terms either of costs or of public benefits. Second, they had to think that imperfections exist in the private small business credit market that prevent the market from delivering the economically efficient amount of credit to small businesses at market prices. Third, they must have believed that the SBA would have the power and expertise to help ameliorate these market imperfections.

Petersen (1999) suggests that small business lending is indeed different from large business lending, on three dimensions: financing costs are different; small businesses pay a higher fixed cost per unit of credit than larger businesses; the availability of information is different. Asymmetric information problems associated with small firms are more severe than with larger firms. The importance of relationships with banking institutions is different. Relationships between banks (typically small ones) and small businesses are much closer than between large companies and banks, and thus are more valuable to both small business and to the banks. However these differences alone are not sufficient to justify government intervention in the small business credit market. The economic rationale for market intervention by the SBA must be linked to some form of market failure. Some suggest that market failure may exist in credit markets because these markets tend to be informationally imperfect. Further the economic literature documents that this market failure may take the form of equilibrium credit rationing.

Market Imperfections and Credit Rationing

The credit rationing literature is one of the more insightful areas in modern economics. Two of the more important papers in this area are Kane and Malkiel (1965) and Stiglitz and Weiss (1981). Stiglitz and Weiss (1981) demonstrate that price alone may not equilibrate demand and supply in credit markets. They also show that the corresponding disequilibrium would unlikely be just a temporary phenomenon.

Importantly Stiglitz and Weiss show that, in equilibrium a loan market may be characterized by credit rationing. They reason that banks making loans are concerned about the interest rate they receive on the loan and the riskiness of the loan. However the interest rate may itself affect the riskiness of the pool of bank loans by either sorting potential borrowers (the adverse selection effect) or influencing the actions of borrowers (the moral hazard effect). Both effects derive directly from the imperfect information that is present in loan markets after banks have evaluated loan applications. When the price (interest rate) affects the nature of the transaction, it is unlikely that price will also clear the market.

The adverse selection aspect of interest rates is a consequence of different borrowers having different probabilities of repaying their loan. The expected return to the bank obviously depends on the probability of repayment, so the bank would like to be able to identify borrowers who are more likely to repay. But it is difficult to identify 'good borrowers'. Typically the bank will use a variety of screening devices to do so. The interest rate that a borrower is willing to pay may act as one such screening device. For example, those who are willing to pay a higher interest rate are likely to be, on average, worse risks. These borrowers are willing to borrow at a higher interest rate because they perceive their probability of repaying the loan to be lower. As the interest rate rises, the average 'riskiness' of those who borrow increases, and this may actually result in lowering the bank's expected profits.

Similarly, as the interest rate and other terms of the contract change, the behavior of the borrower is likely also to change. For instance, raising the interest rate decreases the return on projects which succeed. Higher interest rates may thus induce firms to undertake projects with lower probabilities of success but higher pay-offs when successful. This is the moral hazard problem.

For these reasons, the expected return to the bank may increase less rapidly than the interest rate and, beyond a point, may actually decrease. Clearly, under these conditions, it is conceivable that the demand for credit may exceed the supply of credit in equilibrium. Although traditional analysis would argue that, in the presence of an excess demand for credit unsatisfied borrowers would offer to pay a higher interest rate to the bank, bidding up the interest rate until demand equals supply, it does not happen in this case. This is because the bank would not lend to someone who offered to pay the higher interest rate, as such a borrower is likely to be a worse risk than the average current borrower (Stiglitz and Weiss, 1981). The expected return on a loan to this borrower at the higher interest rate is actually lower than the expected return on the loans the bank is currently making. Hence there are no competitive forces leading supply to equal demand, and credit is rationed.

Of course the interest rate is not the only term of the contract which is important. Stiglitz and Weiss report that the amount of credit extended, and the amount of collateral the bank demands of the borrower, will also affect the behavior of borrowers and the distribution of borrowers. And, as with interest rates, increasing the collateral requirements of borrowers may actually decrease the returns to the lender, by either decreasing the average degree of risk aversion of the pool of borrowers or inducing borrowers to undertake riskier projects.

Consequently it may not be profitable to raise the interest rate or collateral requirements when a bank has an excess demand for credit; instead, banks may deny loans to borrowers who are observationally indistinguishable from those who receive loans. This is what Stiglitz and Weiss (1981) refer to as 'credit rationing'.

Importance of Lending Relationships

Kane and Malkiel (1965) come to a similar conclusion about the possibility of banks rationing credit, but they also suggest that the extent of credit rationing depends on the strength of existing customer relationships; the size, stability and prospects for future growth of deposits; and the existence of profitable future lending opportunities. That is, loans may be rationed to current and prospective borrowers in accordance with the cohesion of the existing relationships along with expectations about the future profitability of those relationships.

Petersen and Raghuram (1994) extended the notion that relationships are important factors in determining credit rationing. They suggested that the causes of credit rationing, adverse selection and moral hazard, may be more prominent when firms are young or small. However, through close and continued interaction, a firm may provide a lender with sufficient information about, and a voice in, the firm's affairs so as to lower the cost and increase the availability of credit. These authors also suggest that an important dimension of a relationship is its duration. Conditional on its positive past experience with the borrower, the bank may expect future loans to be less risky. This should reduce its expected cost of lending and increase its willingness to provide funds.

Petersen and Rajan suggest that, in addition to interaction over time, relationships can be built through interaction over multiple products. That is, borrowers may obtain more than just loans from a bank. Borrowers may purchase a variety of financial services and also maintain checking and savings accounts with the bank. These added dimensions of a relationship can affect the firm's borrowing cost in two ways. First, they increase the precision of the lender's information about the borrower. For example, the lender can learn about the firm's sales by monitoring the cash flowing through its checking account or by factoring the firm's accounts receivables. Second, the lender can spread any fixed costs of producing information about the firm over multiple products. Petersen and Rajan report that both effects reduce the lender's costs of providing loans and services, and the former effect increases the availability of funds to the firm.

Berger and Udell (1995) also study the importance of relationships in the extension of credit to small firms. They find that small firms with longer banking relationships borrow at lower rates and are less likely to pledge collateral than are other small firms. These effects appear to be both economically and statistically significant. According to Berger and Udell, these results suggest that banks accumulate increasing amounts of this private information over the duration of the bank–borrower relationship and use this information to refine their loan contract terms.

Because relationships may be more costly for small businesses to establish relative to large businesses, and because lack of relationships may lead to severe credit rationing in the small business credit market, some form of government intervention to assist small businesses in establishing relationships with lenders may be appropriate. However the nature of intervention must be carefully evaluated. SBA's guaranteed lending programs may well be a reasonable intervention as they serve as a form of substitute for small business collateral. The program also reduces the risk to the lender of establishing a relationship with informationally opaque small business borrowers. Finally the SBA loan guarantee programs may improve the intermediation process by lowering the risk to the lender of extending longer-term loans, ones that more closely meet the needs of small businesses for capital investment. After all, the problem Congress is said to have worried about is long-term credit for small businesses.

THE QUESTIONS, EMPIRICAL STRATEGY AND DATA

Our empirical research focuses on SBA loan guarantees, which are only one of the several ways the government promotes small business lending. Federal Home Loan Banks, for example, are authorized by Congress to accept small enterprise loans as eligible collateral when they extend subsidized advances to banks, which reduces the cost of funding small business loan portfolios.[7] We chose to study the impact of SBA loan guarantees because, if government intervention in the small business credit market is effective, the evidence is likely to be strongest in the SBA programs. This is because

SBA loan guarantees more completely resolve the agency problems that give rise to credit rationing in these markets than do other approaches, like that of the Federal Home Loan Banks. SBA programs also encompass all types of small business lenders, from community banks and thrifts to bigger banks. Finally the SBA has operated for a long time – more than a half a century.

We take as our maintained hypothesis that credit market frictions (primarily in the form of costly information and verification of a small firm's projects) can lead to socially suboptimal credit allocation. To the extent that SBA loan guarantee programs mitigate credit market frictions, there should be a relationship between SBA-guaranteed lending and economic growth and development. Therefore we test whether SBA loan guarantees lessen credit market frictions by testing whether measures of SBA lending are related to local economic growth. Thus our null hypothesis is that SBA lending has no discernible impact on local market economic growth.

To examine this SBA growth hypothesis we utilize data from three sources. The first source is loan-specific data, including borrower and lender information, on all SBA-guaranteed 7(a) and 504 loans from 2 January 1990 to 31 December 2002. A breakdown of loan size, total credit and number of loans under each guarantee program is displayed in Tables 6A.1 to 6A.3 in the appendix. The second source is data on economics conditions from the National Bureau of Economic Research (NBER), the Bureau of Labor Statistics (BLS) and the Bureau of Economic Analysis (BEA) from 1990 to 2001. The third source is data from the Federal Deposit Insurance Corporation's (FDIC) annual summary of deposit data (SUMD) files. All of our data are aggregated to the local market level. We use Metropolitan Statistical Areas (MSAs) to define the relevant local market for urban areas and non-MSA counties as the local market for rural areas. We focus on local markets because we suspect that it is at this level that the SBA-guaranteed lending should have the greatest impact. Hence, our data set consists of approximately 2200 local market observations per year over 12 years (1990 to 2001).

To test our null hypothesis we construct two sets of regression equations in which measures of local economic conditions are related to proxy variables for SBA lending and the structure of the local financial market. Also included are controls for national economic conditions. A second set of regression equations relate proxies for economic growth to levels and changes in SBA lending and market structure variables. Our model is as follows:

$$PICAP_t = \alpha_0\, \alpha_1 PICAP_{t-1} + \alpha_2 SBADEP_{t-1} + \alpha_3 EMPR_t$$
$$+ \alpha_4 NBER_t + \alpha_5 HERF_t + \alpha_6 MSA_t + \alpha_7 SBAG_{t-1}$$
$$+ \alpha_8 SBA7A_{t-1} + \alpha_9 SBAM_{t-1} + \alpha_{10} EMPR_{t-1} + \varepsilon_t. \qquad (6.1)$$

Equation (6.1) uses per capita income ($PICAP$) in the local market level to proxy for economic conditions. The primary variable of interest on the right side of the equation is $SBADEP_{t-1}$ (the total dollar amount of SBA-guaranteed loans scaled by total deposits in the market lagged one year). We scale by total deposits instead of measures of total credit because we cannot construct measures of bank lending at the local market level. Market-level deposit data are available, however, from the SUMD data, and total deposits should be highly correlated with lending. We also include as controls for the impact of SBA lending the share of SBA loans that are 7(a) loans ($SBA7A$), the share of SBA loans provided to manufacturing concerns ($SBAM$) and the SBA's exposure on the outstanding balances of the SBA-guaranteed loans ($SBAG$).

Two variables are included in equation (6.1) to control for the structure of the local market. The first variable is the deposit market Herfindahl index ($HERF$), which provides a measure of the relative concentration, and presumably the relative competitiveness, of the local banking markets. The second variable is a dummy variable (MSA) that captures whether the market is urban ($MSA = 1$) or rural ($MSA = 0$). Finally we include the employment rate ($EMPR$) for the market and a dummy variable for NBER recessions ($NBER = 1$ if the national economy is in a recession, 0 otherwise) to control for local and national economic conditions. The definitions of the variables used in the empirical analysis are in Table 6.1.

Finding a positive and significant relationship between the level of per capita income and SBA-guaranteed loans in a local market is inconsistent with the null hypothesis of no connection between these loans and economic conditions. However we might also observe this positive correlation between economic performance and SBA-guaranteed lending activity if the probability of a lender offering an SBA-guaranteed loan is positively related to local market economic conditions. In other words, the higher level of income might cause the lagged SBA-guaranteed lending rather than the other way around, in part because it incorporates past growth rates. Therefore we investigate whether SBA-guaranteed lending activity is related to local economic growth. To do this we estimate the following regression equation:

$$\Delta LNPI_t = \beta_0 + \beta_1 LPI_{t-1} + \beta_2 \Delta LNSBA_t + \beta_3 \Delta LNDEP_t + \beta_4 \Delta LNEMPR_t$$
$$+ \beta_5 \Delta LNSBA_{t-1} + \beta_6 \Delta LNDEP_{t-1} + \beta_7 NBER_t + \beta_8 MSA_t + \beta_9 HERF_t$$
$$+ \beta_{10} LNSBA_{t-2} + \beta_{11} LNDEP_{t-2} + \beta_{12} LNEMPR_{t-1} + \beta_{12} LNSBAG_{t-2}$$
$$+ \beta_{14} LNSBA7A_{t-2} + \beta_{15} LNSBAM_{t-2} + \mu_t. \tag{6.2}$$

Table 6.1 Variable definitions

Variable	Definition	Source
SBADEP	SBA guaranteed loans per $000 of deposits	SBA, FDIC SUMD
HERF	Deposit market Herfindahl	FDIC SUMD
EMPR	Employment rate	BLS
NBER	Dummy variable = 1 if the year is a recession year, 0 otherwise	NBER
MSADUM	Dummy variable = 1 if observation is an MSA and zero otherwise	BEA
SBAGR	Portion of total SBA guaranteed loan balances covered by SBA guarantee	SBA
SBA7AR	Portion of total SBA guaranteed loan balances that are 7(a) loans	SBA
SBAMR	Portion of total SBA guaranteed loan balances that are loans to manufacturing concerns	SBA
PICAP	Per capita income	BEA
MDUM	Securities to assets ratio	June Call Report
LNPI	Natural log of personal income	BEA
LNSBA	Natural log of total SBA guaranteed loans	SBA
LNDEP	Natural log of total deposits	FDIC SUMD
LNEMPR	Natural log of the employment rate	BEA
ΔLNSBA$_{t-1}$	Natural log of SBA guaranteed loans at $t-1$ minus the natural log of SBA guaranteed loans at $t-2$	SBA
ΔLNDEP$_{t-1}$	Natural log of deposits at $t-1$ minus the natural log of deposits at $t-2$	FDIC SUMD
ΔLNSBA	Natural log of assets at t minus the natural log of assets at $t-1$	SBA
ΔLNDEP	Natural log of deposits at t minus the natural log of deposits at $t-1$	FDIC SUMD
ΔLNEMPR	Natural log of the employment rate at t minus the natural log of the employment rate at $t-1$	BLS
ΔLNPI	Natural log of personal income at t minus the natural log of personal income at $t-1$	BEA

Notes: SBA = small business administration; FDIC SUMD = Federal Deposit Insurance Corporation summary of deposit data; BEA = Bureau of Economic Analysis; BLS = Bureau of Labor Statistics; NBER = National Bureau of Economic Research.

The dependent variable in equation (6.2) is the log change in personal income from $t-1$ to t ($\Delta LNPI_t$).[8] The primary regressors of interest are the log change in small business loans ($\Delta LNSBA_t$), the lagged log change in small business loans ($\Delta LNSBA_{t-1}$) and the log level of small business loans lagged two periods ($LNSBA_{t-2}$). Under our null hypothesis that SBA loan guarantees have no discernable impact on economic growth, we would expect the coefficients on $LNSBA_{t-2}$, $\Delta LNSBA_t$ and $\Delta LNSBA_{t-1}$ to be insignificant. Thus this estimating equation differs from the first in two ways: it shifts the focus from possible past changes of personal income (that contribute to its current level) to a single contemporaneous change, and it also observes more dynamics in the effects of past SBA-guaranteed activity on that contemporary change. Positive and significant coefficients on these SBA lending variables would be evidence consistent with the hypothesis that SBA loan guarantees improve the efficiency of lending markets. As before, we include controls for market structure ($HERF$ and MSA), economic conditions ($LNEMPR$, $\Delta LNEMPR$ and $LNPI_{t-1}$) in equation (6.2), as well as controls for level and growth in deposits ($LNDEP_{t-2}$, $\Delta LNDEP_t$, $\Delta LNDEP_{t-1}$). We also include the values of controls for the type of SBA lending in the market lagged two periods.

THE EMPIRICAL RESULTS

Levels Regression

Equation 6.1 is estimated using weighted least squares at the local market level for every MSA (urban) and non-MSA county (rural) for which we have complete data over the period 1991 to 2001. We start the analysis in 1991 because our SBA loan data begin in 1990 and our empirical specification includes the lagged value of the dependent variable and the lagged small business lending variables on the right side of the equation. Equation (6.1) is re-estimated over the urban and rural samples, excluding the MSA dummy variable. Descriptive statistics for the variables used in the regression can be found in Table 6.2 and the estimation results are presented in Table 6.3.

Consistent with our null hypothesis, the coefficient on the lagged SBA loan-to-deposit ratio is positive but not significantly different from zero for all three samples.[9] This result is not surprising; after all, SBA-guaranteed lending is a small part of the total banking market: less than 7.5 per cent of market deposits on average. SBA-guaranteed lending may be too small economically for the data to yield a statistical relationship between it and per capita income. In other words, while an insignificant coefficient on $SBADEP_{t-1}$ is consistent with SBA loan guarantees having no discernable impact on local economic growth, tests focusing on levels of economic activity may not have the power to reject the null hypothesis.

Table 6.2   Descriptive statistics for equation (6.1) variables

Variable	N	Mean	Std Dev	Minimum	Maximum
PICAP	24 872	18.9273	4.5517	6.09	58.70
$SBADEP_{t-1}$[a]	24 872	7.4450	100.8813	0	8754.2
HERF[b]	24 872	0.5309	0.2884	0.03	1
EMPR (%)	24 872	93.9186	3.2051	61.47	99.30
NBER	24 872	0.1810	0.3850	0	1
MSADUM	24 872	0.1389	0.3458	0	1
$SBAGR_{t-1}$	24 872	0.6205	0.3536	0	1
$SBA7AR_{t-1}$	24 872	0.6737	0.4263	0	1
$SBAMR_{t-1}$	24 872	0.1149	0.2356	0	1
$PICAP_{t-1}$	24 872	18.2244	4.3781	5.50	58.70
MDUM[c]	24 872	0.2378	0.4257	0	1

Notes:
[a]   Guaranteed small business loans per $000 of deposits.
[b]   The Herfindahl index has been normalized to a variable between 0 and 1.
[c]   For markets where there was no recorded SBA guaranteed loan information, we set the value of the SBA lending proxies to 0 and set MDUM = 1 (0 otherwise).

Source: Small Business Administration, Bureau of Economic Analysis, Bureau of Labor Statistics and authors' calculations.

For the full sample and the urban (MSA) sample, the coefficients on $SBAGR_{t-1}$ and $SBA7AR_{t-1}$ are significantly negative, while the coefficient on $SBAMR_{t-1}$ is positive and significant. These results are largely in concert with an explanation that says lenders are relying more heavily on SBA loan guarantees to make loans in more depressed urban markets – ones with lower per capita income. Further results from our urban sample suggest that there are more opportunities for lenders to make loans to small businesses engaged in manufacturing when markets are more economically vibrant. The picture painted by our SBA lending structure variables is somewhat different for the rural (non-MSA) sample, where only the coefficient on $SBAGR_{t-1}$ is significantly different from zero. In other words, lenders in higher-income rural markets rely more heavily on SBA guarantees than lower-income ones. This result is likely due to differences in economic activity across rural markets and the operation of government-subsidized lending programs for agriculture, like the farm credit banks. To the extent that per capita income in rural markets is negatively related to the share

Table 6.3 *Weighted least squares estimation of equation (6.1)*

Dependent variable: PICAP	Full sample Parameter			MSAs Parameter			Non-MSAs Parameter		
	Estimate	t value	Prob > |t|	Estimate	t value	Prob > |t|	Estimate	t value	Prob > |t|
Intercept	−3.4711	−15.22	<0.0001	−4.7193	−6.76	<0.0001	−1.2004	−7.00	<0.0001
$SBADEP_{t-1}$	0.00001	0.10	0.9169	0.0003	0.76	0.4479	0.00000	−0.07	0.947
HERF	−0.0442	−2.01	0.0448	−0.0622	−0.95	0.3446	−0.0967	−5.87	<0.0001
EMPR	0.0506	26.02	<0.0001	0.0659	11.62	<0.0001	0.0110	6.66	<0.0001
NBER	−0.6395	−60.84	<0.0001	−0.6996	−25.13	<0.0001	−0.2661	−23.20	<0.0001
$SBAGR_{t-1}$	−1.3576	−13.53	<0.0001	−1.7138	−5.63	<0.0001	0.1874	2.53	0.0115
$SBA7AR_{t-1}$	−0.2903	−7.74	<0.0001	−0.2950	−2.51	0.0122	−0.0005	−0.02	0.9845
$SBAMR_{t-1}$	0.1781	5.39	<0.0001	0.3857	3.32	0.0009	0.0042	0.22	0.8276
$PICAP_{t-1}$	1.0490	1241.98	<0.0001	1.0488	455.70	<0.0001	1.0449	1120.19	<0.0001
MDUM	−1.2779	−12.02	<0.0001	−1.5420	−4.52	<0.0001	0.2246	2.95	0.0032
MSADUM	−0.0748	−5.28	<0.0001						
Adjusted R-square	0.9910			0.9900			0.9883		
No. of obs.	24 871			3453			21 417		
Root-MSE	927.64			2262.06			388.94		
Dependent mean	26.109			27.129			20.184		
Coeff-var.	3552.88			8338.27			1926.93		

Notes: Observations are weighted by the share of national personal income accounted for by the market in 1990; for equation (6.1), see page 195.

Source: Authors' calculations.

141

of economic activity in agriculture, we would expect demand for SBA loan guarantees to be positively related to income. Hence the positive and significant coefficient on $SBAGR_{t-1}$.

For all three samples the controls for economic activity (NBER dummy, $PICAP_{t-1}$ and $EMPR$) are significant and with the anticipated signs. The coefficient on $HERF$ (deposit market Herfindahl index) is significantly negative for the full sample and for the rural sample. The coefficient on $HERF$ is negative but not significant in the urban sample. These results are in line with the industrial organization literature and may be explained in at least two ways. First, per capita income is higher in more competitive markets, and $HERF$ is a proxy for market competition. Second, the negative correlation is the result of a set of market dynamics in which higher relative per capita income induces more commercial banks to enter the local market. Furthermore, considering the substantial fixed cost associated with market entry, markets with relatively larger aggregate income levels might also experience more entry. Both of these theories would support the perception that urban financial markets are more contestable than rural ones.

Rates of Change Regressions

The results for economic activity and small business lending levels, equation (6.1), provides us with the empirical relationship between the amount of SBA-guaranteed lending scaled by market deposits and the level of per capita income. This, however, is a static view of the relationship between SBA lending and economic activity and an indirect test of the hypothesis that SBA loan guarantees improve social welfare-reducing credit rationing in small business lending markets. A more direct test of this hypothesis is to look at the change in personal income over time as it relates to past levels of SBA lending activity and subsequent changes in SBA-guaranteed lending. To this end we estimate equation (6.2) using the same sample breakdowns as before, but over the 1992–2001 time frame because we need to lag $SBADEP$ by two periods. Descriptive statistics for the variables used in equation (6.2) are found in Table 6.4, and the regression results in Table 6.5.

Table 6.5 shows that SBA-guaranteed lending does affect the growth of income in the market as the coefficient on $LNSBA_{t2}$ (the natural log of SBA-guaranteed loans lagged two periods) is positive and significant for all three samples. Interestingly the impact of SBA-guaranteed lending on income growth is more than 12 times larger in urban than in rural markets. In addition we find no impact of the year-over-year change in SBA lending on income growth as the coefficients on $\Delta LNSBA$ and $\Delta LNSBA_{t-1}$ are not significant in any of our samples.

Table 6.4   Descriptive statistics for equation (6.2) variables

Variable	N	Mean	Std Dev.	Minimum	Maximum
$LNPI_{t-1}$	22 479	13.0605	1.5110	8.48	19.72
$LNSBA_{t-2}$	22 479	10.3557	5.9782	0.00	20.36
$LNDEP_{t-2}{}^a$	22 479	12.1852	1.4866	6.21	19.56
$LNEMPR_{t-1}$ (%)	22 479	4.5411	0.0358	4.12	4.60
$SBAGR_{t-2}$	22 479	0.6239	0.3547	0	1
$SBA7AR_{t-2}$	22 479	0.6749	0.4262	0	1
$SBAMR_{t-2}$	22 479	0.1179	0.2385	0	1
$\Delta LNSBA_{t-1}$	22 479	0.1584	5.7554	−15.26	15.32
$\Delta LNDEP_{t-1}$	22 479	0.0132	0.2561	−5.00	3.71
$\Delta LNSBA$	22 479	0.1493	5.6774	−15.26	15.32
$\Delta LNDEP$	22 479	0.0130	0.2653	−5.00	3.42
$\Delta LNEMPR$	22 479	0.0020	0.0139	−0.16	0.17
$HERF^b$	22 479	0.5352	0.2881	0.03	1.00
NBER	22 479	0.0957	0.2942	0	1
$MSADUM^c$	22 479	0.1394	0.3464	0	1
MDUM	22 479	0.3968	0.4892	0	1
$\Delta LNPI$	22 479	0.0458	0.0481	−0.46	0.43

Notes:
[a] $000.
[b]   The Herfindahl index has been normalized to a variable between 0 and 1.
[c]   For markets where there was no recorded SBA guaranteed loan information we set the
value of the SBA lending proxies to 0 and set MDUM = 1 (0 otherwise).

Source: Small Business Administration, Bureau of Economic Analysis, Bureau of Labor
Statistics, and authors' calculations.

The coefficient on the log level of deposits lagged two periods is negative
and significant for the full sample and the MSA sample. It is positive but
not significant for the non-MSA sample. In other words, growth in personal
income does not appear to be related to the level of local deposits in non-
MSAs. This result is consistent with Craig and Thomson's (2003) finding that
community banks in rural counties are not funding constrained. However in
MSAs we interpret these results as being consistent with an explanation that
says that the fastest-growing markets are able to attract capital from other
regions, including foreign capital. The positive and significant coefficients
on the log change in deposit variables ($\Delta LNDEP$ and $\Delta LNDEP_{t-1}$) for all
three samples suggest that growth in the local funding markets positively
affects income growth.

Table 6.5 Weighted least squares estimation of equation (6.2)

Dependent variable: PICAP	Full sample Parameter			MSAs Parameter			Non-MSAs Parameter		
	Estimate	t value	Prob > |t|	Estimate	t value	Prob > |t|	Estimate	t value	Prob > |t|
Intercept	-1.0419	-34.78	<0.0001	-1.2354	-14.80	<0.0001	-0.3040	-8.94	<0.0001
$LNPI_{t-1}$	0.0015	5.10	<0.0001	-0.0015	-1.65	0.0988	0.0027	7.72	<0.0001
$LNSBA_{t-2}$	0.0027	18.49	<0.0001	0.0050	8.55	<0.0001	0.0004	2.42	0.0155
$LNDEP_{t-2}$	-0.0021	-11.09	<0.0001	-0.0015	-3.30	0.0010	0.0000	0.04	0.9708
$LNEMPR_{t-1}$	0.2414	37.65	<0.0001	0.2870	16.61	<0.0001	0.0694	9.28	<0.0001
$SBAGR_{t-2}$	-0.0295	-12.54	<0.0001	-0.0390	-3.97	<0.0001	-0.0033	-1.42	0.1551
$SBA7AR_{t-2}$	-0.0132	-11.84	<0.0001	-0.0178	-4.71	<0.0001	-0.0051	-4.88	<0.0001
$SBAMR_{t-2}$	-0.0105	-8.51	<0.0001	-0.0224	-5.79	<0.0001	0.0024	2.27	0.0232
$\Delta LNSBA_{t-1}$	0.0000	-0.31	0.7589	0.0031	3.64	0.0003	-0.0001	-1.01	0.3105
$\Delta LNDEP_{t-1}$	0.0027	5.61	<0.0001	0.0031	2.69	0.0072	0.0036	4.47	<0.0001
$\Delta LNSBA$	0.0001	0.57	0.5666	0.0026	2.80	0.0052	0.0000	-0.44	0.6573
$\Delta LNDEP$	0.0016	3.33	0.0009	0.0016	1.42	0.1570	0.0041	5.09	<0.0001
$\Delta LNEMPR$	0.3068	16.81	<0.0001	0.3106	6.39	<0.0001	0.2082	10.58	<0.0001
HERF	0.0020	2.24	0.0252	-0.0004	-0.15	0.8844	0.0031	2.96	0.0031
NBER	-0.0282	-49.41	<0.0001	-0.0302	-21.31	<0.0001	-0.0209	-24.72	<0.0001
MDUM	0.0048	3.06	0.0022	0.0389	2.58	0.0098	0.0011	0.93	0.3540
MSADUM	-0.0016	-2.32	0.0206						
Adjusted R-square	0.1903			0.2582			0.0552		
No. of obs.	22 478			3133			19 344		
Root-MSE	33.32			72.75			20.05		
Dependent mean	0.0532			0.0542			0.0478		
Coeff-var.	62 601.0			134 331.0			41 932.0		

Notes: Observations are weighted by the share of national personal income accounted for by the market in 1990; for equation (6.2), see page 199.

Source: Authors' calculations.

144

The three variables that capture the structure of SBA-guaranteed lending ($SBAGR_{t-2}$, $SBA7AR_{t-2}$ and $SBAMR_{t-2}$), lagged two periods, all enter with significantly negative coefficients for the full sample and MSA sample regressions. For the non-MSA sample regression $SBA7AR_{t-2}$ and $SBAMR_{t-2}$ have significantly negative and significantly positive coefficients, respectively; the coefficient on $SBAGR_{t-2}$ is negative and insignificant. These results suggest that lenders are less likely to rely on SBA loan guarantees when making small business loans, and in particular loans to small manufacturers, in urban markets where they anticipate strong growth. As with the levels results, the positive sign on $SBAMR_{t-2}$ is likely the consequence of higher demand for manufacturing loans in rural markets, where income is growing the fastest. Finally the coefficients on our controls for economic income and local market structure are generally in line with what we found for the levels regressions.

Overall our regression results are consistent with the hypothesis that SBA loan guarantees have positive, albeit small net, social benefits. We find little evidence that the level of SBA-guaranteed lending activity (per $1000 of deposits) is related to the level of per capita income at the local market level. However we find a strong relationship between the level of SBA-guaranteed lending and future income growth in the full sample and the urban and rural market subsamples. This impact of SBA-guaranteed lending on growth appears to be small, as the largest coefficient on the $LNSBA_{t-1}$ regressor is 50 basis points.

CONCLUSIONS AND EXTENSIONS TO THE ANALYSIS

SBA loan guarantee programs are one of many government interventions in markets aimed at promoting small business. The rationale for these guarantees appears to be that credit market imperfections can result in small enterprises being credit rationed, particularly for longer-term loans for purposes such as capital expansion. If SBA loan guarantees indeed reduce credit rationing in the markets for small business loans, there should be a relationship between measures of SBA activities and economic growth. This is what we find. While the data fail to produce a significant positive relationship between SBA-guaranteed lending (adjusted for market size) and per capita income in a market, there is a positive (although small) and significant relationship between the level of SBA lending in a market and future personal income growth.

These results should be considered preliminary, however. The difference between our results for per capita income and for per capita income growth suggests several possible mechanisms. First, the stock of personal income is so large (and so poorly measured) that annual policy regressions will not pick up any effect on it, while the flow of change of personal income might be more clearly measured. On the other hand, the first-differencing of personal income might represent a statistical method to take into account failures in the restrictions that are imposed on the model. There may be unobserved characteristics that are true of counties that influence both the level of personal income and the amount of small business lending. For example, SBA offices could be well developed in areas that are known to have been poorly developed but have a good potential. This 'potential' is an unobserved variable that may bias our regressions of levels of personal income, whereas first-differencing the variables may help with the bias. Further statistical work is needed to clarify the nature of our unobserved error term in order to sharpen our understanding of both the statistical structure of our data and our interpretation of the results.

Our initial estimation imposes other restrictions on the model which may not hold in practice. For instance, we can test the restriction that SBA-guaranteed lending has the same impact on income growth in markets with high and low income (as measured by whether it is above or below the median). Future work will relax these restrictions and thereby more fully utilize the information in our panel data. In addition we plan on extending this work by adding controls for state and regional growth, differences in state taxes and credit cycles. Finally, before we can effectively apply our results to policy restrictions, our estimates need to be posed in the context of a structural model of credit constraints. Identifying such a model, both theoretically and empirically, is tough. This ambitious goal is the aim of our extended research project.

NOTES

1. Ben Craig and James Thomson are economists in the research department at the Federal Reserve Bank of Cleveland. William E. Jackson is an associate professor of finance in the Kenan-Flagler Business School at the University of North Carolina. The views expressed are those of the authors and not those of the Federal Reserve Bank of Cleveland or the Board of Governors of the Federal Reserve System. We thank the Small Business Administration for providing us with the SBA loan-guarantee data and Pat Higgins for outstanding research support. Questions or comments on this paper should be directed to James Thomson at jb.thomson@clev.frb.org.
2. Public Law 163 abolished the RFC and created the SBA. It also clearly stated the necessity for an agency like the SBA, set forth SBA's mission and described the powers the SBA would have at its disposal to carry out that mission.
3. See Public Law 163, s. 207, which empowers the SBA to assist small businesses in obtaining government contracts and to provide technical and managerial aid to small businesses.
4. See Public Law 163, s. 202.

5. Congressional intent is also reflected in Section 204 of Public Law 163 which states, 'In order to carry out the policies of this title there is hereby created an agency under the "Small Business Administration"'. Thus the primary mission of SBA became to '... *aid, counsel, assist, and protect insofar as is possible the interests of small-business concerns'.*

6. Current public policy goals recognized by the SBA are as follows: (1) business district revitalization, (2) expansion of exports, (3) expansion of minority business development, (4) rural development, (5) enhanced economic competition, (6) restructuring because of federally mandated standards or policies, (7) changes necessitated by federal budget cutbacks, (8) expansion of small business concerns owned and controlled by veterans, and (9) expansion of small business concerns owned and controlled by women (SBA, 2004).

7. See Craig and Thomson (2003) for a more complete discussion of the FHLBs' role in supporting small-firm finance.

8. To preserve observations with a value of zero, we add one to all observations prior to taking the natural logarithm.

9. The results are essentially the same when equation (6.1) is estimated with the SBA variables (*SBADEP, SBAMR, SBA7AR* and *SBAGR*) on the right-hand side are lagged two periods.

APPENDIX: CHARACTERISTICS OF LOANS ISSUED UNDER THE SBA 7(a) AND 504 LOAN GUARANTEE PROGRAMS

Table 6A.1 Average SBA loan ($)

Year	Urban 504	Urban 7a	Urban Total	Rural 504	Rural 7a	Rural Total	Total sample
1991	262 159	207 984	213 260	300 958	205 233	213 592	213 345
1992	302 788	244 221	249 582	316 912	232 181	238 305	246 923
1993	325 592	250 624	258 006	346 530	244 144	252 845	256 859
1994	341 261	205 738	218 756	334 919	184 367	195 604	213 855
1995	350 786	150 363	169 179	364 684	125 882	145 227	164 796
1996	376 730	190 938	213 915	341 966	145 963	168 762	206 933
1997	369 753	224 912	238 320	310 629	174 399	188 908	231 171
1998	385 883	236 159	253 764	308 272	199 479	212 395	247 994
1999	412 650	253 674	270 483	335 416	195 475	211 379	263 591
2000	427 095	260 575	277 788	343 140	197 743	213 899	269 633
2001	440 611	241 833	264 551	361 987	195 511	216 531	257 741
Sample	377 773	221 391	237 727	335 527	184 414	199 225	231 391

Source: United States Small Business Administration and authors' calculations.

Table 6A.2   Total SBA loans ($000)

Year	Urban			Rural			Total sample
	504	7a	Total	504	7a	Total	
1991	168 044	1 235 636	1 403 680	58 687	418 265	476 952	1 880 632
1992	380 301	3 043 969	3 424 270	96 975	912 007	1 008 982	4 433 252
1993	564 577	3 978 656	4 543 233	148 315	1 125 014	1 273 329	5 816 562
1994	1 015 593	5 761 698	6 777 291	207 985	1 419 439	1 627 423	8 404 715
1995	1 165 310	4 821 247	5 986 557	234 127	916 799	1 150 926	7 137 483
1996	1 727 682	6 204 515	7 932 197	269 811	874 902	1 144 713	9 076 910
1997	1 219 816	7 273 196	8 493 012	199 424	939 313	1 138 736	9 631 748
1998	1 464 425	6 725 796	8 190 221	191 437	919 600	1 111 037	9 301 258
1999	1 521 028	7 908 288	9 429 316	175 423	797 344	972 767	10 402 083
2000	1 319 722	6 984 461	8 304 183	166 766	768 827	935 593	9 239 776
2001	1 238 118	5 266 396	6 504 514	185 699	694 065	879 765	7 384 279
Sample	11 784 617	59 203 858	70 988 475	1 934 647	9 785 575	11 720 223	82 708 698

Source: United States Small Business Administration and authors' calculations.

149

Table 6A.3 Total number of SBA loans

Year	Urban				Rural			Total sample
	504	7a	Total	504	7a	Total		
1991	641	5941	6582	195	2038	2233		8815
1992	1256	12464	13720	306	3928	4234		17954
1993	1734	15875	17609	428	4608	5036		22645
1994	2976	28005	30981	621	7699	8320		39301
1995	3322	32064	35386	642	7283	7925		43311
1996	4586	32495	37081	789	5994	6783		43864
1997	3299	32338	35637	642	5386	6028		41665
1998	3795	28480	32275	621	4610	5231		37506
1999	3686	31175	34861	523	4079	4602		39463
2000	3090	26804	29894	486	3888	4374		34268
2001	2810	21777	24587	513	3550	4063		28650
Sample	31195	267418	298613	5766	53063	58829		357442

Source: United States Small Business Administration and authors' calculations.

COMMENTARY

Robert Strom

The contribution by Craig, Jackson and Thomson presents an assessment of the impact of the Small Business Administration's (SBA) guaranteed lending on local and regional economic performance. Despite the claims of economists and policy makers that entrepreneurship serves as an engine of economic growth, there is little empirical work on the impact on growth that results from public subsidies to small business. This chapter presents a discussion of the role of one form of public subsidy, SBA loan guarantees, for economic growth.

The chapter is divided into three major parts. First, the authors present background information on the history and structure of the SBA and its guaranteed loan programs. The discussion in this part of the chapter provides the reader with information necessary to understand both the political and economic rationale for the SBA and loan guarantees.

The second part of the chapter deals with a discussion of the literature on the economics of credit markets. In this part, the authors develop a strong case for guaranteed lending within the context of economic theory. Finally the authors present their research questions and empirical work leading to their conclusions. In each of the above parts the authors provide a clear and logical framework for their contribution.

This commentary provides a brief discussion of each part of the chapter. In addition it suggests extensions of the authors' work on the role of public subsidies to entrepreneurship on economic growth.

The discussion of the historical development of the SBA and the attendant legislative activities presents background information necessary to the authors' purpose. The authors cover a wealth of information in a very concise manner. In particular, the information on the 7(a) Guaranteed Loan Program and the 504 Loan Program serves as the basis for the empirical work in the chapter. The authors also include a brief discussion of the Small Business Investment Company (SBIC) Program, noting the important role of the SBIC in providing funds for privately owned and operated venture capital investment firms.

I believe the authors miss an important opportunity in their discussion of the SBIC. The important role the SBIC played in the development of the venture capital industry could serve as an opportunity for the authors to contrast the role of public subsidies for debt versus equity financing of new firms. The SBA website discusses the role that the SBIC program has played in creation of jobs and growth in the US economy over the last half-century. The web site lists a number of success stories from A & W Brands to Xtreme Networks (Small Business Administration, 2004).

The list of firms is quite impressive in terms both of the variety of industries and of geographic locations throughout the country. The firms include America Online, Apple Computer, Callaway, Compaq Computer, Federal Express, Intel and Staples, just to name a few. Surely many of these firms have had a substantial impact on the performance of their local and regional economies.

On the national level, a 2001 study commissioned by the National Venture Capital Association (NVCA) and conducted by DRI-WEFA concluded that companies backed by venture capital funding between 1980 and 2000 have had a substantial impact on employment and output in the US economy. While it is certain that not all of this activity was initiated by SBA support through the SBIC program, the importance of the SBIC program to the development of the venture capital industry cannot be denied.

The authors also miss an opportunity to discuss the institutional arrangements involved in the Small Business Innovation Research (SBIR) program. This program focuses on entrepreneurs because of their propensity for innovation. The program provides start-up and development-stage funds and encourages commercialization of a technology, product or service. Again the impact of bringing these innovations to market may have an important stimulative effect on the economy, both locally and nationally.

I understand that the intent of this chapter is to look more narrowly at the impact of public subsidies to entrepreneurs in the form of SBA loan guarantees. I believe, however, that it would help the reader for the authors to differentiate the intent and impact of SBA programs that are aimed at debt and equity financing, as well as development and commercialization of new technologies.

The authors provide a very insightful discussion of SBA lending and the economics of credit markets to make a theoretical case for SBA intervention. I applaud the thorough manner in which they lead the reader through the economic case for SBA subsidies. My only recommendation here is that they consider including a discussion of the excess of social returns over private returns brought about by entrepreneurial development. Perhaps the case for social returns can be made even more clearly if the authors include the discussion of the innovations generated through SBA programs, such as the SBIR program, that are aimed more directly at innovative activity.

The part of the chapter dealing with authors' research questions, data and empirical work is thoughtful and appropriate for the topic. With respect to the research questions, the authors state that it is their intent to 'shed light on a number of research questions regarding government subsidies directed towards the small business sector. To do this, we focus on one particular government program, SBA loan guarantees'. The authors make a compelling case for choosing the impact of SBA loan guarantees rather than other federally subsidized loan programs such as those of the Federal Home Loan Bank (FHLB). If, however, the relevant research questions involve government subsidies directed toward the small business sector, I would like to see the authors either include the SBIC and SBIR programs of the SBA or make a case similar to the one they did with the FHLB for not including these programs.

If the authors do choose to examine the impact of other SBA programs on economic growth I would suggest a paper by Lerner (1999), 'The Government as Venture Capitalist: The Long Run Impact of the SBIR Program'. In this paper, Lerner asks similar questions regarding the impact on economic growth of public subsidies to small business. Lerner concludes that while SBIR awardees had a greater employment and sales growth than a set of matching firms, the pattern was not uniform. The growth was confined to zip codes with substantial existing venture capital activity and where there were existing high technology industries.

The authors discuss several policy implications of their work. The differential impact of the result for urban and rural areas is particularly interesting and I would like to see the authors more clearly develop the policy questions that relate to those differences.

This is an ambitious contribution with potentially strong policy implications. The authors pose important research questions and have made a good start at a much-needed assessment of the impact of SBA loan guarantees on local and regional growth.

7. Smart places for smart people: cluster-based planning in the 21st-century knowledge economy

Michael Luger

INTRODUCTION

Cluster-based planning for economic development has swept across the USA, Europe and Asia during the past decade. The literature that undergirds the practice goes back over a century, to Alfred Marshall. In short, clusters represent a critical mass of businesses related to each other in different ways. Those relationships create various positive externalities for the members of the cluster, and a basis for policy formation at the local level.

Clearly Marshall's economy in the late nineteenth century was different in fundamental ways from today's economy. His was increasingly dominated by labor-intensive manufacturing businesses and, consequently, he called his clusters 'industrial districts'. He, and a host of successors stretching to the present, have described the importance of business colocation, or 'agglomeration' (Weber, 1929), in terms of what economists now call urbanization and localization economies (Hoover, 1937), increased market power through brokered buying and selling, availability of specialized repair facilities, shared information, reduced risk and uncertainty for entrepreneurs, and tailored infrastructure (Isard, 1956; Lichtenberg, 1960; Vernon, 1960; Carlino, 1978, 1979). Even the earliest theorists recognized the difference between static and dynamic external economies from colocation, where the former arise as a result of reduced costs because of better proximity to suppliers or markets, and the latter are associated with learning, innovation and increased specialization (Bergman and Feser, 1999, p. 8). Bellandi (1989) pointed out that industrial districts are important, not just because of their shared labor pools, opportunities for greater specialization and knowledge spillovers (as intimated by Marshall), but also because of the social and cultural interactions that they allow – the trust, shared customs and social ties that Putnam (1993, 2000) popularized as social capital. Michael Porter picked up on these themes in his influential *The Competitive Advantage of Nations* (1990), the spark for the current intense policy interest in industry clusters.[1]

The conceptual basis for cluster-based planning is as strong in the 'new economy' of the 21st century as it was in the industrial economy of yore, but the different economic landscape of today generates different relationships among businesses, and requires as a consequence different policy responses. For example, instantaneous and ubiquitous communications extend the network among businesses, widening the geographic scope of clusters, even to the point of becoming 'virtual' in some cases (Traxler and Luger, 2000). Another characteristic of the new economy is its tendency to generate ever-widening gaps between more- and less-endowed regions. In short, knowledge resources seek locations with other knowledge resources and support amenities, making it difficult for lagging places to compete. Most recently, Florida (2002) talks about that in regard to the creative class. Finally clusters themselves are becoming more complicated to understand, as new industries emerge at the juncture of several previously distinct technologies. The best example is biotechnology, which is now an umbrella category including such subsets as bio-processing, bio-informatics, bio-engineering, pharmaceuticals and more.

In this chapter I attempt to weave together the major themes introduced above. The central point is that cluster-based planning today must be different from that in the past because of the realities of the new economy. Specifically, first we must define clusters in more than the traditional way (that is, as industrial subgroups linked with other industrial subgroups due to trading relationships), and second we must recognize that regional clusters (such as those defined by Porter's minions in countless studies throughout the world) are not appropriate for all parts of a region (assuming a region is defined as a commuting shed or otherwise broadly integrated economic area), but need to be stepped down to fit the capacity of individual communities.

The chapter is organized into four further sections. In the section that immediately follows, I provide a critique of the 'standard' approach to cluster-based planning and show how it best fits the 'old' economy. Then I draw some contours of the new economy that require new approaches to cluster-based planning, with reference to a sample region. In the third section I summarize an innovative approach to cluster-based planning conducted by a research consortium assembled by a blue-ribbon task force in the Research Triangle region of North Carolina as a follow-up to one of Michael Porter's five regional assessments in the 'Clusters of Innovation' study completed in 2002.[2] The final section summarizes the main points and suggests some directions for future research.

The title of the chapter is 'Smart places for smart people', referring to a growing understanding within the economic development and policy communities that the US cannot compete with low-cost, low-skilled countries for old-economy jobs, but rather, must turn to high-skilled, high-value added jobs appropriate for an advanced, increasingly high-tech economy. The challenge is to find the right types of jobs that can transform all communities into smart places.

THE STANDARD APPROACH TO CLUSTER-BASED PLANNING

The essential feature of industry clusters is the tight connections that bind certain firms and industries together in various aspects of common behavior (Bergman and Feser, 1999, p. 1). Regional clusters are concentrations of businesses that colocate because of trading (buyer–supplier) relationships and/or to share common factor markets (including infrastructure, knowledge resources and labor) and/or common goods markets. As suggested in the introduction, there is a subtle, but important, difference between static agglomeration economies and the more dynamic benefits that accrue to members of a cluster. Informal or formal institutions are often used to leverage the dynamic benefits within a cluster, namely, venues and opportunities for networking, information sharing, collaboration and social learning that aid and encourage continuous innovation, technology upgrading, extension and adaptation to new markets, and so on.

These definitions are unavoidably imprecise. What is meant by tight or colocated? Are colocated firms those in a submetro district, a broader metro area, the same state, the same region? Is there causality implied here? What if firms colocate but do not trade with each other? By the very nature of their colocation they share markets and local resources, but firms may not have chosen their location for the purpose of realizing economies of that sort. Do we only care if they could realize those economies, even if they selected their locations for other reasons? What types of interdependence are most important? If it is knowledge spillovers that we are interested in, by what conduits do they occur? Through conventional product chain ties or labor pools? Through memberships in industry associations or joint linkages with R&D performers such as universities? Are size and critical mass fundamental elements of a cluster and, if so, are rural clusters a theoretical impossibility?

These ambiguities manifest themselves in the operationalization of the concept. There is no single accepted method for identifying clusters. In some cases location quotients on individual industries are used, paradoxically eliminating any notion of sectoral interdependence from the start. More sophisticated approaches rely on factor analyses of input–output or staffing patterns data or discriminant analysis of multiple variables measuring regional industrial characteristics (see DeBresson, 1996; Feser and Bergman, 2000; Hill and Brennan, 2000; Feser and Koo, 2001). The factor analysis approach tends to work better for understanding relationships among mature manufacturing businesses than for smaller businesses, especially those that are service rather than goods-oriented. When factor analysis is performed, the model generates loadings that provide valuable information, but the researcher still must interpret and name the factors. In some instances the loadings make sense, but in others there is often no apparent common feature among the elements. The subjectivity in the approach is no more apparent than when the analyst talks about rotating the factors in order to get loadings that are plausible. The lack of regional input–output and staffing patterns data also limits analysis of localized interdependencies, necessitating tenuous inferences based on national trends.

Emerging and potential clusters are often of greater interest to policy makers than the mature clusters that are the most easily measured. After all, many mature clusters are declining or stagnant and, therefore, not likely to add new jobs in the future. But nascent clusters may be too new or too small to appear in the data. In today's high-tech, high-speed world, several years can be a lifetime. Policy makers also may be more interested in high-tech clusters, as opposed to clusters in general. High-tech businesses are more likely to provide good jobs. That introduces an additional judgment call: how to define high tech. Despite years of debate in the regional science, economics and planning literature, there is still no consensus about the proper definition of that term. (See, for example, Markusen and Glasmeier, 1986; Armington, 1987; Hecker, 1999: Luker and Lyons, 1997; Hadlock *et al.*, 1991).

The challenges inherent in quantitative analysis of secondary data have led to the heavy reliance on interviews, focus groups and surveys of experts. The gathering of expert opinion is the preferred approach of a growing consulting industry that specializes in cluster analysis. The goal is to draw useful information from industry leaders, economic development professionals, chamber of commerce officials, state department of commerce personnel, the manufacturing extension service, academic economists, university scientists and others intimately familiar with the local economy. Stough *et al.*'s assertion (1997, p. 2) that such experts 'are the agents who know the region's industries [best] in terms of basic practice, supply chains, current investment patterns and potential opportunities for new products' is certainly true. Large quantities of subtle and contextual information about a region's business and industry base can be gathered through such largely qualitative methods. Moreover primary data collection of some form is almost always necessary to evaluate adequately key supporting agencies and institutions for which there is often very little high-quality secondary information.

But there are serious risks to the expert-opinion method in cluster analysis as well. First, many such studies implicitly invoke 'know it when you see it' logic; because nothing is being measured in quantitative terms, it is easy to avoid clarifying concepts at the outset. Definitions are likely to shift as information is collected, seriously compromising the objectivity of the findings. Second, experts, like anyone else, are prone to some response bias. Third, the administration of surveys and interviews to convenience samples, as has become the standard practice, very rarely generates data that are representative of the population of experts in a region. Analysts also have a strong incentive to survey and interview those who are receptive to the policy relevance of the study, thus limiting the range of perspectives gathered. Compounding the problem are differences in response rates. Business officials are far less inclined to fill out surveys, grant interviews and attend focus groups. Thus the university and government sectors are usually much better represented than is industry. Finally, because gathering information from experts is time-intensive, comparatively few are consulted. Given that even experts can be myopic in their knowledge of their region's economy, small (and, as we have seen, unrepresentative) samples pose serious problems.

The fact is that neither quantitative nor qualitative methodologies in cluster analysis are without drawbacks. Quantitative studies have probably faced the greatest criticism, but that is largely because they are inherently more transparent. Identifying clusters via the analysis of secondary data requires clear definitions, indicators and decision rules. It is easy to identify weaknesses in specific indicators, existing data sources, industry classifications schemes and statistical models. Qualitative studies, on the other hand, are rarely documented sufficiently to permit a serious validity assessment. It is too easy to assume that experts know best, to trust one's hunch, even in the face of obviously inadequate samples and response bias. The fact that convenience samples, drawn on the basis of an analyst's own views of what is happening in a region, typically confirm that analyst's perspective should come as no surprise. Yet such confirmation is invariably taken as an indicator of the plausibility of the results, not a whole lot different from rotating factors based on their plausibility. Qualitative analysis does indeed have the potential to solve some of the deficiencies of quantitative approaches, but unfortunately that does not make its own deficiencies go away. Likewise the results of quantitative cluster analysis can be seriously misleading if they are interpreted improperly, assumed to be more authoritative than they are, or applied to policy without confirmation via other methods.

In summary, cluster-based planning typically consists of a quantitative analysis of the way individual industries interact through trading, and a qualitative assessment of what industries seem to be emerging. The units of analysis are Standard Industrial Code (SIC) or North American Industrial Classification System (NAICS) groupings and, usually, metropolitan regions. Both the quantitative and qualitative approaches are subject to technical challenges. Most pertinent to this chapter, they fail to account for the growing inappropriateness of SIC/NAICS categories as meaningful aggregates of businesses, they treat regions as undifferentiated spatial units, where all constituent communities have the same workforce and infrastructure capacity, and they do not address the growing need to coordinate among different cluster foci.

IMPLICATIONS OF THE 'NEW ECONOMY'

The Progressive Policy Institute (PPI) in Washington has been the most prominent organization in raising the public's awareness of the 'new economy'. Its biennial 'New Economy Index' ranks states along various dimensions of what the staff considers relevant to new economy places. According to Rob Atkinson, PPI's Vice President,

> The New Economy is about the transformation of all industries and the overall economy. . . [and] represents a complex array of forces. These include the reorganization of firms, more efficient and dynamic capital markets, more economic 'churning' and entrepreneurial dynamism, relentless globalization, continuing economic competition, and increasingly volatile labor markets. (http://www. ppionline.org/ppi_ci.cfm?knlgAreaID=107&subsecID=196&contentID=865)

These forces have at least two consequences that are played out at the local level. One is a growing disparity between the dynamic new economy locations and the more static old economy locations. The second is a breakdown of traditional definitions of industry.

The first of these consequences can be seen in Table 7.1, which contains several indicators for the counties within the Research Triangle Regional Partnership in North Carolina.[3] The counties are divided into three groups: core high-tech counties, containing the densest population settlements, the three research universities, the state capitol, the international airport and related resources; the adjacent non-core metro counties; and the non-adjacent, non-metro counties. 2000 Census data indicate considerable daily commuting from both the adjacent and non-adjacent counties to the

Table 7.1 *Subregional variation in economic outcomes, RTRP*

County	Sub-region	Unemployment rate (percent) 2002	Median household income* 2000	Percent of population >25 years old with high school diploma, 2000	Percent of population >25 with college degree 2000
Chatham	Non-core metro	4.8	$42851	78.5	27.8
Durham	Core metro	5.7	$43337	83.2	40.2
Edgecombe	Non-core metro	12.6	$30983	65.7	8.5
Franklin	Non-core metro	6.4	$38968	74.0	13.3
Granville	Non-metro	6.6	$39965	72.7	13.0
Halifax	Non-metro	12.0	$26459	65.3	11.1
Harnett	Non-metro	8.7	$35105	75.5	12.8
Johnston	Non-core metro	4.9	$40872	76.0	15.9
Lee	Non-metro	7.9	$38900	76.3	17.2
Moore	Non-metro	6.8	$41240	82.7	26.9
Nash	Non-core metro	8.7	$37147	75.3	17.2
Northampton	Non-metro	10.5	$26652	62.4	10.8
Orange	Core metro	3.2	$42372	87.8	51.6
Person	Non-core metro	9.2	$37159	75.0	10.3
Sampson	Non-metro	7.8	$31793	68.8	11.0
Vance	Non-metro	12.4	$31301	67.7	10.7
Wake	Core metro	5.3	$54988	89.4	43.9
Warren	Non-metro	10.0	$28351	67.1	11.5
Wilson	Non-metro	8.3	$33116	69.2	15.0
Core metro counties		*5.1*	*$49899*	*87.7*	*43.9*
Non-core metro counties		*7.2*	*$37997*	*74.4*	*15.9*
Non-metro counties		*8.7*	*$133288*	*72.2*	*15.0*

Note: * Sub-region's median household income is arithmetic average of component counties. Other entries are weighted.

Source: N.C. LINC electronic database – http://data.obsm.state.nc.us/pls/linc/dyn_linc_main.show.

core, though obviously, the intensity of commuting decays somewhat with distance; see Table 7.2.

We see, for example, that 40, 51 and 30 per cent, respectively, of Chatham, Franklin, and Person county workers (adjacent counties) commute to the core, and 35, 23 and 11 per cent, respectively, from Granville, Harnett and Warren counties (non-adjacent).

The main point of Table 7.1 is at the bottom: employment rates, income and educational attainment are progressively worse as we move away from the core of the region. Not shown in the table is that the differences have increased since the last census. Underlying those differences are significant variations in infrastructure and services by county. The widening disparities between more- and less-endowed places, played out within relatively large economic regions/commuting sheds, and between different regions, is a common feature of the new economy (see, for example, Luger, 1998). In short, knowledge businesses require locations with well-developed knowledge resources, and relatively footloose knowledge workers prefer to reside where there is a high level of amenities.

The tradition in regional economics is to consider the metropolitan area as the unit of analysis, and researchers are quite familiar with the appropriate data at that level from the bureaus of the census and labor statistics. Conceptually it makes sense to regard the commuting shed as an integrated whole. And, if we did not construe the region that broadly in impact analyses of policy interventions, we would end up with almost no multiplier effect, since there would be massive leakage to 'the rest of the world'. Finally, in practical terms, it is simply cumbersome to work with individual county data, especially in large regions consisting of many counties.

This tradition of regional analysis undermines the validity of cluster-based planning at that level, given the realities illustrated in Table 7.1. It is unlikely for any target cluster to be appropriate for all locations within a region. For example, a cluster that has advanced skill requirements would be hard to develop in the non-core counties of the Research Triangle region. The *Clusters of Innovation* study (Porter, 2002) did not acknowledge that. The authors recommended particular emphasis on the following four clusters: environmental sciences, biotechnology and information technology, telecommunications and medicine, and biotechnology and agribusiness. That may have resonated with business and government leaders in the core counties, but those outside the core recognized only agribusiness as an appropriate target and, therefore, began to lose interest in the regional planning effort.

A second characteristic of the new economy that poses a challenge for cluster-based planning is the blurring of boundaries between and within clusters. To modify a phrase from a well-known article by Aaron Wildavsky

Economic development through entrepreneurship

Table 7.2   Cross-commuting in 2000

County of residence	Chatham	Durham	Franklin	Granville	Harnett	Johnston	Lee
							County of work
Chatham	**44.69%** **11 018**	11.11% 2739	0.09% 21	0.18% 45	0.11% 26	029% 71	5.73% 1413
Durham	031% 349	**74.94%** **84 262**	0.19% 211	125% 1410	0.00%	0.36% 409	0.16% 178
Franklin	0.21% 47	4.27% 951	**34.93%** **7772**	2.77% 616	0.13% 28	1.27% 282	0.09% 21
Granville	0.06% 12	22.49% 4609	1.16% 238	**53.46%** **10 957**	0.01% 2	0.40% 82	029% 60
Harnett	0.61% 248	1.35% 547	0.06% 24	0.04% 18	**39.20%** **15 916**	3.75% 1521	11.16% 4530
Johnston	0.21% 124	2.80% 1645	0.16% 92	0.18% 107	2.38% 1399	**45.97%** **26 971**	0.32% 187
Lee	6.04% 1383	1.68% 384	0.07% 17	0.14% 31	137% 313	021% 47	**71.56%** **16 382**
Moore	1.24% 398	0.18% 57	0.03% 10	0.05% 17	0.16% 51	0.02% 8	4.50% 1441
Orange	1.30% 792	27.06% 16 470	0.14% 83	0.32% 196	0.01% 9	0.17% 105	0.15% 91
Person	0.26% 43	23.83% 3939	0.05% 8	3.40% 562	0.00%	0.10% 17	0.00%
Vance	0.00%	3.03% 542	2.10% 377	13.10% 2347	0.06% 10	0.12% 22	0.06% 10
Wake	026% 873	12.80% 43 351	0.72% 2430	0.42% 1422	027% 916	1.20% 4050	0.34% 1167
Warren	0.10% 7	2.90% 207	2.74% 196	4.13% 295	0.00%	0.21% 15	0.00%
% commuting out	**55.31%**	**25.6%**	**65.07%**	**46.54%**	**60.80%**	**54.03%**	**28.44%**
# commuting out	**13 639**	**28 171**	**14 476**	**9537**	**24 683**	**31 704**	**6511**

Notes: Cells with no values entered had no workers listed: percentages are rounded. Actual number of workers is shown beneath percentage.

Source: Data taken from the US Census Bureau website at http://www.census.gov/ population/www/cen2000/commuting.html.

Moore	Orange	Person	Vance	Wake	Warren	Total county workforce	Working outside RTRP	Total county workers from RTRP
0.61% 150	17.06% 4206	0.03% 8	0.00%	11.12% 2743	0.00%	24 657	8.99% 2217	**91.01%** 22 440
0.00%	824% 9262	024% 270	0.12% 130	12.39% 13 929	0.01% 8	112 433	1.79% 2015	**98.21%** 110 418%
0.00%	0.24% 54	0.13% 29	4.37% 973	46.51% 10 347	0.27% 60	22 248	4.80% 1068	**95.20%** 21 180
0.03% 7	1.21% 249	1.08% 221	5.01% 1026	12.15% 2489	0.08% 16	20 494	2.57% 526	**97.43%** 19 968
125% 508	0.21% 84	0.00%	0.04% 18	21.78% 8841	0.00%	40 599	20.55% 8344	**79.45%** 32 255
0.01% 8	0.42% 246	0.01% 8	0.05% 30	40.27% 23 628	0.02% 9	58 675	7.19% 4221	**92.81%** 54 454
3.62% 828	1.03% 236	0.00%	0.03% 7	9.15% 2094	0.00%	22 893	5.12% 1171	**94.88%** 21 722
76.10% **24 365**	0.14% 44	0.00%	0.01% 4	0.96% 308	0.00%	32 018	16.60% 5315	**83.40%** 26 703
0.00%	**57.60%** **35 053**	0.23% 142	0.02% 12	6.92% 4212	0.01% 8	60 860	6.06% 3687	**93.94%** 57 173
0.00%	4.06% 671	**58.13%** **9609**	0.44% 73	3.71% 614	0.00%	16 531	6.02% 995	**93.98%** 15 536
0.00%	0.33% 60	0.16% 29	**70.13%** **12 561**	6.56% 1175	1.84% 329	17 911	2.51% 449	**97.49%** 17 462
0.04% 145	1.05% 3552	0.05% 166	0.14% 478	**80.46%** **272 432**	0.01% 18	338 602	225% 7602	**97.75%** 331 000
0.00%	0.70% 50	0.06% 4	24.58% 1757	3.85% 275	**44.87%** 3208	7149	15.58% 1135	**84.12%** 6014
23.90% **7653**	**42.40%** **25 807**	**41.87%** **6922**	**29.87%** **5350**	**19.54%** **66 170**	**55.13%** **3941**			

(1976), 'if clusters are anything, maybe they are nothing'. It is bad enough that the technique of cluster analysis does not produce 'definitive' industry groupings, but in addition, the raw material used in the analyses (SIC/NAICS industries) does not tell the full story of what the constituent business does.

This point is illustrated in Table 7.3. The input–output linkages that generated this loading of industries are from national data. The procedure we used created the grouping shown in the table, which we then had to interpret. Somewhat arbitrarily, we named the set of linked industries the 'chemicals and plastics cluster', recognizing that many non-plastics and non-chemical businesses were included. The table also indicates that the industries included vary in terms of their technology intensiveness.

Economic developers do not seek to recruit clusters to a region, but rather, individual businesses. They like cluster analysis because it can be used to generate a list of industry codes that help them decide which businesses to concentrate on. But there is no guarantee that the particular business they land, even if it belongs to one of the industries in Table 7.3, will have any synergies with other business in the region. Conversely there are likely businesses not included in the table that would be highly linked in the region.

What this means is that industry codes are not the only – and perhaps not the best – business attribute to use when ascertaining the likelihood of business synergies within a region. Some analysts (for example, Feser, 2003) group businesses by the labor they use, understanding that those businesses value the same kinds of education and training, and can draw on a larger labor pool locally, including both unemployed and already employed workers who can move laterally. That is consistent with the volatile nature of the labor market in the new economy referred to by Atkinson above.

In the work conducted for the Research Triangle's cluster task force, summarized in the next section, a third basis was used to group businesses together: their common technologies or applications areas. That is consistent with the role ascribed to science and technology (S&T) in the rapid transformation of new economy businesses, also in the Atkinson quotation above.

CREATING SMART PLACES FOR SMART PEOPLE: CLUSTER-BASED PLANNING FOR THE 21ST CENTURY

When Porter's team left the Research Triangle in 2002, local leaders asked: now what? The project had generated considerable public interest because

Table 7.3 A sample loading of linked industries ('one national benchmark cluster')

SIC	Technology intensive	Description	SIC	Technology intensive	Description
2087		Flavoring extracts and syrups, nec	3069		Fabricated rubber products, nec
2611		Pulp mills	3081		Unsupported plastics film & sheet
2621		Paper mills	3082		Unsupported plastics profile shapes
2631		Paperboard mills	3083		Laminated plastics plate & sheet
2812	✓	Alkalies and chlorine	3084		Plastics pipe
2813	✓	Industrial gases	3085		Plastics bodies
2816	✓	Inorganic pigments	3086		Medical laboratories
2821	✓	Plastics materials and resins	3087		Custom compound purchased resins
2822	✓	Synthetic rubber	3088		Plastics plumbing fixtures
2823	✓	Cellulosic manmade fibers	3089		Plastics products, nec
2824	✓	Organic fibers, noncellulosic	3111		Leather tanning and finishing
2841	✓	Soap and other detergents	3291		Abrasive products
2842	✓	Polishes and sanitation goods	3399		Primary metal products, nec
2843	✓	Surface active agents	3559	✓	Special industry machinery, nec
2844	✓	Toilet preparations	3624	✓	Carbon and graphite products
2851	✓	Paints, varnishes, lacquers, enamels, etc.	3692	✓	Primary batteries, dry and wet
2865	✓	Cyclic crudes and intermediates	3843	✓	Dental equipment and supplies
2869	✓	Industrial organic chemicals, nec	3996		Hard surface floor coverings, nec
2874	✓	Phosphatic fertilizers	8042		Offices and clinics of optometrists
2875	✓	Fertilizers, mixing only	8043		Offices and clinics of podiatrists
2879	✓	Agricultural chemicals, nec	8049		Offices of health practitioners, nec
2891	✓	Adhesives and sealants	8071	✓	Medical laboratories
2893	✓	Printing ink	8072	✓	Dental laboratories
2899	✓	Chemical preparations, nec	8092	✓	Kidney dialysis centers
3011		Tires and inner tubes	8093	✓	Specialty outpatient facilities, nec
3061		Mechanical rubber goods	8099	✓	Health and allied services, nec

of Porter's cachet and had provided some useful advice about the need for a better institutional framework to support new cluster development. But the report was short on implementation.

The cluster task force considered re-engaging the Porter group to take the next step, but instead decided to exploit the considerable local expertise in the Research Triangle region, to ensure sustainability of their efforts. They formed a consortium made up of regional economists from UNC-Chapel Hill's Office of Economic Development (OED) who were knowledgable about industrial clusters; staff of the state's Small Business Technology and Development Center (SBTDC) who understood the needs and capacities of individual businesses; and engineers and technology specialists from RTI, International (RTII), who had just completed a technology assessment of the region's higher education sector.[4]

OED redid the Porter analysis using its own methodology (Porter's is proprietary), including three more years of data. But rather than generating target industrial clusters for the entire 19-county region – as Porter did – OED stepped down the analysis for the three subregions identified in Table 7.1. The results of that analysis are summarized in Table 7.4 (see Luger *et al.*, 2003, for the complete analysis). The table also differentiates between industrial clusters made up of businesses that use a high percentage of high-tech workers, and others (general).

The clusters listed in the first column of the table are those judged to be the most appropriate targets for the region. 'Appropriate target' means the following: indications of competitive local advantage, either by a sizable presence already in the region or by rapid changes in relative national share, and representative of businesses that are adding jobs at best, or at least not losing employment, if the businesses are becoming more productive. These criteria filter out potential clusters that make sense for the region, but do not yet show up in the data.

The *pharmaceuticals and medical technologies cluster* is the strongest cluster target for all counties. However the same activities within that cluster are not appropriate everywhere. The less technological activities, for example bio-processing, are more suited for the non-metro counties, while those or the R&D-intensive functions are appropriate in the core and other metro counties.

Similarly, *food products* appear as appropriate in all subregions, but presumably the activities would be different in different places. For example, within the core counties, there is considerable biotech R&D involving organic products. In non-core metro and non-metro counties there are agricultural and livestock farming operations. The challenge in those farther-flung locations is to apply more biotech R&D in their processes, as well as to undertake more value-added activities on site.

Table 7.4 Summary of appropriate clusters for the region

Cluster	Core metro counties		Sub-region type Non-core metro counties		Non-metro counties	
	general	high-tech	general	high-tech	general	high-tech
Pharmaceuticals and medical technology	✓	✓	✓	✓	✓	
Hospitals, labs, and medical services	✓		✓		✓	
Business support	✓		✓		✓	
Food products	✓		✓		✓	
Information technology	?		?		?	
Communication services and software	?		?			
Chemicals and plastics		✓		✓		
Motor vehicle parts and assembly		✓			✓	
Aerospace		✓		✓		
Industrial machinery		?				
Transportation, shipping, and logistics		?			✓	

167

The data suggest that *hospitals, labs and medical services*, and *business support services* will continue to be strong clusters in all counties. On the one hand, they are good targets because they have absorbed and will continue to absorb workers displaced in traditional manufacturing industries. On the other hand, they are not what the literature refers to as 'traded' clusters: those that bring income into the region from outside. Rather they are focused on the resident population of people and businesses. Some of the occupations in the cluster require mid-tech skills and pay well; others are low-skill and low-pay (more on this below).

Several clusters seemed promising in the 1996–99 period, but shed jobs thereafter, casting their long-term appropriateness in doubt (and, consequently, being given a question mark in the table), notably *information technology* and *communications services and software*. The first of these had a strong representation in all subregions; the second in the core and adjacent metro counties only. *Industrial machinery and metalworking* and *transportation, shipping and logistics* similarly slowed down in the core counties, but not in the other counties in which they were concentrated.

Chemicals and plastics and *aerospace* appear to be promising clusters for high-tech workers and, therefore, would not immediately be appropriate for non-metro counties. The other side of the coin is *transportation, shipping and logistics*, a cluster that looks stronger for non-metro counties than other counties in the region, presumably because of the lower-cost land for space-intensive uses, such as distribution centers, and for location near interstate highways.

Finally, *vehicle parts assembly* appears to be appropriate as a high-tech cluster in core counties, and a general cluster in non-metro counties. That suggests that the companies in Orange, Wake and Durham counties in that cluster are using R&D to improve the design and engineering of products, while those in the outlying counties are more involved in routine production and assembly.

Another way to tailor industrial clusters to subregions with different capacities is through an analysis of the occupational needs of the target businesses. Table 7.5 contains descriptive information about the top five occupations in most of the clusters included in Table 7.4. The lower the educational attainment indexes in the last column, the greater the educational requirement for the occupation. (Compensation data are not included in the table, but they generally correspond to required educational level.) Job openings for any occupation are the sum of new jobs and replacements.

The information in Table 7.5 can be presented in another way: by occupation, showing the projected demand in the whole region for 2008, and the different clusters that would use that labor (see Table 7.6).

*Table 7.5 Top five occupations in selected clusters**

	1998 Empl.	2008 Projected Empl.	Annual Percent Change	Annual Average Openings	Annual Average Growth	Annual Average Replacements	Education Level***
Pharmaceuticals and medical technologies							
1 Packaging and Filling Machine Operators and Tenders	3900	5110	2.74	220	120	100	10
2 Team Assemblers	7140	8920	2.25	310	180	130	11
3 Chemists	1340	1790	2.94	80	50	30	5
4 General and Operations Managers	21 450	26 390	2.09	870	490	380	4
5 Biological Technicians	560	850	4.26	40	30	10	2
Hospitals, labs, and specialized medical services							
1 Registered Nurses	14 240	17 610	2.15	580	340	240	6
2 Nursing Aides, Orderlies, and Attendants	9090	11 770	2.62	400	270	130	11
3 Computer Programmers	7000	7600	0.83	280	60	220	5
4 Licensed Practical and Licensed Vocational Nurses	1290	1890	3.89	90	60	30	11
5 Computer Software Engineers, Applications	5740	8810	4.38	350	310	40	5
Information technology and equipment							
1 Computer Programmers	7000	7600	033	280	60	220	5
2 Computer Software Engineers, Applications	5740	8810	4.38	350	310	40	5
3 Computer Support Specialists	4290	7850	6.23	390	360	30	5
4 Computer Systems Analysts	n/a	n/a	n/a	n/a	n/a	n/a	n/a
5 Computer Software Engineers, Systems Software	n/a	n/a	n/a	n/a	n/a	n/a	n/a
Communication services and software							
1 Computer Programmers	7000	7600	0.83	280	60	220	5
2 Computer Software Engineers, Applications	5740	8810	4.38	350	310	40	5
3 Computer Support Specialists	4290	7850	6.23	390	360	30	5
4 Computer Systems Analysts	n/a	n/a	n/a	n/a	n/a	n/a	n/a
5 Civil Engineers	n/a	n/a	n/a	n/a	n/a	n/a	n/a
Business support services							
1 Tellers	2690	2770	0.29	130	10	120	11
2 Lawyers	2830	3630	2.52	110	80	30	1
3 Legal Secretaries	1640	1970	135	60	30	30	7
4 Paralegals and Legal Assistants	170	210	2.14	0	0	0	6
5 Customer Service Representatives	1470	1720	1.58	70	30	40	11
Chemicals and plastics							
1 Molding, Coremaking, and Casting Machine Setters, Operators, and Tenders, Metal and Plastic	860	1130	2.77	40	30	10	10
2 Team Assemblers	7140	8920	2.25	310	180	130	11
3 Extruding and Drawing Machine	660	840	2.44	40	20	20	10
4 First-Line Supervisors/Managers of Production and Operating Workers	3960	4940	2.24	190	100	90	8
5 Dental Laboratory Technicians	1160	1550	2.94	60	40	20	10

Table 7.5   continued

	1998 Empl.	2008 Projected Empl.	Annual Percent Change	Annual Average Openings	Annual Average Growth	Annual Average Replace-ments	Educa-tion Level***
Metalworking and industrial machinery							
1 Team Assemblers	7140	8920	2.25	310	180	130	11
2 Inspectors, Testers, Sorters, Samplers, and Weighers	3900	4040	0.35	100	10	90	8
3 First-Line Supervisors/Managers of Production and Operating Workers	3960	4940	2.24	190	100	90	8
4 Multiple Machine Tool Setters, Operators, and Tenders, Metal and Plastic	300	410	3.17	20	10	10	10
5 Maintenance/Repair Workers, General	7700	8900	1.46	290	120	170	9
Vehicle parts and assembly							
1 Team Assemblers	7140	8920	2.25	310	180	130	11
2 Molding, Coremaking, and Casting Machine Setters, Operators, and Tenders, Metal and Plastic	860	1130	2.77	40	30	10	10
3 Machinists	1590	1920	1.90	60	30	30	9
4 Aerospace Engineers	**	**	**	**	**	**	**
5 Extruding and Drawing Machine Setters, Operators, and Tenders, Metal and Plastic	660	840	2.44	40	20	20	10
Transportation, shipping, and logistics							
1 Truck Drivers, Heavy and Tractor-Trailer	7600	9300	2.04	280	170	110	11
2 Truck Drivers, Light or Delivery Services	6230	7920	2.43	260	170	90	11
3 Laborers and Freight, Stock, and Material Movers, Hand	960	1180	2.08	40	20	20	10
4 Reservation and Transportation Ticket Agents and Travel Clerks	1220	1360	1.09	40	10	30	11
5 Motor Vehicle Operators	1580	1330	−1.71	30	0	30	11

* The selection of top 5 occupations within specific clusters is based on 2001 US. data. The current and projected employment data are for the 13 counties in the Research Triangle Regional Partnership only and come from ESC's 1998 'North Carolina Occupational Trends': eslmi12.esc.state.nc.us/projections/.
** Indicates suppressed employment lower than 50.
*** 1 = first professional degree, 2 = doctoral degree, 3 = master's degree, 4 = work experience plus bachelor's degree, 5 = bachelor's degree, 6 = associate's degree, 7 = post-secondary vocational training, 8 = work experience in a related occupation, 9 = long-term on-the-job training (>12 months), 10 = mid-term on-the-job training (1–12 months), 11 = short-term on-the-job training.

To connect the Table 7.6 information to that in Table 7.4, read down the columns. For example, Table 7.4 indicates that transportation, shipping and logistics is more appropriate for non-metro counties than elsewhere. For non-metro counties to be able to cash in on that promise, they must have an adequate supply of truck drivers and motor vehicle operators, for example. The region as a whole needs computer programmers and software engineers, nurses and nurses' aides, and lab technicians. Those occupations serve clusters that are appropriate for all counties. On the other hand, textile machine operators and woodworking machine setters will not be in demand by any of the target clusters.

The ultimate purpose of this exercise was to identify appropriate targets for policy to help grow quality jobs in all the counties of the extended Research Triangle region. Particular emphasis was given to clusters that seemed to have a competitive advantage in the region, and that represented sectors that were growing. The standard approach is to use national benchmark clusters – statistically generated groups of linked industries. Assuming that trading patterns (input–output linkages) among industries are related more to the technical requirements of those businesses than to features of the local economy, we can expect the composition of clusters to be similar from region to region. A less-than-representative share of a component industry in a particular region's cluster therefore may represent a target of opportunity for economic developers, to recruit or help grow that industry.

Figure 7.1 contains the industries that make up the national benchmark cluster in information technology and instruments (IT). A region with a fully developed IT cluster would have a sizable presence of all components shown in the figure. We see that the Research Triangle Regional Partnership (RTRP) region is not fully developed in this cluster: it has a sizable presence of businesses in the seven industries listed in the left-hand column, but is missing a sizable presence of businesses in the nine industries listed in the right-hand column. Businesses in the underrepresented industries (the right-hand column) constitute possible targets of opportunities for recruiters. Those businesses can be sold a location that should provide a rich local network of buying and selling possibilities (based on national experience).

Cluster	Major Components	Missing Components
Information technology and instruments	Data processing and preparation	Electronic computers
		Computer storage devices
	Computer peripheral equipment, nec	Computer terminals
	Engine electrical equipment	Calculating and accounting equipment
	Computer related services, nec	Semiconductors and related devices
	Computer programming services	Electronic connectors
		Search and navigation equipment
	Electronic components, nec	Optical instruments and lenses
	Environmental controls	Electromedical equipment
	National benchmark cluster	

Figure 7.1   Targets of opportunity in the information tech and instruments cluster

Table 7.6 *Projected demand, by occupation and cluster, 2008*

Occupation	Projected demand	Pharmaceuticals and medical technologies	Hospitals, labs, spec. med. services	Information technology and equipment	Communication equipment and software	Business support services	Chemicals and plastics	Metalworking and industrial machinery	Vehicle parts and assembly	Transportation, shipping, and logistics	Food products
Bakers	80										✓
Biological Technicians	70	✓									
Chemists	130	✓									
Computer Programmers	340			✓	✓						
Computer Software Engineers, Applications	660			✓	✓						
Computer Support Specialists	750			✓	✓						
Customer Service Representatives	100		✓			✓					
Dental Laboratory Technicians	1000		✓								
Extruding/Drawing Machine Setters; Operators; Tenders, Metal and Plastic	60						✓	✓			
First-Line Supervisors/Managers of Production and Operating Workers	290						✓	✓			
General and Operations Managers	1360	✓									
Inspector, Testers, Sorters, Samplers, and Weighers	110						✓		✓		
Laborers and Freight, Stock, and Material Movers, Hand	60									✓	
Lawyers	190					✓					
Legal Secretaries	90					✓					

Occupation	Number
Licensed Practical and Licensed Vocational Nurses	150
Machinists	90
Maintenance and Repair Workers, General	410
Meat, Poultry, and Fish Cutters and Trimmers	110
Molding, Coremaking, Casting Machine Setters, Operators, Tenders, Metal/Plastic	70
Motor Vehicle Operators	30
Multiple Machine Tool Setters, Operators, and Tenders, Metal and Plastic	30
Nursing Aides, Orderlies, and Attendants	670
Packaging and Filling Machine Operators and Tenders	340
Packers and Packages, Hand	960
Paralegals and Legal Assistants	0
Registered Nurses	920
Reservation and Transportation Ticket Agents and Travel Clerks	50
Sewing Machine Operators	20
Slaughterers and Meat Packers	20
Team Assemblers	490
Tellers	140
Textile Knitting and Weaving Machine Setters, Operators, and Tenders	10
Textile Winding, Twisting, Drawing Out Machine Setters, Operators, Tenders	0
Truck Drivers, Heavy and Tractor-Trailer	450
Truck Drivers, Light or Delivery Services	430
Woodworking Machine Setters, Operators, and Tenders, Except Sawing	10

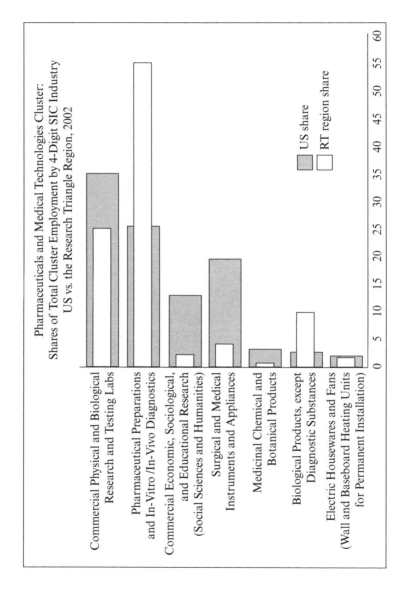

Figure 7.2   Targets of opportunity in the pharma and medical technologies cluster

Figure 7.2 tells the same story for the pharmaceutical and medical technologies cluster, using a different graphic. The Research Triangle region is very strong in pharmaceutical preparations and biological products; however it is underrepresented in surgical and medical instruments and appliances, commercial labs and in medicinal chemicals and botanical products relative to the USA. Businesses in those industries constitute targets of opportunity.

OED's project report includes more charts like Figure 7.2, as well as the accompanying data for each of the clusters that are part of the analysis (as listed in Table 7.4). Table 7.7 summarizes the important observation from

Table 7.7 Potential targets of opportunity to strengthen existing clusters

SIC(s)	Description	Cluster(s) in which it figures
8734, 3577, 7379	Computer programming, processing and data preparation	Hospitals, labs, med. svcs. IT and instruments Communications/software
8042, 3678, 8712	Information retrieval services	Hospitals, labs, med svcs. IT and instruments
8049, 3827	Computer integrated systems and facilities management	Hospitals, labs, med. svcs. IT and instruments
2731	Specialty hospitals, other than psychiatric	Hospital, labs, med. svcs.
2869	Soaps and specialty cleaning agents	Chemicals and plastics
3061, 3821	Primary metal products	Chemicals and plastics Metalworking and industrial machinery
8072	Plastics and plastic products	Chemicals and plastics
7375	Engineering and architectural services	Communications services and software
3511	Motor vehicles and passenger car bodies	Vehicle parts assembly
3229	Special dies and tools, die sets, and industrial molds	Vehicle parts assembly
2048	Frozen foods	Food products
6062	Insurance carriers and foreign institutions	Business support services
6321	Savings institutions	Business support services

those exhibits: the industries that are underrepresented components of key clusters. It includes the SIC codes, a brief description and the name of the associated cluster(s).

The fact that a region is underrepresented in an industry relative to the USA does not necessarily mean that industry is a good target for recruitment. It may be a declining sector globally, or the region may have a substitutable strength in another industry. For example, as Figure 7.2 shows, the Research Triangle region is relatively low on *commercial* economic, sociological and educational research, but clearly a leader in university research in those and other areas.

The information on projected employment growth and wage levels, shown in Table 7.8, can help identify those industries likely to be more promising employers for the region. Once this screen of employment growth is imposed, industries such as cleaning agents, primary metal products, frozen foods and savings institutions are eliminated as good targets to help grow the clusters they are in. Nonetheless, plastics parts and motor vehicles – two manufacturing sectors – may be appropriate targets for the non-metro areas.

RTI International (RTII) provided a complementary way to identify targets of opportunity. It assessed existing and emerging *areas of applied technology strength*,[5] regardless of the industry in which that technology is used. That approach was particularly well suited to the Research Triangle region, which has a density of university-based and government-funded applied research. It is the type and quality of such research that draws many diverse industries to the region. In some cases, researchers have identified a priori the industry or industries that will apply their work, but in other cases they do not. In the fluid technological world in which we live today, it is difficult for any expert to know what technologies businesses are using, and how they are applying them. The creative and productive use of technology is what defines 'innovation'.

Figure 7.3 presents RTII's major applied technology areas as column headings. They include pharmaceutical processes, research about biological agents and infectious disease, advances in medical care, analytical instrumentation, nanoscale technologies, pervasive computing, informatics and agricultural biotechnology. (Fuller descriptions of these, and the rationale for their inclusion, are presented in the RTII report; see note 5).

Figure 7.3 also contains OED's industrial clusters as row headings. They represent businesses that, to varying degrees, tend to use the technologies defined by RTII. We show the intensity of application of each of RTII's technologies by our industry clusters, as follows: the darkest shade indicates above-average use, the medium shade signifies average use, and the lightest shade indicates some use. A blank cell represents little application of technology within the designated industry. The scores in the matrix were

Table 7.8 Most promising industry targets within clusters

SIC	Description	2000 US Employment	2010 US Employment	Projected Percentage Change	2001 Mean Annual Income of Workers
7379	Computer programming, processing and data preparation	2 256 900	4 162 000	45.7	$59 740
8069	Specialty hospitals, other than psychiatric	4 000 000	4 510 000	11.3	$38 150
2814	Soaps and specialty cleaning agents	218 000	190 200	(14.6)	$48 080
3399	Primary metal products	44 600	43 300	(3.0)	$35 730
3089	Plastics and plastic products	746 300	902 000	17.3	$30 410
8711	Engineering and architectural services	1 098 200	1 419 000	22.6	$52 790
3711	Motor vehicles and passenger car bodies	1 017 600	1 104 000	7.8	$44 810
3544	Special dies and tools, die sets, and industrial molds	330 901	331 000	0.0	$38 500
2037, 2053	Frozen foods	301 700	282 900	(6.6)	$29 930
6311, 6321, 6351, 6361, 6399	Insurance carriers and foreign institutions	1 589 400	1 632 000	2.6	$44 880
6035, 6036	Savings institutions	2 032 300	2 002 000	(1.5)	$33 150

Note: The shaded rows are those with projected employment growth nationally.

Sources: Bureau of Labor Statistics: 2001 National Industry-Specific Occupations Employment and Wage Estimates; and Industry Output and Employment Projections for the Year 2010.

assigned by the research team, based on its knowledge of the industrial economy, and on input solicited from industry experts at RTII and elsewhere around North Carolina.

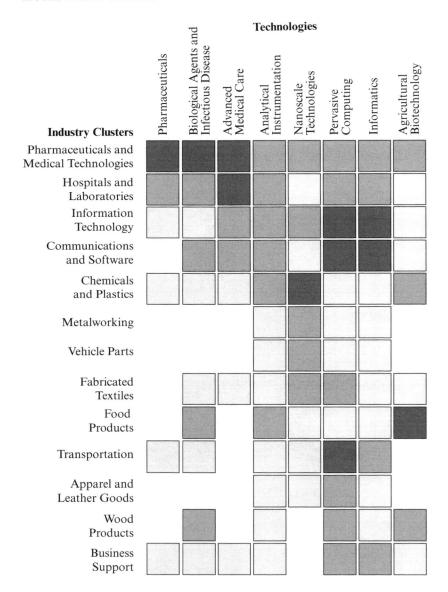

Figure 7.3   Combining industrial and technology clusters

One role for the third partner in the research consortium (SBTDC) was to identify specific businesses (by name and location) that fall into the dark cells in Figure 7.3, develop fuller profiles on them and pass the best prospects on to recruiters. SBTDC's use of the two-way filter represented in Figure 7.3 should reduce the false positives in recruitment that occur when a business is approached because it falls into a target SIC/NAICS group, but turns out not to have connections with the regional economy.

In addition, if economic developers added to their recruitment strategy the general marketing of the region as a world leader in the technologies shown across the top of Figure 7.3, they would also reduce false negatives. These occur because businesses that use, or plan to use those technologies, but are not in the industry aggregations along the left-hand side of Figure 7.3, would find location in the region attractive, but are not recruited and do not know about the strength of the region in their area of application. They are not recruited because their current or planned use of the technology is not widely known, and could even be proprietary. Once made aware of the support available in their technology area, some of those businesses are likely to self-select into the region, even without a recruitment visit.

CONCLUSION

Globalization has resulted in a massive loss of lower-skilled jobs from US regions to China, Malaysia, Vietnam and various offshore locations. That exodus will continue, even accelerate, as trade barriers are lowered through WTO and other compacts, and developing countries become more responsive to the needs of multinational corporations.

The response by regions across the USA affected by this large-scale displacement has been mixed. Smart places understand their place in the new economy of the 21st century. They recognize that there is no future in low-skilled, low-tech jobs, but also that all subregions are not yet appropriate for the highest-end R&D. They know that 'one size does not fit all'. Smart regions also understand that new economy businesses are dynamic, and succeed by adopting new technologies that may not be commonly associated with the industry in which they are placed for statistical purposes.

This chapter describes an innovative approach to industrial development by one of the country's smart regions: the Research Triangle of North Carolina. As in so many other regions around the world, leaders commissioned a cluster-based planning effort that identified strong and growing targets for recruitment and expansion, but, rather than stopping there, the task force formed a consortium of researchers to implement the plan in a way that recognized intraregional differences in capacity, and the ever-changing technology content of businesses. The research team proceeded by redoing and stepping down Michael Porter's original analysis to the subregional level, and by defining clusters, not just around industry codes, but also around occupations and technologies.

It is too early to judge whether this approach will result in more and better economic development than otherwise would have occurred. That is a topic for further research. But the approach has generated considerable enthusiasm from a broad spectrum of stakeholders in the region, notably those in non-core and non-adjacent counties that previously felt left out of technology-oriented planning.

NOTES

1. See Feser and Luger (2003) for a fuller literature review.
2. Council on Competitiveness, 'Monitor Group, and on the Frontier', *Clusters of Innovation: Research Triangle* (Washington, DC: Council on Competitiveness, January 2002).
3. The U.S. Bureau of Economic Analysis describes the Raleigh–Durham economic area as including Chatham, Durham, Edgecombe, Franklin, Granville, Halifax, Harnett, Johnson, Lee, Nash, Northampton, Orange, Person, Sampson, Vance, Wake, Warren and Wilson counties, and the Porter team used this definition for the Research Triangle region. Twelve of these counties are served by the Research Triangle Regional Partnership, along with Moore county.
4. The Office of Economic Development was renamed the Carolina Center for Competitive Economies (C3E) during the time this chapter was being prepared.
5. Amy Witsil and Dan Winfield (RTI International), *R&D Inventory and Growth Opportunity Analysis*, for the Research Triangle Regional Partnership, July 2003.

COMMENTARY

Hunter Morrison

Michael Luger writes, as both an academic and a practitioner, about cluster-based planning and its application to understanding and managing the 21st-century knowledge-based economy. As an academic, he grounds the techniques of economic cluster analysis championed by Michael Porter in the rich history of economic geography developed to explain the agglomeration or 'clustering' of economic activities in the industrial cities of the late 19th and early 20th centuries. As a practitioner, Luger takes Porter's broad, descriptive approach to the analysis of economic activity in contemporary communities and develops methods that allow economic development professionals to move from analysis to action.

Luger's work represents a significant advance in the use of cluster-based analysis to address the needs of specific communities and their unique local economies. He addresses the challenge faced by local economic development practitioners to use cluster-based analysis, not simply to describe a region's economy, but also to craft specific policies and programs that are well-tailored to the place and its people.

Luger begins by recounting the origins of cluster-based economic analysis in the analysis of industrial districts characterized by the agglomeration of related businesses in a defined geographic area. Such districts dominated the industrial cities of Europe and the United States, creating unique places that are remembered in many older cities today as the 'warehouse district', the 'jewelry district' or 'printer's row'. These close-packed business districts, often served by rail lines, were tangible evidence of the economic activity that created the wealth of individual communities.

With the advent of trucking and advances in telecommunication, economic agglomerations that once were discrete and visible have been dispersed across broad regional landscapes. Understanding the interactions between firms located within the same region has become more complex and challenging. Porter and his colleagues addressed this challenge by promoting the analysis of economic clusters at a multijurisdictional or regional level. No longer could a local economy be understood as being defined by the economic activities taking place within a single city. Only by examining the activities of firms and workers operating within large commuter sheds could an economist understand the nature of a local economy.

Porter's contribution to the field of economic development has been significant. By changing the focal length of analysis from compact urban districts to broad regional geographies, Porter has enabled today's economic development practitioners to identify agglomerations of like and related industries on a regional scale, much as their predecessors were able to identify industrial concentrations within discrete districts on an urban scale.

Perhaps the most cited example of the application of Porter's regional approach is that of the California wine industry and the cluster of firms, from barrel manufactures to shippers, established with the expansive geography of the wine country to support the vineyards. This approach has been used to explain the clustering of high-tech firms in the Silicon Valley and underpins the strategy many communities have adopted when trying to grow new industrial clusters in industries such as bio-technology.

Luger, as an economic development practitioner working within the context of North Carolina's Research Triangle, addresses the limitations of Porter's broad-brush approach when it confronts the diversity within a specific regional economy. While the Research Triangle is known for its intellectual horse power and technological innovation, driven by the cluster of public and private universities, it sits within a 19-county regional economy that includes significant 'old economy' activities such as metal working, auto assembly and industrial machinery. While some of the region's economic activities, particularly in pharmaceuticals, medical technology and aerospace, can be characterized as high-tech, a significant proportion of the region's economic activities are of a more general or traditional nature.

As an economic development practitioner, Luger is concerned, not just with describing the local economy, but with interviewing in it. Specifically he and his colleagues are concerned with driving the analysis to specific conclusions regarding workforce composition, projected employment and educational/training needs. By moving beyond Porter's broad-brush analysis of the 19-county region as a whole and instead focusing on the economic activities taking place within the region's constituent counties and municipalities, they are able to develop a much more specific understanding of the dynamics of their regional economy and develop strategies tailored to meet the needs of a diverse workforce.

Luger's study supports cluster-based regional economic development analysis, but points out the limitations of this approach when applied to the needs of a complex local economy. He describes a methodology used in the North Carolina Research Triangle to build on the findings of a cluster-based regional approach by undertaking a finer-grained analysis of the broad range of economic activities taking place within the region. As such, Luger's work provides valuable insights for economic development practitioners and others interested in understanding and creating 'smart places for smart people' in the 21st century.

8.   Regional wealth creation and the 21st century: women and 'minorities' in the tradition of economic strangers

John Butler

THEORETICAL CONSIDERATIONS

The study of wealth creation and economic prosperity and its related formulas that predict success, stands at the center of scholarship that is concerned with how countries, regions and cities prosper. When Adam Smith penned *The Wealth of Nations* in 1776, he posited the nation state as the unit of analysis for an understanding of prosperity. Jan Jacobs, in *Cities and the Wealth of Nations*, posits the city as the major contributor to wealth creation within nation states. In a real sense, these works are indicative of theoretical debates that have been discussed within the academy for years. The purpose of this chapter is to understand, within the context of nation states, cities and regions, the contribution of women and minority-owned enterprises in America.

The theoretical tradition for the study of women and 'minority' enterprises lay in the early scholarship of George Simmel, whose work brings together the importance of the city and the development of entrepreneurship. Writing in the late 1800s, he tried to account for the structures that produced people who were more likely to start enterprises as societies were moving from hunting and gathering to market economies. Using Europe as a laboratory, he noted that people who brought market economies to early hunting and gathering societies were distinct ethnic groups who were never from the existing economic structure of the established society, but were merchants from city life. To the established society, these merchants represented cosmopolitan life and were viewed as alien, as was the art of trading. Thus Simmel's famous statement, the stranger as trader and the trader as stranger, was born. To Simmel, entrepreneurs were 'strangers' who for different reasons had been denied opportunities in established societies, and became catalysts for entrepreneurial development in the western world.

Max Weber, a German scholar writing at the turn of the last century, also had an intense interest in understanding the development of entrepreneurship, or the fundamental basis of the work ethic. His ideas appear in *The Protestant Ethic and the Spirit of Capitalism,* and can be seen as a natural extension of Simmel's work. His theoretical legacy is the idea that religious or ethnic minorities who have little opportunity to serve the state are driven into economic activity with peculiar force. He noted that this had been true of the Huguenots of France, the Poles under Lewis XIV, and the Jews for hundreds of years. In a real sense, the groups that appear in Weber's work can be seen as representing Simmel's strangers.

Simmel's strangers and Weber's excluded groups are what we now called immigrant, minority and women entrepreneurs. The theoretical word that binds these groups is 'strangers'. It is certainly true that each immigrant group has its own unique history, a history that could differ greatly from other groups. For example, immigrant Russians and Chinese have different experiences of market economies and of course different historical experiences. White females, in the aggregate, certainly have different experiences than have female immigrants or other females who are non-white. Black Americans, who are not immigrants, share a unique experience within America. Although there is certain overlap among these groups, they share the reality of having differential opportunities in the history of America. Or, as Simmel would say, established societies create 'strangers' out of them because of their historical exclusion from the opportunity structure. In the case of some modern strangers, this might be due to racial differences, the mastery of the host language, or the reality of gender exclusion within the established society.

Also related to our discussion is the emphasis on regions, or how certain regions tend to outperform other regions. In an interesting kind of way, scholarship that examines the importance of regions has connected Simmel's strangers with economic prosperity throughout history. When we pay attention to business history, this relationship can almost be seen as a scientific pattern, a pattern that can be seen in the ancient world. In a major research effort, Karl Moore and David Lewis (1999) tie together the historical importance of regions, strangers in foreign lands and economic development:

> Long before their armies marched up and down the Tigris and Euphrates to terrorize the ancient world, groups of talented Assyrian traders [peacefully] took up residence in foreign countries hundreds of kilometers away from home, being

welcomed by the princes of Babylon, Aram and even distance Anatolia as a blessing and not a scourge. As they formed their numerous commercial colonies in foreign lands, these Old Assyrian merchants of the second millennium BC perfected a thousand-year-old system of private enterprise inherited from Sumner and Babylon. Living and trading near the dawn of civilization, these corporate traders, moreover, were innovative to a startling degree, for the commercial structures they created may rightly be described as one of the first attempts at the 'entrepreneurial government' being celebrated in the 1990s.

Systematic, strong and predictive observations were made by scholars such as Simmel, who observed 'strangers' immigrating to foreign lands and engaging in enterprise. These basic ideas allow us to understand how regions prosper as newcomers settle in certain regions. More importantly they show us how present-day groups of women and 'minorities', who are not immigrants, but 'strangers', can enhance communities through entrepreneurial behavior.

Studies of regions that prosper, thanks to the presence of 'strangers', have a strong tradition that is being revitalized in the context of American scholarship. As noted by Butler and Kozmetsky (2004) in *Immigrant and Minority Entrepreneurship: The Continuous Rebirth of American Communities,* understanding regional prosperity also means understanding the contributions of newcomers and 'strangers'. As early as 1953, a Presidential Commission on Immigration and Naturalizations noted, 'The richest regions are those with the highest proportion of immigrants'. Their industry, their skills and their enterprises were major factors in the economic development that made these regions prosperous. Also, in *Immigrants and the American City,* Thomas Muller (1993) examines how immigrants create entrepreneurial activities for wealth creation in gateway cities such as Miami, Florida, New York City and San Francisco. These cities owe their population growth, especially since the1970s, exclusively to immigration. For generations, however, immigrants have flocked to these cities, revitalizing them and contributing to their continued economic stability.

As noted earlier, the study of women and minority groups can also be seen in the tradition of 'strangers'. But, in order to do this one has to treat the development of entrepreneurial activities as a lag effect within an equation, and return to the days when the 'stranger' effect was the strongest. For example, Black Americans who will never assimilate have a strong tradition of new venture development as they have moved, as Abram Harris (1936) notes in *The Negro as Capitalist,* from slavery to business enterprise. One also has to control for time periods (for example, free Blacks in the north and south before the Civil War and entrepreneurial efforts after the Civil War in the south). More importantly, white females and Black Americans, groups that have been discriminated against in certain ways, can be seen as 'strangers' in the tradition of Simmel. In this chapter the theoretical tradition of the stranger is applied to recent immigrant groups within prosperous regions, Black Americans within regions with a tradition of economic security, and women entrepreneurs.

REGIONAL PROSPERITY AND IMMIGRANT ENTREPRENEURSHIP

As noted above, cities with a rich tradition of immigrant entrepreneurs also tend to be cities that are associated with entrepreneurial growth. In some cases newcomers immigrate on their own and in other cases they are forced out of a country. For example, when Castro noted that there would be a new Havana, he had no idea that the new Havana would be in Miami, Florida. This is because free-thinking Cubans left that island and created what has been called the 'Cuban Miracle' in Dade Country, Florida. Instead of being a burden on the city, these strangers, in the tradition of Simmel, placed new venture development at the very center of community and made Dade County one of the fastest growing entrepreneurial counties in America. Scholars have produced excellent literature describing the process of business creation within the original ethnic enclave of Miami.

Setting the pace for this scholarship on Miami is Alejandro Portes and Robert L. Bach's (1985) *Latin Journey.* Using Miami as a laboratory, this work shows how different labor markets were created and how entrepreneurs created jobs for other immigrants. It also contrasted the labor market experiences of Cubans and Mexican Americans, and, along with Ivan Light's (1972) *Ethnic Enterprise in America,* reintroduced scholars to the importance of studying the new strangers of America.

Official statistics (U.S. Department of the Census, 2002) place Cuban Americans in the Hispanic category, a group which has recently received significant attention in America. From a theoretical point of view, one understands that not all Hispanic enterprises are driven by immigration. But the tradition of Miami, and the value structure set there, can clearly be been seen when the data on Hispanic firms are broken up by city. States with the largest percentage of Hispanic-owned firms include California (28 per cent), Texas (20 per cent) and Florida (16.2 per cent).

Within the Hispanic category, Mexican–Americans had the greatest overall number of firms, followed by those from Latin America, other Hispanics, Cubans, Puerto Ricans and Spaniards. The Census reported that these enterprises 'totaled 1.2 million firms, employed over 1.3 million people and generated $186.3 billion in revenues in 1997'. The report also noted that 'The largest number of Hispanic-owned firms (1 million) were sole proprietorships, unincorporated businesses owned by individuals. C corporations, all legally incorporated businesses except for Subchapter S corporations (whose shareholders elect to be taxed as individuals rather than as corporations), numbered 78,500. But C corporations ranked first in receipts ($71.8 billion) among all Hispanic-owned firms, the report showed. C corporations were included in the Hispanic portion of the Survey of Minority-Owned Business Enterprises, source of the data, for the first time in 1997.'

As can be seen from the above, most of the research coming out of the Commerce Department notes that most activity in the tradition of immigrants is generated by small enterprises. Indeed most of the research on immigrant entrepreneurship examines how small enterprises develop a sense of economic stability for newcomers. The recent explosion of wealth in certain regions of America shows the importance of Simmel's 'strangers'. This research brings together newcomers, technology development, technology transfer and wealth creation.

During the latter part of the 20th century, Silicon Valley emerged as the natural laboratory for the study of wealth creation and best business practices in the world. The rapid amount of economic activity and growth in a region without an already established industrial economy attracted planning bodies from cities around the world to see how the miracle was performed. As noted by Timothy Stugeon, the model of Silicon Valley became the Holy Grail of economic development.

Annalee Saxenian (1994), in *Regional Advantage: Culture and Competition in Silicon Valley and Route 128,* notes that this region has its origins in the migration of scientists and entrepreneurs from Route 128 in Boston to the open-arm culture in the San Francisco area, and academic institutions such as Stanford University. Everett Rogers and Judith Larsen's (1984), *Silicon Valley Fever: Growth of High-Technology Culture,* details entrepreneurial spirit and growth of firms within the valley. It should also be pointed out that, prior to the development of present day Silicon Valley, the San Francisco area had given birth to the Federal Telegraph in 1909, engaged in early vacuum tube developments and saw the development of enterprises such as RCA, Magnavox, Fisher Research Laboratories and Litton Industries.

One of the major variables for the development of Silicon Valley was the arrival of talent from the 'old' region that had dominated the technology (semiconductor industry) development and start-up companies in America, Route 128 in the Boston area. As companies such as Sun Microsystems and Conner Peripherals were developing alongside established companies such as Hewlett-Packard and Intel in Silicon Valley, Route 128 was in decline. Silicon Valley thus became the new region in America for creativity and business success. By 1994, it was home to one-third of the 100 largest technology firms that had been created in America since 1965. Between 1986 and 1990, the market value of these firms increased by $25 billion, making it without regional competitors in America. The electronics industry, in 1990 alone, exported more that $11 billion in products (one-third of the nation's total); and Silicon Valley was the home of 39 of America's 100 fastest-growing electronics companies.

Silicon Valley is also home to, and its creation was helped by, Simmel's 'strangers'. Consider the following observation by Annalee Saxenian and Jumbi Edulbehram (1998):

> Silicon Valley is widely known for its most revolutionary product, the integrated circuit, or IC. However, the saying in the local technology community that 'Silicon Valley is run by ICs' refers not to semiconductors, but to Indians and Chinese. Immigrants make up a growing share of the professional and technical workforce in Silicon Valley, and many of these skilled immigrants are becoming entrepreneurs. Chinese and Indian engineers, in particular, have started some of the region's most successful technology companies, including Sun Microsystems, Cirrus Logic, Vitelic, Gateway Design, Solectron and Network Peripherals, as well as hundreds of less well-known firms that make up the region's dense industrial infrastructure.

The above quotation captures the fact that Simmel's 'strangers', or what are called 'immigrant entrepreneurs', are central to regions that are prosperous. As a matter of fact, one has to ask whether regions such as Silicon Valley can be prosperous without immigrant entrepreneurs. All relevant data support the fact that strangers are present when regions or cities develop an entrepreneurial culture and create wealth and jobs.

When the numbers are put to the analysis, the contribution of newcomers to the wealth creation in this region is impressive. 'Almost one-quarter (23 per cent) of Silicon Valley's high-tech firms are run by Chinese or Indians. … Of the 7769 high-tech firms started in Silicon Valley from 1980 through 1996, 1350 (17 per cent) were run by Indians. … All told, Chinese and Indian-run firms accounted for a total of $12.5 billion in sales and 46290 jobs in Silicon Valley in 1996 (Saxenian and Edulbehram, 1998).

The impact that newcomers have on the education of children has also been documented in the literature. This theme runs through early research on immigration entrepreneurs in the sense that the self-employed have a tendency to educate their children. Regions like Silicon Valley also tend to attract highly educated people. Thus, among the population that helped to create Silicon Valley, 56 per cent of the adult Indians and 47 per cent of the Chinese possess a four-year college degree (for whites the figure is 30 per cent). These immigrants earned MS and PhDs at a far greater rate than their white counterparts: 32 per cent of Indians and 23 per cent of the Chinese have advanced degrees, as compared to only 11 per cent for the white population. The relationship between education and entrepreneurship, especially the education of children, has been associated with immigrant entrepreneurs within success regions.

Chinese and Indians in Silicon Valley lead a tradition of immigrants from those parts of the world. The Official U.S. Census (2002) on Asian and Pacific Islander-owned enterprises shows that they created over 900 000 enterprises and employed more than 2.2 million people. The Census estimates that these enterprises produced $306.9 billion in revenues (2002). Enterprises owned by this group made up 4 per cent of all enterprises in America and generated 2 per cent of receipts in the country. (As expected, 71 per cent of these firms were sole proprietorships or unincorporated enterprises by individuals.) One-half of all revenues of Asian and Pacific Islander-owned enterprises were generated by incorporated enterprises, or C corporations, which produced $145.8 billion dollars (from 127 000 enterprises).

Of course the Census data do not distinguish between immigrant and non-immigrant populations, but when combining the results of different data sets, we get a better picture of Americans in this cultural tradition. The Census data does dovetail with the scholarship that has been done on Asian entrepreneurship, and the regional component of gateway cities is apparent. For example, on mainland America, Asian and Pacific Islanders produced over 12 per cent of all enterprises in California. This is followed by New York's 8.2 per cent. Min Zhou's work shows how immigration helps to revitalize China Town in New York, turning it from a declining ghetto into a thriving business section of the city.

The documentation of newcomers in a strange land that contribute to economic stability is convincing. Immigrant Cubans' contribution to the development of South Florida, and immigrant Japanese's contribution to California are plentiful in the case studies of America. An interesting question is, can regions prosper without strangers?

BLACK AMERICANS AND REGIONAL ADJUSTMENT: INTERNAL VARIATION ON THE STRANGER CONCEPT

The oldest 'strangers' to opportunities within America are Black Americans, who are of all racial descents. Also the oldest documentation in America on the development of business enterprise within this tradition relates to Black Americans. More importantly, the majority of most black success today, however measured, is standing on the shoulders of black visionaries who took the race, in the words of Abram Harris, from slavery to business enterprise. Thus, in order to understand black entrepreneurship today, one needs to have at least some understanding of black business history.

Prior to the Civil War, free Blacks in the north and south set the stage for entrepreneurship as a means of adjustment to America. Early research stresses a regional component to this business development. Related to that development are the creation of community, the building of colleges and universities, and thus a value structure that is grounded in economic stability and the education of children. Perhaps the first documentation of this process was published in 1830: entitled 'A Register of Trades of Colored People in the City of Philadelphia and Districts', it listed 656 entrepreneurs engaged in 57 enterprises. This community developed the enterprise of catering, produced one of the wealthiest merchants of its time (James Forten's company manufactured sails for seagoing ships) and created the African Methodist Church. This church produced Wilberforce College and many private colleges and universities in America and Africa. Mutual aid societies and private banking also developed in Philadelphia.

Other northern cities where free Blacks created a significant entrepreneurial enterprise were New York City and Cincinnati, Ohio. Prior to the Civil War, Blacks dominated the restaurant business in New York; in Cincinnati they were active in building trades. By the end of slavery, free Blacks had established a tradition of business enterprise in America that was in the tradition of Simmel's 'strangers', or people who had to make a living in hostile circumstances.

Blacks coming out of slavery continued the tradition of business enterprises throughout the south and in other parts of the country. By 1910, less than 60 years after emancipation, the group had developed entrepreneurial enclaves in cities throughout the south. As noted by Margaret Levenstein (2004) in a work entitled 'African–American Entrepreneurship: The View from the 1910 Census', 'One of the most striking findings of this study is that, in 1910, African Americans were more likely than white Americans to be employers, and almost as likely as whites to be self-employed.'

After the Civil War, this entrepreneurial miracle was carried, for the most part, by Blacks in the southern region of American. Organized by Booker T. Washington and his Negro Business League, entrepreneurship was placed at the very center of community as segregation and other legal laws of hostility were put in place. Scholarship has done an excellent job in documenting this tradition of Black America, which is quite different from the history of northern Blacks in factories during the heyday of the industrial economy of America.

In Robert Kenzer's (1997) *Enterprising Southerners: Black Economic Success in North Carolina, 1865–1915*, a community that understood the relationship between business enterprise, economic stability and living well in American under difficult circumstances was addressed. He also linked Black Americans who were free during the days of slavery to those who received freedom. As noted by Kenzer, 'Even with the newly insurmountable problems … it appears that at least half of the 1870 landowners may have been antebellum freemen. Furthermore, these antebellum freedmen owned a substantial share of all of the land owned by blacks in 1870.'

The documentation of black enterprise in North Carolina would dominate the literature on race and entrepreneurship between 1900 and the late 1950s. These works include William Kenneth Boyd's (1927) *The Story of Durham*, Booker T. Washington's 'Durham, North Carolina: a city of negro enterprises', E. Franklin Fraziers' (1925) 'Durham: capital of the black middle class' and S. Huntington Hobbs' *North Carolina: An Economic and Social Profile*. When Professor W.E.B. Dubois (1953) visited Durham, North Carolina at the turn of the century, he noted the following: 'There is in this city a group of five thousand or more colored people, whose social and economic development is perhaps more striking than that of any similar group in the nation.' A sociological analysis of the city compared the emphasis on entrepreneurship to the creative life in New York City:

> Durham offers none of the color and creative life we find among Negroes in New York City. It is a city of fine homes … and middle-class respectability. It is not the place where men write and dream; but a place where men calculate and work. … As we read the lives of the men in Durham who have established the enterprises there, we find stories paralleling the most amazing accounts of the building of American Fortune. We find them beginning their careers without much formal education and practicing the old-fashioned virtues of the old middle class. … These men have mastered the technique of modern business and acquired the spirit of modern enterprise.

The historical Durham was known throughout the literature as 'Black Wall Street', a name that was tagged on many black communities that placed entrepreneurship at the center of activity. From a regional point of view, these communities were mostly southern, and reflected the fact that legal segregation created a process of business, economic and educational achievement that was foreign to the great majority of Blacks who lived outside the south during most of the 20th century.

The children of present-day Durham, whose parents and grandparents were dismissed as the Black Bourgeoisie and despised by many Blacks because they developed a sense of economic stability, have been busy placing self-employment at the center of the community. After years of concentration on civil rights activity, which was needed to secure basic rights in America, the leadership of the community has been focusing on new venture development.

As the center for enterprise in North Carolina, Durham has become, like many southern cities, a best-practice place of historical significance.

Of all of the economies that did well in the south, Atlanta, Georgia has stood at center stage since the turn of the century. When W.E.B. Dubois (1953) wrote *The Souls of Black Folk,* one of the chapters was entitled 'The Wings of Atlanta'. The Wings of Atlanta were universities that would provide the region with excellent people. Dubois noticed how the entire city, at the turn of the 20th century, was gearing up for business enterprise and was determined to be a great city of the south, Sherman having burned the city during the Civil War. In terms of Black America, Dubois (1953) noted:

> The old leaders of Negro opinion, in the little groups where there is a Negro social consciousness, are being replaced by new; neither the black preacher nor the black teacher leads as he did two decades ago. Into their places are pushing the farmers and gardeners, the well-paid porters and artisans, the business-men – all those with property and money. And with all this change, so curiously parallel to that of the Other-world, goes too the same inevitable change in ideals. The South laments to-day the slow, steady disappearance of a certain type of Negro, the faithful, courteous slave of other days, with his incorruptible honesty and dignified humility. He is passing away just as surely as the old type of Southern gentleman is passing, and from not dissimilar causes – the sudden transformation of a fair far-off ideal of Freedom into the hard reality of bread-winning and the consequent deification of Bread.

As noted by Joseph Jewell (2004), there was a relationship between the decline of skilled manual labor and the development of self-employment by Blacks in the developing city of Atlanta. Jewell, in a major effort entitled 'Race, social reform and the making of a black middle class: Atlanta, 1870–1900', found that Atlanta Blacks who turned to self-employment within a decade of entering the market as free laborers were better off economical than those who sought employment alongside Whites. Between 1870 and 1890, 40 to 55 per cent of Black Atlantics listed in the Fulton County tax records as possessing more than $1000 in personal or real property were self-employed. Of that number, almost two-thirds were operating enterprises based on skilled manual trades.

Between 1900 and the 1960s, Atlanta's black entrepreneurs operated under an economic detour, or segregation laws which made it impossible for them to operate in the white market. When Joseph A. Pierce (1947) wrote the definitive work on black entrepreneurship in the middle of the century, *Negro Business and Business Education,* of all the 12 cities surveyed,

Atlanta had the greatest number of enterprises. Through the years the city's black colleges and universities, or what Dubois called the 'Wings of Atlanta', would produce entrepreneurs and help brand the city as a Mecca for black entrepreneurship and black educational success. Although other cities would develop a strong black middle-class with the self-employed at the very center, Atlanta carried the brand for black entrepreneurship within the research literature. These internal newcomers developed a value structure that would be passed from generation to generation.

Modern work on Atlanta shows how civil rights legislation affected a city with a strong historical emphasis on new venture development. This legislation made it possible for black enterprises to move from the segregated market, and more importantly, for the first time bid on projects by the city of Atlanta. In the first definitive study of black Atlanta since the early days, Thomas D. Boston (1999) noted the following:

> the first wave of affirmative action programs ... planted the seeds for the emergence of a new generation of black business owners. ... For example, between 1992 and 1995, firms receiving prime construction contracts in Atlanta awarded $163,477,896 in subcontracts. Of this amount, $72.5 million went to black-owned firms, but not all of this was in construction, $13 million was for procurement of commodities and supplies, $7.5 million was for the procurement of professional services. ... Between 1992 and 1995, 816 black-owned firms received awards from the City of Atlanta, bid on awards, or were certified by the Compliance Office. Of this number, 31.2 per cent of firms were in construction services, 10.5 per cent were in architectural and engineering services, 23.3 per cent were in professional services, 10.7 per cent were in general services, and 24.3 per cent were goods suppliers.

As noted by Boston (1999), there is a lot of 'fuss' about present-day Atlanta because black enterprises produce about 6 per cent of the current workforce. The transformation of Atlanta was effective because Blacks were standing on the shoulders of a community that built colleges and universities and had an understanding of the importance of entrepreneurship for a degree of economic stability.

It is important to understand that today's entrepreneurial history within Black America is a continuation of a tradition that is as old as the country. Data from the US Census Bureau (1997) *Survey of Minority Owned Enterprise* present the ten states with the largest number of Black-owned firms compared to all firms and population for the latest data, 1997. The data column, 'black as a percentage of all' is important to draw a relationship between value structures developed at the turn of the century. States from the south have the highest percentage of Black-owned firms. Black entrepreneurs in Maryland created 11.9 per cent of all firms in that state; Maryland is followed by Georgia (9.8), North Carolina (7.0) and Virginia (7.0). New York black entrepreneurs produced 5.7 per cent of firms in that state and those in Ohio produced 3.5 per cent of firms. When number of firms is considered, New York had the most, followed by California and Texas.

Data from the Census notes that the more than 8 million enterprises owned by Black Americans employed over 700 000 people and produced over $71 billion in revenues for the year 1997. These enterprises make up 4 per cent of the 20.8 million non-farm enterprises and 0.4 per cent of the $18.6 trillion in receipts for all enterprises. The data also note that the vast majority of African–American-owned firms, 90 per cent, or 737 100, were sole proprietorships, unincorporated businesses owned by individuals. C corporations (all legally incorporated businesses except for Subchapter S corporations, whose shareholders elect to be taxed as individuals rather than as corporations) numbered 42 700. But C corporations ranked first in receipts among all African–American-owned firms, reporting $28.5 billion. The 1997 Survey of Minority-Owned Business Enterprises was the first to include C corporations, from which the current tabulations are derived.

Perhaps the transformation of black enterprises over the years can best be seen in the work of Timothy Bates. In *Race, Self-Employment and Upward Mobility* (1977), he shows how black enterprises have made the transition from traditional enclave enterprises to emerging enterprises that are located all over the city. He notes that, although popular notions associate black enterprises with 'ghetto' communities, data on emerging black enterprises are inconsistent with this notion. In Bates's words, 'College-educated African Americans tend to avoid such businesses because they can earn higher returns elsewhere. Running a small retail store in the ghetto, bluntly, is a waste of their time.'

Bates uses data from 'The Characteristics of Businesses Owners' that allow scholars to have a better understanding of 'minority'-owned enterprises. Compiled by the U.S. Bureau of the Census in 1992, it is the first national database that describes the traits of the self-employed in America. Bates notes that gains in higher education show how reductions in traditional discriminatory barriers can be translated into significant progress for Black Americans.

WOMEN ENTREPRENEURS AS ECONOMIC STRANGERS

Women entrepreneurs have entered the market place as a special kind of stranger. It is safe to say that not even Simmel, who coined the stranger concept, could imagine that females would come to play an important role in the development of business enterprises. Although females have always played a role in business development of immigrant groups, they can be placed under the theoretical banner of 'stranger' because only in the last decades have they begun to start and manage enterprises in significant numbers. As noted by Jeanne Coughlin (2002) in *The Rise of Women Entrepreneurs*,

> Women everywhere are becoming entrepreneurs. In greater numbers than ever before, women are stepping away from traditional economic roles and venturing out to start their own businesses. In every field imaginable, even the most 'masculine', you don't have to look hard to find female entrepreneurs who have overcome seemingly impossible odds to achieve success.

Understanding women entrepreneurs also means moving from the racial and ethnic ties, that bound men and women in the same group, to a gender orientation (where female is the major organizing variable; race is recorded as female) that sees women as moving away from 'traditional' gender roles. For example, 1996 data show that one in eight, or 13 per cent, of the women-owned enterprises in America are owned by a woman of color. Research shows that, for the year 2002, women were majority owners of at least a 50 per cent share in 10.1 million businesses, or 46 per cent of all privately held firms in the United States. Between 1997 and 2002, the number of women-owned firms increased at more than 1.5 times the national rate. Even more striking, larger businesses led by women (100 or more employees) grew by 18.3 per cent. Women launched new businesses in every industry, sector and geographic region of the United States.

The official survey of the U.S. Census revealed that there were 5.4 million women-owned businesses in America, employing 7.1 million people and generating $818.7 billion in receipts for the year 1997. The survey also shows that there were 3.6 million husband–wife (jointly owned) firms with $943.9 billion in receipts. Finally the data note that, 'As of 1997, privately held majority women-owned firms made up 26 per cent of the nation's 20.8 million non-farm businesses and 4.4 per cent of the $18.6 trillion in receipts for all businesses.'

According to the Census, states having the greatest percentage of women-owned businesses were California (12.9 per cent), New York (7.3 per cent) and Texas (2.7 per cent). The only deep south states represented in the analysis are Florida and Georgia, where women own 6.2 per cent and 2.7 per cent, respectively, of firms. This is very different from the black data, where southern states were so prominent when one looked at the percentage of black enterprise by state. This of course reflects different histories between Black Americans and all women in America. Four states – California (700 500), New York (394 000), Texas (381 500) and Florida

(337 800) – accounted for 33 per cent of the firms that were 51 per cent or more owned by women.

The majority of firms owned by women (4.6 million or 85 per cent) were unincorporated businesses owned by individuals or sole proprietorships. Some 6 per cent (or 314 700) of these firms were C corporations (defined as legally incorporated businesses, except for subchapter S corporations, whose shareholders elect to be taxed as individuals rather than as corporations), but this 6 per cent accounted for $366.8 billion or 45 per cent of the receipts from all enterprises owned by women.

CONCLUSION

The literature on what we have been calling 'strangers' stands as a unique tradition in the study of business enterprise. Scholarship has documented the fact that, since antiquity, certain ethnic groups have moved into regions and cities and endowed them with economic activity. Indeed one can say almost with scientific certainty that regions that do not have 'strangers' as entrepreneurs are less likely to be prosperous. From Ancient Assyria to Silicon Valley, for example, strangers have been present. New York City, Atlanta and San Franciso have all benefited from the presence of people who develop entrepreneurial activity.

Contained within the experiences of immigrant, minority and women entrepreneurs are the variables that make enterprises successful. While the research reported in this work has been concerned with receipts in the aggregate, one question is what makes successful entrepreneurs in America. Or, to put it another way, are the variables different that predict success between native-born Americans, immigrants, women and minority groups? The answer to this question begins to bridge theoretical traditions that concentrate on immigrants or strangers and native born entrepreneurs.

In a major research effort, Timothy Bates notes that, while many people in what we are calling the 'stranger' tradition start enterprises, not all are successful. This type of research bridges the stranger tradition by concentrating on variables that make entrepreneurs successful. Bates' (1977) major conclusion is that

> the ingredients for success in self-employment vary little between immigrants and nonimmigrant or across racial-ethnic groups in contemporary America. People most likely to pursue self-employment are highly educated and skilled, often possessing significant personal financial resources. Likewise, those lacking the requisite skills and capital, whether immigrant or otherwise, are unlikely to start small businesses. Among people who choose self-employment without appropriate education, skills, and financial resources, business failure and self-employment

exit rates are high. The patterns typify black, Asian, and white Americans, men and women, immigrants and the native born.

Bates' work informs us that success in the business world depends on certain kinds of knowledge, skills and capital. Research around the globe shows that strangers are enhancing countries by bringing skills and capital. Robert Kloosterman and Jan Rath's book, *Immigrant Entrepreneurs: Venturing Abroad in the Age of Globalization* (2003), looks at experiences of newcomers in 11 countries. The process of regional economic revival is a continuing process.

9. Universities, entrepreneurship and public policy: lessons from abroad

Bo Carlsson

INTRODUCTION

The purpose of this chapter is to review the recent literature on academic entrepreneurship and public policy, to compare and contrast the research findings in the United States and overseas and to draw out the policy lessons.[1]

It is clear from the start that there are fundamental differences between the United States and its foreign competitors in this arena, namely (1) that the legal environment for academic entrepreneurship in the USA differs from that elsewhere, and (2) that the US economy is much more entrepreneurial than most societies elsewhere. This means that the mechanisms used to transfer ideas and research findings from the academy to business and then to transform them into new businesses are different. Thus the US literature focuses primarily on technology transfer and on examining the institutional features, particularly on the university side, of the university–industry interface. In most of the rest of the world, by contrast, until recently there have been very few technology licensing or tech transfer offices at universities. This is largely a reflection of differences in intellectual property rights. In continental Europe, the inventor (not the university) is the owner of the intellectual property resulting from academic research. As a result, the literature focuses more on other mechanisms of spillover from academic research and examines a broader set of university–industry links, particularly in the form of university spin-offs and industrial liaison offices. There is also more focus on regional economic development and on regional and national innovation systems.

The chapter is organized as follows. We begin with a review of technology transfer at US universities following the Bayh–Dole Act in 1980. This is followed by an examination of academic entrepreneurship/university spin-offs outside the United States. We then take a look at spillovers and university–industry linkages in a broader context (particularly innovation systems). The chapter concludes with a review of policy issues and a discussion of lessons to be drawn.

THE BAYH–DOLE ACT AND ITS CONSEQUENCES

Impact on Technology Transfer, Patenting and Start-ups

University patenting and licensing activities in the United States have increased sharply in the last two decades. One of the reasons is the Bayh–Dole Act, which was enacted by the US Congress in 1980 and became effective on 1 July 1981. The Act transferred the rights to intellectual property generated under Federal grants from the funding agencies to the universities, thus providing the latter with opportunities to exploit research results commercially. One of the major arguments for the Act was that stronger protection of publicly funded research would lead to a faster and more efficient technology transfer, stimulating innovation and generating economic growth.

What has been the impact of Bayh–Dole on technology transfer? Sampat and Nelson (2002) traced the evolution of university patenting and licensing procedures in the United States over the last century. They found that, at the beginning of the twentieth century, universities avoided patenting and licensing activities. Commercialization of university research occurred through informal spillover. Today, in contrast, all research universities have technology transfer or licensing offices to patent and market faculty inventions.

The number of technology transfer offices at US universities increased dramatically, from 25 in 1980 to 200 in 1990 (Carlsson and Fridh, 2002, pp. 200–201). In 2003, the number exceeded 300. Meanwhile the number of patents issued to US universities also increased sharply. The number of such patents issued annually more than doubled (from 264 to 551) between 1979 and 1984; between 1984 and 1989 it more than doubled again (to 1228) (Mowery *et al.*, 2001, p. 104). The increase continued, though at a somewhat slower pace; in 2002, 3673 patents were issued to US universities, hospitals and research institutes. The number of start-up companies formed on the basis of licenses from US universities in 2002 was 450. The total number of such companies started in 1994–2002 was 3151, compared to 1169 in the period 1980–1993 (Association of University Technology Managers (AUTM) 2002 Licensing Survey).

Even though it is clear that Bayh–Dole has played an important role in this development, it is only one of several important factors behind the rise of university patenting and licensing activity. Other contributing factors were increased federal financial support for basic biomedical research in universities, beginning in the late 1960s, and the related rise of research in biotechnology, beginning in the early 1970s, as well as court rulings and shifts in federal policy that made it easier to patent research results (Mowery *et al.*, 2001, p. 100).

Academic Concerns about Impact on Research Quality and Content

While it is beyond dispute that there has been a dramatic increase in the rate of commercialization of academic research since the early 1980s, there have also been questions and concerns raised about its influence on the nature and content of academic research. According to Derek Bok, the former president of Harvard University, 'the new-found concern with technology transfer is disturbing not only because it could alter the practice of science in the university but also because it threatens the central values and ideals of academic research' (Weiner, 1986, quoted in Stephan and Levin, 1996, p. 184).[2]

But so far, the research does not seem to provide support for these concerns. For example, Mowery *et al.* (2001) examined the records of faculty inventions, patents and licenses at Stanford, Columbia and the University of California over the 1980s and 1990s and found that Bayh–Dole appears to have had little effect on the content of academic research. The patent and licensing portfolios of these three universities were found to be remarkably similar ten years after the passage of the Bayh–Dole Act. This result is confirmed by Thursby and Thursby (2002) who found that increased licensing is due primarily to an increased willingness of faculty and administrators to license as well as to increased business reliance on external R&D rather than a shift in faculty research.

Stephan and Levin (1996) examined the relationship in science between the reward structure and entrepreneurial activity. They drew a distinction between two types of property rights: basic science is fostered by a mechanism of reputational rights, whereas technological advances (and the products and processes they produce) are fostered by a mechanism of proprietary rights. The two forms of property rights differ markedly in terms of the incentives they provide to share information in a timely fashion. The authors argue that, because of a host of factors, university-based scientists in certain fields are more likely to 'privatize' (that is, commercialize) knowledge today than in the past, trading reputational rights for proprietary rights. They argue further that the exchange of scientific information may have been restricted as universities and scientists have tried to protect patentable research results, that the willingness to publish, or publish quickly, has diminished and that the willingness to share information has decreased.

They concluded that the movement towards commercialization of research results may be more beneficial to product development and the scientists engaged in the activity than to basic science.

Addressing similar concerns, Mowery *et al*. (2002) found little evidence of a decline in the importance of patents issued after 1980 that are assigned to experienced patenters. They also found that the importance of patents issued to institutions that had not patented previously increased during the later 1980s and 1990s. Thus they found little support for the argument that the internal 'research culture' in US universities has changed after Bayh–Dole and that this has triggered a decline in the importance of academic patents. On the contrary, Shane (2004) explored the university share of patents from 1969 to 1996 across 117 lines of business. He showed that the university share of patents has increased in the post-Bayh–Dole period relative to the pre-Bayh–Dole period and that this increase is correlated with the effectiveness of licensing in each line of business.[3] This suggests that the Bayh–Dole Act has provided incentives for universities to increase patenting in those fields in which licensing is an effective mechanism for acquiring new technical knowledge,[4] but it does not necessarily mean that the direction of research has shifted.

In another paper, Shane (2002a) examined the conditions under which university inventions will be licensed or commercialized. He showed that university inventions are more likely to be licensed when patents provide effective protection of intellectual property rights and that, when patents are effective, university technology is generally licensed to non-inventors. He also showed that the effectiveness of patents increases royalties earned for inventions licensed to non-inventors.

Jaffe and Lerner (2001) examined the initiatives since 1980 to encourage patenting and technology transfer at the *national laboratories* (as distinct from universities). They found that the policy changes had a substantial impact on the laboratories' patenting: they have gradually reached parity in patents per R&D dollar with research universities. Unlike the case of universities, laboratory patent quality has remained constant or even increased despite this growth.

Owen-Smith (2003) studied the relationships between commercial and academic systems for the dissemination and use of new scientific findings. He found that increased patenting and commercial engagement on US campuses has altered the rules that govern inter-university competition. Whereas commercial and academic standards for success were once separate systems with distinct stratification orders, they have become integrated into a hybrid regime where achievement in one realm is dependent upon success in the other.

Office of Technology Transfers (OTTs) and Institutional Factors at Universities

Several papers have studied various aspects of offices of technology transfer (OTTs) in universities. For example, Carlsson and Fridh (2002) examined the organization and place of OTTs within the university structure, the process of technology transfer and the staffing and funding of the office. The findings suggest that technology transfer from universities to the commercial sector needs to be understood in its broader context. The primary purpose of a technology transfer program is for the university to assist its researchers in disseminating research results for the public good. Success in this endeavor is only partially reflected in income generated for the university (in fact, most universities make little or no money in technology transfer) or the number of business start-ups. The degree of success depends not only on the nature of the interface between the university and the business community but also on the receptivity in the surrounding community as well as the culture, organization and incentives within the universities themselves.

Siegel *et al.* (2003) found that OTT activity is characterized by constant returns to scale and that environmental and institutional factors explain some of the variation in performance. They concluded that the most critical organizational factors are faculty reward systems, OTT staffing/compensation practices and cultural barriers between universities and firms. This was confirmed by Jensen *et al.* (2003), who studied the determinants of invention disclosures by faculty and the resulting license contract terms. They also examined how the portion of inventions disclosed at different stages varies with faculty quality. Quality was found to be inversely related to the share of license income allotted to faculty.

Feldman *et al.* (2002) studied the role of equity in newly established companies as a technology transfer mechanism that offers advantages for both generating revenue and aligning the interests of universities, industry and faculty. They found that the recent rise in university equity holdings is a function of behavioral factors related to the university's prior experiences with licensing, success relative to other institutions and the organization of the technology transfer office, as well as structural characteristics related to university type. DiGregorio and Shane (2003) show that intellectual eminence and the policies of making equity investments in start-ups and maintaining a low inventor's share of royalties increase new firm formation.

It should be clear from this brief review that the focus of academic research on technology transfer in the United States has been primarily on the organization of technology transfer activities at universities and on the impact of the increase in these activities over the last 20 years or so on the nature and content of academic research. It is evident that there has been a substantial increase in university patenting activity post Bayh–Dole and that the academic share of total patenting has increased. But there is not much evidence that the nature of research in academic institutions has changed.

What I find striking and intriguing is that this review of the recent literature has found no analyses of the impact in the United States of technology transfer from universities on the economy in terms of job creation, new firm formation and economic growth. It is possible that such studies were made earlier (prior to the 1990s), but the lack of recent studies suggests a potentially important opportunity for further research.

TECHNOLOGY TRANSFER OUTSIDE USA

In Europe, until recently, there have been very few technology licensing or technology transfer offices at universities, primarily because of differences in intellectual property rights. As mentioned already, in contrast to the case of the United States, intellectual property rights to academic research in continental Europe belong to the inventors, not the universities. Since the universities cannot commercialize property that they do not own, there have been limited incentives for universities to establish technology transfer units. As a result, most European countries have adopted a general targeted spillover model (as distinct from a model found specifically on technology transfer) of commercializing academic research. That is now changing, as national governments charge universities with a 'third task' in addition to teaching and research: interaction with the business community to promote economic growth. But, until recently, the non-US literature on academic entrepreneurship has focused more on spillovers from academic research (as distinct from specifically on technology transfer) and has examined a broader set of university–industry links than the US literature, particularly in the form of university spin-offs and industrial liaison offices.

The European Spillover Model

In a study that illustrates the importance of institutional arrangements for academic entrepreneurship, Jones-Evans *et al.* (1999) examine the role that universities play in the regional economic development in two contrasting small countries of Europe: Sweden and Ireland. Given their different innovation profiles, especially the relative resources allocated to R&D (much larger in Sweden than in Ireland), it is not surprising that the organization and development of technology transfer from universities to industry differ between the two countries. In both countries, the main vehicle is industrial liaison offices (ILOs) which have responsibilities much broader than technology transfer. In Sweden, the ILOs tend to be part of a network of technology-transfer organizations, often acting as a gateway to areas of expertise, such as patenting, within the university. The system appears to be more centralized in Ireland, with ILOs being more directly responsible for the technology transfer function. The higher complexity of the Swedish system means that the main barriers to further collaboration with the business community involved incremental improvements to the technology-transfer process, whereas in Ireland there were more fundamental problems of a lack of finance and resources to develop the role of ILOs further. The authors conclude that the primary role of the industrial liaison office is to operate as a strategic focus for overall university–industry collaboration, as well as to provide easy access for industry to knowledge, research expertise and services within the university.

From the 1990s, universities in several European countries have been charged with the 'Third Task' of generating economic growth through interaction with the business community. One of these countries is Sweden. Substantial efforts have been made to transform national research policy into a policy for innovation. One of the bottom-up responses to this top-down initiative has been an attempt on the part of some Swedish universities to transform themselves into entrepreneurial institutions. Jacob *et al.* (2003) did a case study of the transformation reflecting the new research policy at one Swedish university, Chalmers University of Technology. Chalmers' journey was examined against the backdrop of the changing national climate for universities as well as local factors within the university itself.

The authors drew two types of conclusions. One is that the university needs to develop a more comprehensive and coherent (purposive) institutional framework for entrepreneurial activity. A positive attitude among faculty and students to commercialization of research results, well-developed alumni networks and regular contacts between faculty and industry representatives are not enough; a more formal and purposive structure is needed to foster successful academic entrepreneurship. The other conclusion is that a value shift (cultural change) is necessary within the university toward embracing and not merely tolerating entrepreneurial values.

A German study draws similar conclusions: Krucken (2003) notes the intensification of university–industry relations and the increased role of universities in a knowledge society and that economic development through technology transfer has become a 'third academic mission' on a par with universities' traditional missions of teaching and research. But he finds, based on empirical evidence from technology transfer offices at German universities, that there are institutional barriers to the diffusion of that mission and that they are largely ignored.

Goldfarb and Henrekson (2003) compare the policies and institutional arrangements promoting the commercialization of university-generated knowledge in Sweden and the United States. Both countries expend large resources on university R&D but they follow very different models for commercialization. Despite the fact that Sweden has a leading academic record in terms of level of spending (the highest R&D/GDP ratio in the world) as well as outcomes in the form of research publications and citations of research results, the rate of commercialization of academic research results seems to be low. Goldfarb and Henrekson argue that this is due in part to the top-down nature of Swedish national policies aimed at commercializing these innovations (the 'third task' mandate) as well as an academic environment that discourages academics from actively participating in the commercialization of their ideas. They contrast this with the institutional setting in the USA in which there is competition among universities for research funds and research personnel. This in turn has led to significant academic freedom to interact with industry, including substantial involvement in new firms. Braunerhjelm *et al.* (2003) argue similarly that the shortcomings of the Swedish innovation systems are due to weak links between universities and industry when market-based mechanisms have been replaced by central direction within the universities. Together with generally weak incentives for firm start-ups, this leads to a low degree of academic entrepreneurship and weak links in the Swedish innovation systems.

Academic Spin-offs

Given the lack of university ownership of intellectual property rights, the main vehicle of technology transfer from academic institutions is spin-offs. A number of studies are focused on defining and analyzing various types of university spin-offs (USOs). Pirnay *et al.* (2003) define USOs as new firms created to exploit commercially knowledge, technology or research results developed within a university. They propose a typology based on two factors, namely the status of individuals involved in the new business venturing process (researchers or students), and the nature of knowledge transferred from university to the new venture (codified or tacit), inducing the nature of the USO activities (product or service-oriented). Perez and Sanchez (2003) study how active in network development and technology transfer USOs are during their early years to overcome initial disadvantages. They also look at the relationship between early network development and knowledge creation and technology transfer in university spin-offs. Using data from companies spun off from a Spanish university in the 1990s, they find that technology transfer and networking at university spin-offs decreased after their early years, while at the same time the relationships with customers increased.

Locket *et al.* (2003) examine technology-based spin-out companies in the United Kingdom, focusing on the difference between those universities that have been most active in the area and those that have been least active. Their results indicate that the more successful universities have clearer (more purposive) strategies towards the spinning out of companies and the use of surrogate entrepreneurs in this process. In addition, the more successful universities were found to possess a better infrastructure in the form of greater expertise and more established networks helpful in fostering spin-out companies.

These findings are echoed in another UK-based study. Vohora *et al.* (2004) investigated nine USOs in seven UK universities. Their findings highlight

the importance of path dependencies in the development of USOs and suggest a key role for practitioners in helping academic entrepreneurs acquire the appropriate resources from the earliest phases. Practitioners should, therefore, consider carefully where and how universities could add the most value to new USOs. Many of the VCs interviewed expressed frustration that universities still had some way to go in learning how to present viable investment propositions. It was considered rare for proposals to present details of how ventures would achieve proof of market and proof of technology. Nor was there widespread evidence that TTOs were carrying out effective IP due diligence prior to submitting proposals. This highlights the importance of obtaining the capability to synthesize scientific knowledge with an understanding of the relevant market and in iterating towards the appropriate commercial proposition. Practitioners within universities need either to develop the skills to carry out these tasks effectively or to develop high levels of social capital with surrogate entrepreneurs who do have the skills.

Our research also highlights the need to acquire the resources early on that will enable the venture to be launched with adequate and appropriate resources that will provide the basis for continuing development. Key to this aspect is the need for appropriate entrepreneurial commitment to the venture. There is a need for greater career support and entrepreneurial training to be provided to academics who wish to participate in the commercialization of their academic research. Whether academics choose an entrepreneurial career path by acquiring the patents to their research and commercializing it themselves, or prefer to remain in their research post, their commitment to the entrepreneurial team engaged in the commercialization process is fundamental. Without this commitment, the vital knowledge necessary to make the technology function in the marketplace is likely to be missing and the chances of the USO becoming a sustainable venture are therefore likely to be slim. As some academics may not wish to become committed full time to the venture, or may not [have] the appropriate skills to lead the venture successfully, practitioners may again need to develop social capital to identify suitable surrogate entrepreneurs. (Vohora *et al.*, 2004, p. 173)

The idea of path dependence and the need for continual interaction between university researchers and the business environment is reflected in several studies. For example, Grandi and Grimaldi (2003) analyzed 40 Italian academic spin-offs and their external relationships. They found that the founding teams' frequency of interaction with external agents is influenced by the frequency of interaction with external agents of the research groups of origin and by their scientific and technological excellence.

More generally, we realized ... that it is extremely difficult for newly established companies to make themselves known on the market and to create their first contacts with clients. In the majority of cases, their first contacts are inherited from their university of origin. This happens mainly for two reasons: (a) because academic entrepreneurs keep on networking with external companies or public institutions that they had met when they were still working at the university; (b) because the universities from which new companies have spun off provide academic entrepreneurs with some work (applied research or development), that they could not take on by themselves, either because they had no time, or because they are concerned that developmental activities might reduce their commitment towards more fundamental types of research. (Grandi and Grimaldi, 2003, p. 339)

Monjon and Waelbroeck (2003) assess the importance of information flows from universities to innovative firms and investigate the relative contribution of formal collaboration and pure knowledge spillovers in this process. The study is based on French firm-level data. The authors find that spillovers provide the most benefit to firms that imitate existing technologies or those that are involved in incremental innovation. On the other hand, they find, interestingly, that highly innovative firms appear to derive most benefit from collaborative research with universities – but *foreign* universities, not domestic (French) ones. Indeed highly innovative firms are at the frontier of the academic knowledge in their industry. Therefore they only benefit marginally from aggregate (or industry-wide) spillovers. They require new forms of academic knowledge that they acquire through formal cooperation with foreign universities.

Saez *et al.* (2002) study the reasons why Spanish companies cooperate with universities and research centers and the characteristics of these relationships. Their results indicate that cooperation with centers is a nationwide phenomenon involving basic research, conducted under the sponsorship of different research support schemes promoted by central and regional administrations in Spain.

Mora-Valentin *et al.* (2004) analyzed the impact of a series of contextual and organizational factors on the success of 800 cooperative agreements between Spanish firms and research organizations between 1995 and 2000. Their findings show that the most important factors for the firms are commitment, previous links, definition of objectives and conflict. For research organizations, previous links, communication, commitment, trust and the partners' reputation are the most important.

A German study (Czarnitzki and Spielkamp, 2003) raises the interesting idea that knowledge-intensive business service firms can fill some of the functions of university–industry liaison. By taking advantage of information and communication technologies, such business service firms can play the role of 'converters' of technological information within the economy, functioning as providers, purchasers or partners in the context of innovation. A sound innovation capacity, especially knowledge, creativity, market and management skills, allows them to become bridges for innovation.

Science Parks

One institutional arrangement that has frequently been used to foster both technology transfer and entrepreneurship is science parks. Science parks may be defined as sites near a university on which high-technology industrial businesses are housed, so that they can benefit from the research expertise of the university's scientists. The first science parks were built in the United States in the early 1950s, but most of the growth has occurred since 1980. According to Link and Scott (2003, p. 1326), there were 127 science parks in the United States in 1998. This represents more than half of the 250 or so current membership in the International Association of Science Parks.

In spite of the large number of science parks in the United States, there seem to be few studies of science parks in the USA in recent years. However there are numerous studies in other parts of the world. Perhaps the most thoroughly studied country is Sweden (see Dahab and Cabral, 1998, Löfsten and Lindelöf, 2001, 2002, 2003; Lindelöf and Löfsten, 2002, 2003). In a series of studies, Lindelöf and Löfsten have examined 134 firms in 11 Swedish science parks and 139 firms outside the parks. Their general findings are that new technology-based firms (NTBFs) in science parks have a higher rate of job creation and sales growth than other NTBFs, but they are not generally more profitable. While there are few formal linkages between NTBFs and universities, the science park-based NTBFs have more links with universities than do other NTBFs. But the links are at a low level, primarily involving recruiting university graduates and informal contacts. There is no evidence that science park NTBFs have greater R&D 'output' in the form of patents than comparable NTBFs elsewhere.

While the results for Sweden are mixed, at best, those in the United Kingdom do not appear to be much more encouraging. Siegel *et al.* (2003a) reviewed some recent evidence comparing the performance of firms located on and off UK science parks. The evidence they found suggests that the returns to being located on a science park are negligible. This finding is confirmed by Romijn and Albu (2002), whose research indicated that the regional science base has played a key role in nurturing new high-tech ventures but that science parks have not contributed to this. They also found that interaction with parties with complementary capabilities such as suppliers and service providers is also associated with high innovative performance. However the findings do not support the current policy of encouraging regional networks revolving around firms in similar business activities and close customer relations.

The experience has been similar in Canada. According to Shearmur and Doloreux (2000), over the last 25 years, 17 science parks have opened in Canada, but the authors found no link between the opening of a science park and employment growth in high-tech sectors.

The results are somewhat more positive for Italy. Colombo and Delmastro (2002) compared a sample of Italian firms on and off science park locations.

> The empirical results confirm the conventional wisdom that input and output measures of innovative activity are only marginally different between on- and off-incubator firms. Nonetheless, they also show that Italian parks managed to attract entrepreneurs with better human capital, as measured by educational attainments and prior working experience. In addition, on-incubator firms show higher growth rates than their off-incubator counterparts. They also perform better in terms of adoption of advanced technologies, aptitude for participating in international R&D programs and establishment of collaborative arrange-ments, especially with universities. Lastly, they find it easier to get access to public subsidies. Altogether, such findings support the view that science parks are an important element of a technology policy in favor of NTBFs. (Colombo and Delmastro, 2002, p. 1103)

Sadowski *et al.* (2003) examined the process by which technological competencies and resources of large firms evolve and its effects on the characteristics of their collaboration with smaller companies. In focusing on the issue of complementarity between local and international sourcing of capabilities and resources in the mobile telecommunication industry, they combined an empirical analysis of the structure of Finnish science parks with an examination of internationalization strategies of large Finnish companies. They found that Finnish telecommunications giant Nokia has increasingly become engaged in sourcing capabilities internationally rather than locally. This may well pose some long-term problems for the local embeddedness of the company in Finland.

Bakouros *et al.* (2002) studied three science parks in Greece. They found that informal links have been established between the firms and the local university. However only the firms located at one science park have developed formal links, while the formal links of the companies at the other two parks are still at the infant level. Synergies between the on-park companies are limited to commercial transactions and social interactions; research synergies were found to be completely absent in all three parks.

While not specifically studying science parks (but rather SMEs and NTBFs), Storey and Tether (1998) found that there has been a major shift in the last 15 years in almost all EU economies towards establishing stronger links between research institutions and the commercial sector. However they found these links to be strongest between universities and larger, rather than smaller, firms. Nevertheless there is considerable interest in most countries in enhancing the links between universities and SMEs. Partly these involve dismantling the barriers that universities have traditionally established and that prevent academics from establishing their own businesses. But if the prime objective of outreach activities is to generate income for the university, it is almost inevitable that the prime links are likely to remain with larger, rather than smaller, enterprises. The authors conclude that for these reasons it is easy to exaggerate the strength of links between SMEs in general, or NTBFs in particular, and universities. In most instances these links are not given high priority within the institution.

Using a study of the Singapore Science Park, Phillips and Yeung (2003) found that the 'institutional thickness' and 'local embeddedness' were inadequate for all but a small number of R&D firms in the park. They also found that spatial proximity to R&D institutions and organizations did not automatically result in collaborative R&D efforts. They concluded that, for science parks to be more than a form of glorified property development, there is an urgent need for a fundamental transformation in the prevailing thinking of economic planning, R&D policies and urban development.

Science parks have also been established in Russia in the last decade. Kihlgren (2003) studied science parks in St Petersburg and found that they have been rather successful in securing financing for their tenants but deficient in providing management assistance. The transfer of technology to industry has been weak because of the limited demand for high-tech products. Many firms survive in an embryonic state. This explains why, despite the difficulties, the number of jobs created has been substantial, although presumably many are low paid.

While experience around the world with respect to science parks has not been encouraging, it is noteworthy that there are no studies examining the US experience. At least, I have not found any in connection with this survey. Given that about half of the science parks in the world are in the United States, is it possible that US science parks have been more successful than those elsewhere? There is certainly room for more research here.

International Spillovers and the Role of Multinational Firms

An important source of new technology in an increasingly knowledge-based and globalized economy is international knowledge spillovers. The most important technology transfer mechanism here is foreign direct investment (FDI) by multinational firms. While this mechanism is mostly ignored in the US literature, it has received considerable attention elsewhere. For example, Howells and Nedeva (2003) study the growth of industry–academia links and in particular the growth of cross-border collaboration and funding, especially involving UK entities. Veugelers and Cassiman (2004) note that

> [the] use of foreign direct investment as a channel of international spillovers is by now fairly established in the empirical literature on innovation and growth. It is often argued that subsidiaries of foreign multinational enterprises are a mechanism through which technological know-how flows across borders. For foreign subsidiaries to be channels of international spillovers, these subsidiaries need to source know-how internationally and transfer their know-how to the local economy. (Veugelers and Cassiman, 2004, p. 455)

Using direct firm-level evidence from the Belgian Community Innovation Survey on the occurrence of technology transfers, Veugelers and Cassiman find that foreign subsidiaries are indeed more likely than other firms to acquire technology internationally. But, after controlling for the superior access to the international technology market that foreign subsidiaries enjoy, they also find that these firms are not more likely than local firms to transfer technology to the local economy. Apparently additional mechanisms are required in the host environment.

Similar results are reported for Sweden by Ivarsson (2002), who found that foreign-located affiliates of multinational corporations generate technological competencies, both internally and through organized cooperation with external business partners in the host country. He found that technological integration is especially associated with affiliates operating in competitive host country clusters. This indicates that a large pool of indigenous technological competence may be necessary as a pull factor for inward asset-seeking FDI. However technological linkages between foreign multinationals and host country partners do not come automatically. Instead they need substantial and long-term investments in personal and non-personal resources.

A Scottish study (Siler *et al.*, 2003) examined the extent to which technology generated in US parent firms is transferred to their Scottish affiliates in the form of productivity gains. The empirical results, based on a firm-level panel dataset, show that the labor productivity growth of Scottish subsidiaries is positively linked to the R&D activity of their US parents. It is noteworthy, however, that the R&D variable was found to be less significant than the subsidiary's own human capital in explaining productivity growth. The impact of human capital was found to be particularly important in smaller firms competing in the process industries. In contrast, technical knowledge appears to be transferred more readily to larger subsidiaries, those that have already achieved a relatively high level of productivity, and those that compete in industries based on product technology.

What the literature seems to suggest is that FDI can be an important mechanism of technology transfer but that positive results are obtained only when the local host community has a high level of absorptive capacity so that it can take advantage of spillovers. In this regard there is really no difference between technology transfer via direct foreign investment and that via universities. Some kind of cluster of competencies and/or firms may be necessary.

Culture and Environment

It is clear from the preceding analysis that technology transfer from universities needs to be understood in its broader context. The degree of success depends not only on the nature of the interface between the university and the business community but also on the receptivity in the surrounding community as well as the culture, organization and incentives within the universities themselves.

As pointed out in the European literature cited above, the institutional context within the universities matters a great deal. This is certainly true in the United States as well, as shown in a paper by Feldman and Desrochers (2003). They examined the evolution of university practices and policies towards technology transfer at the Johns Hopkins University, a leading research university and one of the largest recipients of federal research funding. The authors explored 'the university's founding mission, the expectation regarding patenting and the ownership of intellectual property, the types of funding sources and their expectations regarding what constitutes appropriate activity and the success or lack of success of institutional experiences, degree of risk aversion and commitment to change' (p. 20). They found several reasons why

> Hopkins has not generated highly visible economic benefit for the local area. One of the most important … is that it was never one of the university's objectives. Consequently there was a general lack of incentives and encouragement for commercial activity that might have potentially benefited the local area. This mission and academic culture institutionalized the norms of open science and stand in sharp contrast to the economic extension orientation of the Morrell Act land grant institutions or the decidedly more commercial orientation of MIT or

the economic development mission put forward by Leland Stanford. Another possible reason ... is that the type of basic work conducted at Hopkins was less amenable to direct technology transfer than the work conducted at institutions with a much stronger engineering curriculum, such as Stanford and MIT ... When industrial activities occurred through the initiative of individuals or through personal circumstances, there is no evidence of success. This appears to have only reinforced the norm that this more applied commercial work was not an activity suitable for the university. (Feldman and Desrochers, 2003, pp. 20–21)

The interface between the university and the business community is another important institutional factor. One dimension is the degree and nature of collaboration between the university and the entrepreneurial firms in its environment. Shane (2002b) discusses four dimensions of university–entrepreneurial firm collaboration: (1) industry-sponsored contract research, (2) consulting, (3) technology licensing and (4) technology development and commercialization. In each area Shane identifies how entrepreneurial firms behave vis-à-vis universities and how they differ from large established companies.

Owen-Smith and Powell (2003) have explored another dimension, namely network ties between universities and industry. They found that well-connected institutions develop higher-impact patent portfolios. 'Reaping the benefits of such connections, however, requires experience in balancing academic and corporate priorities to avoid the danger of "capture" by industrial interests as overly tight connections limit patent impact. This pattern of diminishing returns to connectivity is robust across multiple citation measures of patent quality' (p. 1695).

Research also indicates that the industry environment matters. For example, Nerkar and Shane (2003) find empirical evidence that industry concentration plays an important role. Specifically they find that, in order to compete successfully with established firms, new technology-based firms need to exploit radical technologies with broad scope patents.

Similarly, Gans and Stern (2003) have studied the 'commercialization environment', the microeconomic and strategic conditions facing a firm that is translating an idea into a value proposition for customers. They tried to identify the central drivers of start-up commercialization strategy and the implications of these drivers for industrial dynamics. Their analysis suggests that competitive interaction between start-up innovators and established firms depends on the presence or absence of a 'market for ideas'.

While there is a large literature on industry clusters – much too large to review here – it is interesting to note that the technology transfer literature in the United States makes very few references to it. In order to identify the relevant findings, one would have to use different keywords and concepts than those used here. What this suggests is that technology transfer between academia and industry is only one component, although probably an important one, in regional economic development, and that the links may be indirect. The analyses of Silicon Valley in California and Route 128 in Boston are highly suggestive examples (Saxenian, 1994; Bresnahan *et al.*, 2001).

Only two of the studies reviewed here mention clusters. One is Sorenson (2003) who notes that, in many industries, production resides in a small number of highly concentrated regions. While most explanations for this phenomenon have focused on how the colocation of firms in an industry might increase the efficiency of production, Sorenson argues that industries cluster because entrepreneurs find it difficult to retrieve the information and resources they require when they reside far from the sources of these inputs. Since existing firms often represent the largest pools of these important factors, the existing geographic distribution of production places important constraints on entrepreneurial activity. As a result, new firms tend to arise in the same areas as existing ones and hence reproduce the industrial geography. Sorenson reviews empirical evidence from the shoe manufacturing and biotechnology industries in support of this thesis.

A paper by Stuart and Sorenson (2003) develops another but similar explanation for firm colocation in high-technology industries that draws upon a relational account of new venture creation. The authors argue that industries cluster because entrepreneurs find it difficult to leverage the social ties necessary to mobilize essential resources when they reside far from those resources. Therefore opportunities for high tech entrepreneurship mirror the distribution of critical resources. The same factors that enable high-tech entrepreneurship, however, do not necessarily promote firm performance. The empirical analysis focuses on biotechnology and investigates the effects of geographic proximity to established biotechnology firms, sources of biotechnology expertise (highly skilled labor) and venture capitalists on the location-specific founding rates and performance of biotechnology firms. The authors find that the local conditions that promote new venture creation differ from those that maximize the performance of recently established companies.

Access and proximity to the necessary resources are certainly important determinants of the location of economic activity, including new start-ups. Culture is also important for entrepreneurship, generating differences across national and regional boundaries. A supportive national or regional culture will, *ceteris paribus*, increase the entrepreneurial potential of a country or region. This suggests that, in addition to support from political, social and business leaders, there needs to be a supportive culture to cultivate the mind and character of the potential entrepreneur. Some cultures are more conducive to entrepreneurship than others. Mueller and Thomas (2001) studied culture and entrepreneurial potential in a nine-country comparison of locus of control and innovativeness.

> In individualistic cultures we found an increased likelihood of an internal locus of control orientation. There was also support for the hypothesis that an entrepreneurial orientation, defined as internal locus of control combined with innovativeness, is more likely in individualistic, low uncertainty avoidance cultures than in collectivistic, high uncertainty avoidance cultures. (Mueller and Thomas, 2001, p. 51)

CONCLUSIONS AND POLICY IMPLICATIONS

There are two major conclusions of this study. The first is that institutional arrangements matter hugely for the relationships between universities and their environment and therefore for the impact of academic research on the economy and on the society in general. The ownership of intellectual property rights is of fundamental importance. The assignment to the universities of intellectual property rights to the results of federally funded research through the Bayh–Dole Act led to a reorganization and formalization of technology transfer from US universities in the form of technology licensing or transfer offices. This provided a form of shock to the US system that has stimulated university patenting and licensing activity. No similar shock has occurred in Europe, although charging universities with the 'third task' of fostering economic growth (in addition to the traditional tasks of teaching and research) is a step in a similar direction.

It is noteworthy, but perhaps not surprising, given the Bayh–Dole shock, that most of the US literature reviewed here focuses on the technology supply side, particularly academic research, its commercialization via technology transfer from the universities and the particular arrangements (technology transfer offices) facilitating transfer. The European literature, on the other hand, focuses more on the demand side, the general and less formal spillover effects of academic research and the institutional environment outside the universities.[5] As indicated already, this reflects differences in intellectual property rights and the institutional arrangements for formal technology transfer as compared with more informal technological spillovers.

The second conclusion of this study is the need to examine entrepreneurial activity resulting from academic research in a systemic framework that takes both supply and demand for technology into account. It is clear that entrepreneurship and innovation, particularly in the area of high technology, are increasingly being related to a receptive environment in the form of clusters and networks. These are made up of many component organizations – private, public, non-profit and others – that are interrelated in complex ways.

Understanding the role of public policy in this setting requires viewing the system as a whole rather than the component parts individually. One of the primary challenges for policy makers is to create a favorable climate for private entrepreneurship, often related to the formation of clusters. However cluster formation cannot be directed, only facilitated. Planning cannot replace the imaginative spark that creates innovation. Still, once clusters have been formed, a comprehensive set of facilitating policies, from information provision and networking to tax codes and labor laws, may be necessary (Carlsson and Mudambi, 2003).

A great deal of policy thinking in the last 15 years has been driven by the insights gained from the so-called 'new (or endogenous) growth theory' (Romer 1986, 1990; Lucas, 1988). In the previous neoclassical model of economic growth, the idea was that capital investment was the main driver of growth. The intellectual breakthrough contributed by the new growth theory was the recognition that investments in knowledge and human (as distinct from physical) capital generate economic growth through the spillover of knowledge. The main policy implication is that investment in knowledge and human capital is the best way to stimulate growth. But endogenous growth theory does not explain how or why spillovers occur; it simply assumes that they do. As pointed out by Acs *et al.* (2004), there is a missing link in the argument, namely the mechanism that converts knowledge into economic growth. There are actually two missing elements: not all knowledge is economically relevant and economic knowledge does not always result in successful economic activity. The conversion of knowledge into economically useful knowledge is the task of the entrepreneur who recognizes economic opportunity and takes action to exploit it. The success of the entrepreneurial activity depends partly on the economic conditions, especially how receptive the economic environment is. Some countries and regions are quite receptive, while others are not: it is as though there is a thick filter screening out entrepreneurial activity. Acs *et al.* (2004) have developed a model that introduces a filter between knowledge and economic knowledge and identifies entrepreneurship as a mechanism that reduces the thickness of the knowledge filter. The main policy implication is that public policies facilitating knowledge spillovers through entrepreneurship are important in promoting economic growth. Generating new knowledge is not enough.

Thus the most important policy implication of the analysis in this chapter is that it is necessary to bring the supply side and the demand side of technology together rather than treating them separately. This is true for both the analysis itself and the discussion of policy implications. In other words, a systems approach is needed.[6]

Europe can learn from the USA about more formal and purposive arrangements for technology transfer, while the USA can learn from Europe about external arrangements (institutions and policies). Even though technology spillovers have had only limited success in Europe, there are still arrangements that may be worthy of consideration in a US context, especially in view of the fact that there are huge local and regional differences within the USA. Much more research on culture and the business environment for technology transfer has been done in Europe than in the USA.

Close collaboration between universities and the business community is essential, but science parks may not be the vehicle. At least, they do not seem to work well outside the USA, but we do not know much about how they work in the USA. Internal factors within universities have been studied more in the USA than elsewhere, but there is still much to be learned.

Two areas have been identified where more research is needed: analyses of the impact of technology transfer and university spillovers on the economy, particularly in the USA; also the role of science parks in promoting economic growth in the USA is poorly understood.

NOTES

1. The review is focused primarily on studies published in 2000 or later.
2. Similarly Richard Nelson has argued that 'To try to make universities more like industrial labs will tend to take attention away from their most important functions, which are to be a major source of new public technological knowledge and societies' most effective vehicle for making technological knowledge public' (Nelson, 1989, p. 240, quoted in Stephan and Levin, 1996, p. 184).
3. 'Effectiveness' here refers to the establishment and enforcement of intellectual property rights.
4. It should perhaps be pointed out that patenting remains a minority activity: a majority of faculty never patent, and publication rates far outstrip patenting rates. In a study of MIT, Agrawal and Henderson (2002) found that most faculty members estimate that patents account for less than 10 per cent of the knowledge that transfers from their labs. Their results also suggest that in two important ways patenting is not representative of the patterns of knowledge generation and transfer from MIT: patent volume does not predict publication volume, and the firms that cite MIT papers are in general not the same firms as those that cite MIT patents.
5. I have found only a handful of studies referring to regions other than the United States and Western Europe.
6. For an overview of the innovation systems literature, see Carlsson (2003, forthcoming).

References

Acs, A. and D. Audretsch (1990), *Innovation and Small Firms*, Cambridge, MA: MIT Press.

Acs, Z.J., D.B. Audretsch, P. Braunerhjelm and B. Carlsson (2004), 'The missing link: the knowledge filter and entrepreneurship in endogenous growth', working paper, Case Western Reserve University, Cleveland, OH.

Adams, J. and Z. Griliches (1996), 'Research productivity in a system of universities', NBER working paper, no. 6120.

Agrawal, A. and R. Henderson (2002), 'Putting patents in context: exploring knowledge transfer from MIT', *Management Science*, **48**(1), 44–60.

Aldrich, H. (1999), *Organizations Evolving*, London: Sage.

Armington, C. (1987), 'The changing geography of high-technology business', in J. Rees (ed.), *Technology Regions and Policy*, Totowa, NJ: Rowman & Littlefield.

Association of University Technology Managers (2003), 'AUTM Licensing Survey: FY2002'.

Atack, J. and F. Bateman (1987), *To Their Own Soil: Agriculture in the Antebellum North*, Ames, IA: Iowa State University Press.

Audretsch, D. (2003), 'Standing on the shoulders of midgets: the US Small Business Innovation Research Program (SBIR)', *Small Business Economics*, **20**, 129–35.

Audretsch, D. and P. Stephan (1996), 'Company–scientist locational links: the case of biotechnology', *American Economic Review*, **86**(3), 641–52.

Audretsch, D., A. Link and J. Scott (2002), 'Public/private technology partnerships: evaluating SBIR-supported research', *Research Policy*, **31**, 145–58.

Audretsch, D., J. Weigand and C. Weigand (2000), 'Does the small business innovation research program foster entrepreneurial behavior? Evidence from Indiana', in C. Wessner (ed.), *The Small Business Innovation Research Program*, Washington, DC: National Academy Press, pp. 160–93.

Bakouros, Y.L., D.C. Mardas and N.C. Varsakelis (2002), 'Science park, a high tech fantasy? An analysis of the science parks of Greece', *Technovation*, **22**(2), 123–8.

Bania, N., M. Fogarty and S. Kauffman (1987), 'An assessment of Cleveland's scientific and engineering base and its role in the economy', working paper, Case Western Reserve University, Cleveland, OH.

Barker, E. (1999), 'Hot zones: the best cities in America for starting and growing a business', *Fortune*, December, 67–90.

Bates, T. (1977), *Race, Self-Employment and Upward Mobility: An Illusive American Dream*, Baltimore, MD: Johns Hopkins University Press.

Battelle Memorial Institute (2001), 'State government initiatives in biotechnology', Columbus, OH.

Baumol, W. (2004), 'Education for innovation: entrepreneurial breakthroughs vs. corporate incremental improvements', National Bureau of Economic Research, Working Paper 10578, Cambridge, MA.

Becker, G.S. (1975), *Human Capital*, New York: National Bureau of Economic Research.

Bellandi, M. (1989). 'The industrial district in marshall', in E. Goodman, J. Bamford and P. Saynor (eds), *Small Firms and Industrial Districts in Italy*, London: Routledge, pp. 136–52.

Berger, Allen N. and Gregory F. Udell (1995), 'Relationship lending and lines of credit in small firm finance', *Journal of Business*, **68**(3), 351–81.

Berglund, D. and C. Coburn (1995), *Partnerships*, Columbus, OH: Battelle.

Bergman, E.M. and E.J. Feser (1999), 'Industrial and regional clusters: concepts and comparative applications', Regional Research Institute, West Virginia University, Morganton, WV.

Bernstein, E. (2003), 'Want to go to Harvard Law?', *The Wall Street Journal*, 16 September.

Bingham, R. (1998), *Industrial Policy American Style*, New York: M.E. Sharpe.

Birch, D. (1987), *Job Creation in America: How Our Smallest Companies Put the Most People to Work*, New York: Free Press.

Blair, D. and D. Hitchens (1998), *Campus Companies – UK and Ireland*, Aldershot, UK: Ashgate.

Bok, D. (2003), *Universities in the Marketplace: The Commercialization of Higher Education*, Princeton, NJ: Princeton University Press.

Borjas, G. (1996), *Labor Economics*, 2nd edn, New York: Irwin McGraw-Hill.

Boston, T.D. (1999), *Affirmative Action and Black Entrepreneurship*, New York: Routledge.

Boyd, W.K. (1927), *The Story of Durham*, Durham, NC: Duke University Press

Bozeman, B. and J. Dietz (2002), 'Strategic research partnerships: constructing policy relevant indicators', *Journal of Technology Transfer*, **26**, 385–93.

Braunerhjelm, P., P. Svensson and F. Westin (2003), 'Akademiskt entreprenörskap', *Ekonomisk Debatt*, **31**(3).

Bresnahan, T.F., A. Gambardella and A. Saxenian (2001), '"Old economy" inputs for "new economy" outcomes: cluster formation in the new Silicon Valleys', *Industrial and Corporate Change*, **10**(4), 835–60.

Brooks, H. and L. Randazzese (1998), 'University–industry relations: the next four years and beyond', in L. Branscomb and J. Keller (eds), *Investing in Innovation: Creating a Research and Innovation Policy that Works*, Cambridge, MA: MIT Press.

Brown, G. and J. Turner (1999), 'Reworking the federal role in small business research', *Issues in Science and Technology*, Summer.

Butler, J. and G. Kozmetsky (2004), *Immigrant and Minority Entrepreneurship: The Continuous Rebirth of American Communities*, Westport, CT: Praeger.

Buttel, F., M. Kenney, J. Kloppenburg, Jr, T. Cowan and D. Smith (1986), 'Industry/land grant university relationships in transition', in L. Busch and W. Lacey (eds), *The Agricultural Scientific Enterprise*, Boulder, CO: Westview Press, pp. 296–312.

Carlino, G.A. (1978), 'Economies of scale in manufacturing location', Martinus Nijhoff Social Science Division, Boston.

Carlino, G.A. (1979), 'Increasing returns to scale in metropolitan manufacturing', *Journal of Regional Science*, **19**, 363–73.

Carlsson, B. (forthcoming), 'Innovation systems: a survey of the literature from a Schumpeterian perspective', in H. Hanusch and A. Pyka (eds), *Elgar Companion to Neo-Schumpeterian Economics*, Cheltenham, UK and Northampton, MA, USA: Edward Elgar.

Carlsson, B. (2003), 'Internationalization of innovation systems: a survey of the literature', paper presented at the conference in honor of Keith Pavitt: 'What Do We Know about Innovation?', SPRU, University of Sussex, Brighton, UK, 13–15 November.

Carlsson, B. and A. Fridh (2002), 'Technology transfer in United States universities – a survey and statistical analysis', *Journal of Evolutionary Economics*, **12**(1–2), 199–232.

Carlsson, B. and R. Mudambi (2003), 'Globalization, entrepreneurship and public policy: a systems view', *Industry and Innovation*, **10**(1), 103–16.

Casson, M. (1987), 'Entrepreneur', in J. Eatwell, M. Milgate and P. Newman (eds), *The New Palgrave: A Dictionary of Economics*, vol. 2, London: Macmillan Press, pp. 151–3.

Census Report (2003), 'Migration of the young, single and college educated: 1995–2000', US Census Bureau, Washington, DC.

Charles, D. and C. Conway (2001), 'Higher education–business interaction survey', Centre for Urban and Regional Development Studies, University of Newcastle upon Tyne, UK.

Charney, A. and G. Libecap (2003), 'The contribution of entrepreneurship education: an analysis of the Berger Program', *International Journal of Entrepreneurship Education*, **1**(3).

Chu, J. (2004), 'How to plug Europe's brain drain', *Time Europe*, http://www.time.com/time/europe/html/040119/brain/story.html, January.

Clark, B. (1998), *Creating Entrepreneurial Universities*, Oxford, UK: Elsevier Science.

Clark, V. (1929), *History of Manufactures in the United States*, vol. 1, New York: Carnegie, Institution of Washington.

Coburn, C. (1995), *Partnership: A Compendium of State and Federal Cooperative Technology Programs*, Columbus, OH: Batelle Memorial Institute.

Cohen, W. (1995), 'Empirical studies of innovative activity', in P. Stoneman (ed.), *Handbook of Economics and Technological Innovation*, Oxford, UK: Blackwell, pp. 182–264.

Cohen, W. (2000), 'Taking care of business', *ASEE Prism Online*, January, 1–5.

Cohen, L. and R. Noll (1991), *The Technology Pork Barrel*, Washington, DC: Brookings Institution.

Cohen, W., R. Florida and W.R. Coe (1994), *University–Industry Research Centers in the United States*, Pittsburgh, PA: Carnegie-Mellon University.

Collins, S. and H. Wakoh (2002), 'Universities and technology transfer in Japan: recent reforms in historical perspective', *Journal of Technology Transfer*, **25**, 213–22.

Colombo, M.G. and M. Delmastro (2002), 'How effective are technology incubators? Evidence from Italy', *Research Policy*, **31**(7), 1103–22.

Cooper, A. (2003), 'Entrepreneurship: the past, the present, the future', in Z. Acs and D. Audtretsch (eds), *Handbook of Entrepreneurial Research*, Boston: Kluwer Academic Publishers, pp. 21–34.

Cornwell, C., D. Mustard and D. Sridhar (2002), 'The enrollment effects of merit-based financial aid: evidence from Georgia's HOPE Scholarships', University of Georgia, Economics Working Paper 00–480, resubmitted to *Journal of Labor Economics*.

Coughlin, J. (2002), *The Rise of Women Entrepreneurs: People Processes and Global Trends*, Westport, Conn.: Quorum Books.

Craig, B. and J. Thomson (2003), 'Federal home loan bank lending to community banks: are targeted subsidies desirable?', *Journal of Financial Services Research*, **23**(1), 5–28.

Czarnitzki, D. and A. Spielkamp (2003), 'Business services in Germany: bridges for innovation', *Service Industries Journal*, **23**(1), 1–30.

Dahab, S.S. and R. Cabral (1998), 'Services firms in the Ideon Science Park', *International Journal of Technology Management*, **16**(8), 740–50.

DaVanzo, J. (1983), 'Repeat migration in the United States: who moves back and who moves on?', *The Review of Economics and Statistics*, **65**(4), 552–9.

Davis, S., J. Haltiwanger and S. Schuh (1996), *Job Creation and Destruction*, Cambridge, MA: MIT Press.

Davis, S., J. Haltiwanger and S. Schuh (2000), 'Small business and job creation: dissecting the myth and reassessing the facts', *Advances in Entrepreneurship*, **2**, 476–94.

de Crevecoeur, J.H. St. John (1981), *Letters from an American Farmer*, New York: Penguin Books.

De Voretz, D. and S. Laryea (1998), 'Canadian human capital transfers: the USA and beyond', paper presented to The Fraser Institute's conference, 'The Brain Drain: Causes, Consequences and Policy Response', Vancouver, BC, 13 November.

DeBresson, C. (ed.) (1996), *Economic Interdependence and Economic Activity*, Cheltenham, UK and Brookfield, USA: Edward Elgar.

Deloitte and Touche (2004), 'Pennsylvania Manufacturing Study'.

DeLorean, J. and J. Wright (1980), *On a Clear Day You Can See General Motors*, New York: Avon Books.

Denison, E. (1962), *The Sources of Economic Growth in the United States and the Alternatives Before Us*, New York: Committee for Economic Development.

Dertouzous, M., R. Lester and R. Solow (1989), *Made in America*, Cambridge, MA: MIT Press.

Detroit Free Press (2004), 'Program that helps manufacturers gets election-year attention', http://www.freep.com/news/statewire/sw105541_20041012.htm, 12 October.

DiGregorio, D. and S. Shane (2003), 'Why do some universities generate more start-ups than others?', *Research Policy*, **32**(2), 209–27.

Dimanescu, D. and J. Bodkin (1986), *The New Alliance*, Cambridge, MA: Ballinger Publishing.

Dubois, W.E.B. (1953), *The Souls of Black Folk*, New York: Fawcett Publication.

Dynarski, S. (2000), 'Hope for whom? Financial aid for the middle class and its impact on college attendance', *National Tax Journal*, **53**(3), 2 September, 629–62.

Eisinger, P. (1988), *The Rise of the Entrepreneurial State*, Madison, WI: University of Wisconsin Press.

Ergas, H. (1987), 'The importance of technology policy', in P. Dasgupta and P. Stoneman (eds), *Economic Policy and Technological Performance*, New York: Cambridge University Press, pp. 51–96.

Etzkowitz, H. (1989), 'Entrepreneurial science in the academy: a case of the transformation of norms', *Social Problems*, **36**(1), 14–29.

Feldman, M. (1994), 'The university and economic development: The case of Johns Hopkins University and Baltimore', *Economic Development Quarterly*, **8**(1), 67–76.

Feldman, M. (2001), 'Trends in patenting, licensing, and the role of equity at selected US universities', presentation to the National Academies Board on Science, Technology and Economic Policy Committee on Intellectual Property Rights in the Knowledge-Based Economy, 17 April.

Feldman, M. and P. Desrochers (2003), 'Research universities and local economic development: lessons from the history of the Johns Hopkins University', *Industry and Innovation*, **10**(1), 5–24.

Feldman, M. and M. Kelley (2002), 'How states augment the capabilities of technology-pioneering firms', *Growth and Change*, **33**(2), 173–95.

Feldman, M. and M. Kelley (2003), 'Leveraging research and development: assessing the impact of the US Advanced Technology Program', *Small Business Economics*, **20**(2), 153–65.

Feldman, M., I. Feller, J. Bercovitz and R. Burton (2002), 'Equity and the technology transfer strategies of American research universities', *Management Science*, **48**, 105–21.

Feller, I. (1990), 'University–industry R&D relationships', in J. Schmandt and R. Wilson (eds), *Growth Policy in the Age of High Technology*, Boston: Unwin Hyman, pp. 313–43.

Feller, I. (1999), 'The American university system as a performer of basic and applied research', *Industrializing Knowledge*, 65–101.

Feller, I. and G. Anderson (1994), 'A benefit–cost approach to the evaluation of state technology development programs', *Economic Development Quarterly*, **8**, 127–40.

Feller, I., C. Ailes and D. Roessner (2002), 'Impacts of research universities on technological innovation in industry: evidence from engineering research centers', *Research Policy*, **31**, 457–74.

Feser, E.J. (2003), 'What regions do rather than make: a proposed set of knowledge based occupation clusters', *Urban Studies*, **40**(10), 1937–58.

Feser, E.J. and E.M. Bergman (2000), 'National industry cluster templates: a framework for applied regional cluster analysis', *Regional Studies*, **34**(1), 1–19.

Feser, E.J. and J. Koo (2001), 'Labor-based industry clusters', unpublished manuscript, Chapel Hill.

Feser, E.J. and M. Luger (2003), 'Cluster analysis as a mode of inquiry: its use in science and technology policymaking in North Carolina', *European Planning Studies*, **11**(1), 11–24.

Florida, R. (2002), *The Rise of the Creative Class*, New York: Basic Books.

Florida, R. and M. Kenney (1990), *The Breakthrough Illusion*, New York, Basic Books.

Floud, R. (1994), 'Britain, 1860–1914, a survey', *The Economic History of Britain Since 1700, vol. 2, 1860–1939*, 2nd edn, Cambridge, UK: Cambridge University Press, pp. 1–28.

Fogarty, M. (1998), 'Cleveland's emerging economy: a framework for investing in education, science and technology', working paper, Case Western Reserve University, Cleveland, OH.

Fogarty, M. and A. Sinha (1999), 'Why older regions can't generalize from Route 128 and Silicon Valley', in L. Branscomb, F. Kodama and R. Florida (eds), *Industrializing Knowledge*, Cambridge, MA: MIT Press.

Fogarty, M., A. Jaffe and A. Sinha (2002), 'ATP and the US innovation system: a methodology for identifying enabling R&D spillover networks with applications to microelectro-mechanical systems (MEMS) and optical recording', forthcoming from the Advanced Technology Program, National Institute of Standards and Technology.

Fogarty, M., A. Sinha and A. Jaffe (2000), 'Sustaining the "new economy": California as a source of new technology', working paper, Case Western University, Cleveland, OH.

Frazier, E.F. (1925), 'Durham: capital of the black middle class', in W. Reiss (ed.), *The New Negro*, New York: Albert and Charles Boni.

Gans, J.S. and S. Stern (2003), 'The product market and the market for "ideas": commercialization strategies for technology entrepreneurs', *Research Policy*, **32**(2), 333–50.

Geiger, R. (1993), *Research and Relevant Knowledge: American Research Universities Since World War II*, Oxford, UK: Oxford University Press.

Geiger, R. and C. Sa (2004), 'Beyond technology transfer, US state policies to harness university research for economic development', *Minerva*.

Gittleman, M. (2000), 'Building a knowledge-based industry: scientists, firms and institutions in biotechnology in the United States and France', working paper, New York University.

Goldfarb, B. and M. Henrekson (2003), 'Bottom-up versus top-down policies towards the commercialization of university intellectual property', *Research Policy*, **32**(4), 639–58.

Goldman, M. (1984), 'Building a Mecca for high technology', *Technology Review*, May–June.

Golub, E. (2003), 'Generating spin-offs from university-based research: the potential of technology transfer', PhD dissertation, Columbia University, NY.

Gottlieb, P. (2001), 'The problem of brain drain in Ohio and Northeastern Ohio', Center for Regional Economic Issues, Cleveland, Ohio.

Gottlieb, P. (2003), 'Brain drain policies in the US States: treating the symptom instead of the disease?', working paper, Rutgers University, NJ.

Grandi, A. and R. Grimaldi (2003), 'Exploring the networking characteristics of new venture founding teams', *Small Business Economics*, **21**(4), 329–41.

Gray, D., M. Lindblad and J. Rudolph (2001), 'Industry–university research centers, a multivariate analysis of member retention', *Journal of Technology Transfer*, **26**, 247–54.

Greater Boston Chamber of Commerce Report (2003), 'Preventing a brain drain: talent retention in greater Boston'.

Greenwood, M. (1985), 'Human migration: theories, models and empirical studies', *Journal of Regional Science*, **25**(4), 521–44.

Grigg, T. (1994), 'Adopting an entrepreneurial approach in universities', *Journal of Engineering and Technology Management*, **11**(3–4), 273–98.

Hadlock, P., D. Hecker and J. Gannon (1991), 'High technology employment: another view', *Monthly Labor Review*, July, 26–30.

Harden, B. (2003), 'Brain-gain cities attract educated young', *Washington Post*, 9 November.

Hariharan, V. (2004), 'Can India plug its brain drain?', *Technology Review*, http://www.technologyreview.com, 30 March.

Harris, A. (1936), *The Negro as Capitalist*, New York: Arno Press.

Hebert, R. and A. Link (1988), 'In search of the meaning of entrepreneurship', *Small Business Economics*, **1**, 39–49.

Hecker, D. (1999), 'High-technology employment: a broader view', *Monthly Labor Review*, **122**, 18–28.

HEI (2004), 'Higher education infomation systems – the electronic query system of the Ohio Board of Regents', http://www.regents.state.oh.us/hei/.

Helper, S. and J. Kiehl (2004), 'Developing supplier capabilities: market and non-market approaches', *Industry and Innovation*, **11**(1–2), 89–107.

Hill, E.W. and J.F. Brennan (2000), 'A methodology for identifying the drivers of industrial clusters: the foundation of regional competitive advantage', *Economic Development Quarterly*, **14**(1), 65–96.

Honeck, J. (1998), 'Industrial policy for old industrial regions: a comparative study of Ohio and the Basque Country', unpublished PhD dissertation, University of Wisconsin–Madison.

Hoover, E.M. (1937), *Location Theory and the Shoe and Leather Industries*, Cambridge, MA: Harvard University Press.

Hopkins, J. (2004), 'Entrepreneurs are born, but can they be taught?,' *USA Today*, 7 April 2002, 1B ff.

Howells, J. and M. Nedeva (2003), 'The international dimension to industry–academic links', *International Journal of Technology Management*, **25**(1–2), 5–17.

Hoxby, C. (1997), 'How the changing market structure of US higher education explains college tuition', NBER Working Paper.

Hsu, D. and T. Bernstein (1997), 'Managing the university technology licensing process', *Journal of the Association of Technology Managers*, **9**, 1–33.

Hughes, J. (1977), *The Governmental Habit*, New York: Basic Books.

Hughes, T. (1989), *American Genesis*, New York: Viking Penguin.

Huntington Hobbs, S. (1958), *North Carolina: An Economic and Social Profile*, Chapel Hill: The University of North Carolina Press.

Industrial Research Institute, Inc. (2001), 'Industry–university intellectual property', External Research Directors Network, position paper.

Isard, W. (1956), *Location and Space Economy*, New York: John Wiley.

Ivarsson, I. (2002), 'Transnational corporations and the geographical transfer of localised technology: a multi-industry study of foreign affiliates in Sweden', *Journal of Economic Geography*, **2**(2), 221–47.

Jacob, M., M. Lundqvist and H. Hellsmark (2003), 'Entrepreneurial transformations in the Swedish university system: the case of Chalmers University of Technology', *Research Policy*, **32**(9), 1555–68.

Jaffe, A.B. and J. Lerner (2001), 'Reinventing public R&D: patent policy and the commercialization of national laboratory technologies', *Rand Journal of Economics*, **32**(1), 167–98.

Jaffe, A., M. Trajtenberg and M. Fogarty (2000), 'Knowledge spillovers and patent citations: evidence from a survey of inventors', *AEA Proceedings*, pp. 215–18

Jarmin, R. (1999), 'Evaluating the impact of manufacturing extension on productivity growth', *Journal of Policy Analysis and Management*, **18**(1), 99–119

Jensen, R.A., J.G. Thursby and M.C. Thursby (2003), 'Disclosure and licensing of university inventions: "the best we can do with the s**t we get to work with"', *International Journal of Industrial Organization*, **21**(9), 1271–300.

Jensen, R. and M. Thursby (2001), 'Proofs and prototypes for sale: the tale of university licensing', *American Economic Review*, **91**, 240–59.

Jewell, J. (2004), 'Race, social reform and the making of a black middle class: Atlanta, 1870–1900', unpublished manuscript, Department of Sociology Texas A&M University, College Station, Texas.

Jones-Evans, D., M. Klofsten, E. Andersson and D. Pandya (1999), 'Creating a bridge between university and industry in small European countries: the role of the industrial liaison office', *R & D Management*, **29**(1), 47–56.

Kane, E.J. and B.G. Malkiel (1965), 'Bank portfolio allocation, deposit variability, and the availability doctrine', *Quarterly Journal of Economics*, **79**(1), 113–34.

Kennedy, P. (1987), *The Rise and Fall of the Great Powers*, New York: Random House.

Kenney, M. (1986), *Biotechnology: The University–Industrial Complex*, New Haven: Yale University Press.

Kenney, N. and W. Goe (2004), 'The role of social embeddedness in professional entrepreneurship: a comparison of electrical engineering and computer science at UC Berkeley and Stanford', *Research Policy*, **33**, 691–707.

Kenzer, R. (1997), *Enterprising Southerners: Black Economic Success in North Carolina, 1865–1915*, Charlottesville, VA: University Press of Virginia.

Kihlgren, A. (2003), 'Promotion of innovation activity in Russia through the creation of science parks: the case of St. Petersburg (1992–1998)', *Technovation*, **23**(1), 65–76.

Kloosterman, R. and J. Rath (2003), *Immigrant Entrepreneurs: Venturing Abroad in the Age of Globalization*, Guilford, UK: Biddles Ltd.

Kneller, R. (2003), 'University–industry cooperation and technology transfer in Japan compared with the United States: another reason for Japan's economic malaise?', *University of Pennsylvania Journal of International Economic Law*, **24**(2), 329–449.

Krucken, G. (2003), 'Mission impossible? Institutional barriers to the diffusion of the "third academic mission" at German universities', *International Journal of Technology Management*, **25**(1–2), 18–33.

Lanjouw, J. and M. Shankerman (1997), 'Stylized facts of patent litigation: value, scope, and ownership', NBER Working Paper, no. 6297.

Lerner, J. (1999), 'The government as venture capitalist: the long run impact of the SBIR program', *The Journal of Business*, **72**(3).

Leslie, S. (1993), *The Cold War and American Science: The Military–Industrial–Academic Complex at MIT and Stanford*, New York: Columbia University Press.

Levenstein, M. (2004). 'African–American entrepreneurship: the view from the 1910 Census', in J. Butler and G. Kozmetsky (eds), *Immigrant and Minority Entrepreneurship: The Continuous Rebirth of American Communities*, London: Praeger.

Lichtenberg, R.M. (1960), *One-tenth of a Nation*, Cambridge, MA: Harvard University Press.

Light, I. (1972), *Ethnic Enterprise in America*, Berkeley, CA: The University of California Press.

Lin, B.W. (2003), 'Technology transfer as technological learning: a source of competitive advantage for firms with limited R&D resources', *R & D Management*, **33**(3), 327–41.

Lindelöf, P. and H. Löfsten (2002), 'Growth, management and financing of new technology-based firms – assessing value-added contributions of firms located on and off science parks', *Omega-International Journal of Management Science*, **30**(3), 143–54.

Lindelöf, P. and H. Löfsten (2003), 'Science park location and new technology-based firms in Sweden – implications for strategy and performance', *Small Business Economics*, **20**(3), 245–58.

Link, A.N. and J.T. Scott (2003), 'US science parks: the diffusion of an innovation and its effects on the academic missions of universities', *International Journal of Industrial Organization*, **21**(9), 1323–56.

Livingston, S. (2003), 'Brain drain: grads with advanced degrees are flowing out of Ohio', *The Cleveland Plain Dealer*, 23 February.

Lockett, A., M. Wright and S. Franklin (2002), 'Technology transfer and universities' spin-out strategies', working paper, Nottingham Business School, UK.

Lockett, A., M. Wright and S. Franklin (2003), 'Technology transfer and universities' spin-out strategies', *Small Business Economics*, **20**(2), 185–200.

Löfsten, H. and P. Lindelöf (2001), 'Science parks in Sweden – industrial renewal and development?', *R & D Management*, **31**(3), 309–22.

Löfsten, H. and P. Lindelöf (2002), 'Science parks and the growth of new technology-based firms – academic–industry links, innovation and markets', *Research Policy*, **31**(6), 859–76.

Löfsten, H. and P. Lindelöf (2003), 'Determinants for an entrepreneurial milieu: science parks and business policy in growing firms', *Technovation*, **23**(1), 51–64.

Lowe, R. (2002), 'Invention, innovation, and entrepreneurship: the commercialization of university research by inventor-founded firms', PhD dissertation, University of California, Berkeley, CA.

Lucas, R. (1988), 'On the mechanics of economic development', *Journal of Monetary Economics*, **22**, 3–39.

Luger, Michael (1998), 'Technology development programs, intergovernmental relations and balanced regional growth', in A.A. Summers and L. Sen (eds), *Comparisons of Urban Economic Development in the US and Western Europe*, Washington, DC: The Urban Institute Press, pp. 493–529.

Luger, M., L. Stewart and G. Androney (2003), 'Identifying "targets of opportunity" competitive clusters for RTRP and its sub-regions', for the Research Triangle Regional Partnership, December.

Luker, B. and D. Lyons (1997), 'Employment shifts in US high technology industries, 1988–1996', *Monthly Labor Review*, **120**(2), 12–26.

Luria, D. (1996a), 'Toward lean or rich? Small-manufacturer performance, and some implications for extension centers', *The Bench Press*, **3**, 1–5.

Luria, D. (1996b), 'Why markets tolerate mediocre manufacturing', *Challenge*, **39**(4), 11–16.

Luria, D. (1997), 'Toward lean or rich? What performance benchmarking tells us about SME performance and some implications for extension center services and mission', in P. Shapira and J. Youtie (eds), *Manufacturing Modernization: Learning from Evaluation Practices and Results*, Atlanta, GA: Georgia Institute of Technology.

Luria, D. and E. Wiarda (1996), 'Performance benchmarking and measuring program's impacts on customers: lessons from the Michigan Manufacturing Technology Center', *Research Policy*, **25**(2), 233–46.

Luria, D., R.J. Cole, A. Baum and E. Wiarda (1994), 'Fixing the manufacturing base: the allocation of manufacturing extension', *Journal of Policy Analysis and Management*, **13**(3), 571–80.

Lynch, R. (2004), 'Rethinking growth strategies: how state and local taxes affect economic development', Economic Policy Institute, Washington, DC.

Markusen, A.R. and A. Glasmeier (1986), *High Tech America: The What, How, Where and Why of the Sunrise Industries*, New York: HarperCollins.

Matkin, G. (1990), *Technology Transfer and the University*, New York: Macmillan.

McDougall, W. (2004), *Freedom Just Around the Corner*, New York: HarperCollins.

McQueen, D. and J. Wallmark (1991), 'University technical innovation: spin-offs and patents in Goteborg, Sweden', in A. Brett, D. Gibson and R. Smilor (eds), *University Spin-off Companies*, Savage, MD: Rowman and Littlefield pp. 103–15.

Monjon, S. and P. Waelbroeck (2003), 'Assessing spillovers from universities to firms: evidence from French firm-level data', *International Journal of Industrial Organization*, **21**(9), 1255–70.

Moore, K. and D. Lewis (1999), 'Birth of the multinational: 2000 years of ancient business history from Ashur to Augustus', Copenhagen Business School, Denmark.

Mora-Valentin, E.M., A. Montoro-Sanchez and L.A. Guerras-Martin (2004), 'Determining factors in the success of R&D cooperative agreements between firms and research organizations', *Research Policy*, **33**(1), 17–40.

Mortenson, T. (ed.) (2002), 'Interstate migration of college freshmen, 1986–2000', *Post Secondary Education Opportunity*, October, no. 124.

Mortenson, T. (ed.) (2004), 'Mobility and interstate migration for the young, single and college educated, 1995–2000', *Post Secondary Education Opportunity*, July, no. 125.

Mount Auburn Associates (2001), 'An evaluation of EDA's University Center Program, Somerville, MA', report to Economic Development Administration, award #99–06–07452.

Mowery, D. (2001), 'Trends in patenting, licensing, and the role of equity at selected US universities', presentation to the National Academies Board on Science, Technology and Economic Policy Committee on Intellectual Property Rights in the Knowledge-Based Economy, 17 April.

Mowery, D. and N. Rosenberg (1993), 'The US national innovation system', in R. Nelson (ed.), *National Innovation Systems*, New York: Oxford University Press, pp. 29–75.

Mowery, D., and B. Sampat (2001), 'University patents and patent policy debates in the USA, 1925–1980', *Industrial and Corporate Change*, **10**(3), 781–814.

Mowery, D., R. Nelson, B. Sampat and A. Ziedonis (2001), 'The growth of patenting and licensing by US universities: an assessment of the effects of the Bayh–Dole Act of 1980', *Research Policy*, **30**, 99–119.

Mowery, D., R. Nelson, B. Sampat and A. Ziedonis (2004), *Ivory Tower and Industrial Innovation*, Stanford, CA: Stanford Business Books.

Mueller, S.L. and A.S. Thomas (2001), 'Culture and entrepreneurial potential: a nine country study of locus of control and innovativeness', *Journal of Business Venturing*, **16**(1), 51–75.

Muller, T. (1993), *Immigrants and the American City*, New York: New York University Press.

Mustar, P. (1997), 'Spin-off enterprises. How French academics create high-tech companies: conditions for success or failure', *Science and Public Policy*, **24**(1), 37–43.

National Governor's Association (2004), 'A governor's guide to strengthening state entrepreneurship policy', NGA Center for Best Practices, Washington, DC.

National Science Board (2003), *The Science and Engineering Workforce – Realizing America's Potential*, Washington, DC: National Science Foundation.

National Science Foundation (2001), 'Strategic research partnerships', in J. Jankowski, A. Link and N. Vonortas (eds), *Proceedings from an NSF Workshop*, Washington, DC: National Science Foundation.

National Science Foundation (2002), *Science and Engineering Indicators*, Washington, DC: United States Government Printing Office.

National Science Foundation (2004), *Science & Engineering Indicators – 2004*, Washington, DC: National Science Board.

Nelson, R. (1989), 'What is private and what is public about technology', *Science Technology and Human Values*, **14**(3), 229–41.

Nerkar, A. and S. Shane (2003), 'When do start-ups that exploit patented academic knowledge survive?', *International Journal of Industrial Organization*, **21**(9), 1391–410.

Newton, D. and M. Hendricks (2003), 'Can entrepreneurship be taught?', *Entrepreneur*, April.

Office of the Governor of Ohio (2000), 'Governor announces $14.5 million in technology action fund awards', Press release, 30 March.

Ohio Board of Regents (2004), http://www.regents.state.oh.us/sgs/choice-grant.htm.

Ohio Board of Regents, Ohio's Colleges and Universities (2001), 'Profile of student outcomes, experiences and campus measures', 12 December.

Owen-Smith, J. (2003), 'From separate systems to a hybrid order: accumulative advantage across public and private science at research one universities', *Research Policy*, **32**(6), 1081–104.

Owen-Smith, J. and W.W. Powell (2003), 'The expanding role of university patenting in the life sciences: assessing the importance of experience and connectivity', *Research Policy*, **32**(9), 1695–711.

Payne, A. and A. Siow (2003), 'Does federal research funding increase university research output?', *Advances in Economic Analysis and Policy*, **3**(1), 1–25.

Perez, M.P. and A.M. Sanchez (2003), 'The development of university spin-offs: early dynamics of technology transfer and networking', *Technovation*, **23**(10), 823–31.

Petersen, M.A. (1999), 'The small business lending relationship', Conference on Consumer Transactions and Credit, Federal Reserve Bank of Philadelphia, Philadelphia, PA.

Petersen, M.A. and G.R. Raghuram (1994), 'The benefits of lending relationships: evidence from small business data', *Journal of Finance*, **49**(1), 3–37.

Phillips, S.A.M. and H.W.C. Yeung (2003), 'A place for R&D? The Singapore Science Park', *Urban Studies*, **40**(4), 707–32.

Pierce, J.A. (1947), *Negro Business and Business Education*, New York: Harper Brothers.

Pirnay, F., B. Surlemont and F. Nlemvo (2003), 'Toward a typology of university spin-offs', *Small Business Economics*, **21**(4), 355–69.

Pollard, S. (1994), 'Entrepreneurship, 1870–1914', in *The Economic History of Britain Since 1700, Volume 2, 1860–1939*, 2nd edn, Cambridge, UK: Cambridge University Press, pp. 62–89.

Porter, M.E. (1990), *The Competitive Advantage of Nations*, New York: Free Press.

Porter, M.E. (2002), *Clusters of Innovation: Research Triangle*, Washington, DC: Council on Competitiveness.

Portes, A. and R. Bach (1985), *Latin Journey*, Berkeley, CA: University of California Press.

President's Commission on Immigration and Naturalization (1953), *Report of the President's Commission on Immigration and Naturalization*, Washington, DC: Government Printing Office.

Pressman, L. (ed.) (1999), *AUTM Licensing Survey: FY 1999*, Northbrook, Il: Association of University Technology Managers.

Pressman, L. (ed.) (2002), *AUTM Licensing Survey: FY 2002*, Northbrook, Il: Association of University Technology Managers.

Pressman, L., S. Guterman, I. Abrams, D. Geist and L. Nelsen (1995), 'Pre-production investment and jobs induced by MIT exclusive patent licenses: a preliminary model to measure the economic impact of university licensing', *Journal of Association of University Technology Managers*, **7**, 49–81.

Putnam, R.D. (1993), *Making Democracy Work: Civic Traditions in Modern Italy*, Princeton, NJ: Princeton University Press.

Putnam, R.D. (2000), *Bowling Alone: The Collapse and Revival of American Community*, New York: Simon and Schuster.

Rege, M. (2003), 'Networking strategy: cooperate today in order to meet a cooperator tomorrow', working paper, Department of Economics, Case Western Reserve University, Cleveland, OH.

Rhyne, E.H. (1988), *Small Business, Banks, and SBA Loan Guarantees: Subsidizing the Weak or Bridging a Credit Gap?*, New York: Quorum Books.

Rivette, K. and D. Kline (2000), *Rembrandts in the Attic: Unlocking the Hidden Value of Patents*, Boston: Harvard Business School Press.

Roberts, E. and R. Malone (1996), 'Policies and structures for spinning off new companies from research and development organizations', *R&D Management*, **26**(1), 17–48.

Rogers, E. and J. Larsen (1984), *Silicon Valley Fever: Growth of High-Technology Culture*, New York: Basic Books.

Romer, P. (1986), 'Increasing returns and economic growth', *American Economic Review*, **94**, 1002–37.

Romer, P. (1990), 'Endogenous technical change', *Journal of Political Economy*, **98**, 71–102.

Romijn, H. and M. Albu (2002), 'Innovation, networking and proximity: lessons from small high technology firms in the UK', *Regional Studies*, **36**(1), 81–6.

Rosenberg, N. and R. Nelson (1994), 'American universities and technical advances in industry', *Research Policy*, **23**(3), 323–48.

Rosenthal, S. and W. Strange (2003), 'The micro-empires of agglomeration economies', in R. Arnott and D. McMillen (eds), *Blackwell Companion to Urban Economics*, Oxford, UK: Blackwell.

Ruegg, R. and I. Feller (2003), 'A toolkit for evaluating public R&D investments', Washington, DC, NIST NIST GCR 03–857.

Sadowski, B.M., K. Dittrich and G.M. Duysters (2003), 'Collaborative strategies in the event of technological discontinuities: the case of Nokia in the mobile telecommunication industry', *Small Business Economics*, **21**(2), 173–86.

Saez, C.B., T.G. Marco and E.H. Arribas (2002), 'Collaboration in R&D with universities and research centres: an empirical study of Spanish firms', *R & D Management*, **32**(4), 321–41.

Sampat, B.N. and R.R. Nelson (2002), 'The evolution of university patenting and licensing procedures: an empirical study of institutional change', *New Institutionalism in Strategic Management – Advances in Strategic Management: A Research Annual*, **19**, 132–64.

Samuel, Y. (2004), 'Holden ties student loan forgiveness to jobs in life sciences: plan seeks to promote state as the place for a quality work force', *St. Louis Post-Dispatch*, 13 February.

Saxenian, A. (1994), *Regional Advantage: Culture and Competition in Silicon Valley and Route 128*, Cambridge, MA: Harvard University Press.

Saxenian, A. and J. Edulbehram (1998), 'Immigrant entrepreneurs in Silicon Valley', *Berkeley Planning Journal*, **12**, 33–40.

Schmidt, P. (2004), 'Programs that pay tuition in exchange for work are unproved, report says', *The Chronicle of Higher Education*, 27 February.

Schmiemann, M. and J. Durvy (2003), 'New approaches to technology transfer from publicly funded research', *Journal of Technology Transfer*, **28**, 9–15.

Scott, J. (2001), 'Strategic partnerships, what have we learned?', working paper, Dartmouth College.

Shaker Heights Schools (2004), 'Wall Street Journal recognizes Shaker as a top feeder school for elite colleges', News Release, 2 April.

Shane, S. (2002a), 'Executive forum: university technology transfer to entrepreneurial companies', *Journal of Business Venturing*, **17**(6), 537–52.

Shane, S. (2002b), 'Selling university technology: patterns from MIT', *Management Science*, **48**(1), 122–37.

Shane, S. (2003), *A General Theory of Entrepreneurship: The Individual–Opportunity Nexus*, Cheltenham, UK and Northampton, MA, USA: Edward Elgar.

Shane, S. (2004), 'Encouraging university entrepreneurship? The effect of the Bayh–Dole Act on university patenting in the United States', *Journal of Business Venturing*, **19**(1), 127–51.

Shane, S. and T. Stuart (2002), 'Organizational endowments and the performance of university start-ups', *Management Science*, **48**(1), 154–70.

Shane, S. and S. Venkataraman (2000), 'The promise of entrepreneurship as a field of research', *Academy of Management Review*, **25**, 217–26.

Shapira, P. (1995), 'Manufacturing extension: performance, challenges and policy issues', in L. Branscomb and J. Keller (eds), *Investing in Innovation: Creating a Research and Innovation Policy*, Cambridge, MA: MIT Press.

Shapira, P. (2003), 'Evaluating manufacturing extension services in the United States: experiences and insights', in P. Shapira and S. Kuhlman (eds), *Learning from Science and Technology Policy Evaluation*, Cheltenham, UK and Northampton, MA, USA: Edward Elgar, pp. 260–92.

Shearmur, R. and D. Doloreux (2000), 'Science parks: actors or reactors? Canadian science parks in their urban context', *Environment and Planning A*, **32**(6), 1065–82.

Sheban, J. (2003), 'Bill targets high-tech grad students', *Columbus Dispatch*, 15 October.

Siegel, D., D. Waldman and A. Link (1999), 'Assessing the impact of organizational practices on the productivity of university technology transfer offices: an exploratory study', NBER Working Paper No. 7256.

Siegel, D.S., P. Westhead and M. Wright (2003a), 'Assessing the impact of university science parks on research productivity: exploratory firm-level evidence from the United Kingdom', *International Journal of Industrial Organization*, **21**(9), 1357–69.

Siegel, D.S., P. Westhead and M. Wright (2003b), 'Science parks and the performance of new technology-based firms: a review of recent U.K. evidence and an agenda for future research', *Small Business Economics*, **20**(2), 177–84.

Siler, P., C.Q. Wang and X.M. Liu (2003), 'Technology transfer within multinational firms and its impact on the productivity of Scottish subsidiaries', *Regional Studies*, **37**(1), 15–25.

Slaughter, S. and L. Leslie (1997), *Academic Capitalism*, Baltimore, MD, Johns Hopkins University Press.

Small Business Administration (2004), 'Webpage for Small Business Administration', www.sba.gov, 8 March.

Smith, B. (1990), *American Science Policy Since World War II*, Washington, DC, Brookings Institution.

Smith, H. (1989), *The Power Game: How Washington Works*, New York: Ballentine Books.

Sommers, D. (2003), 'Brain drain or weak attraction?', a briefing for the Ohio Governor's Commission on higher education and the economy, Ohio Board of Regents, Columbus, OH.

Sorenson, O. (2003), 'Social networks and industrial geography', *Journal of Evolutionary Economics*, **13**(5), 513–27.

Stanley, M. and S. Helper (2003), 'Industrial clusters, social capital and international competition in the US component manufacturing industry', presented to 'Clusters, Industrial Districts and Firms: the Challenge of Globalization', conference in honor of Professor Sebastiano Brusco, Modena, Italy, September.

Steffensen, M., E.M. Rogers and K. Speakman (2000), 'Spin-offs from research centers at a research university', *Journal of Business Venturing*, **15**(1), 93–111.

Stephan, P. (2001), 'Educational implications of university–industry technology transfer', *Journal of Technology Transfer*, **26**, 199–205.

Stephan, P.E. and S.G. Levin (1996), 'Property rights and entrepreneurship in science', *Small Business Economics*, **8**(3), 177–88.

Stiglitz, J.E. and A. Weiss (1981), 'Credit rationing in markets with imperfect information', *American Economic Review*, **71**(3), 393–410.

Storey, D.J. and B.S. Tether (1998), 'Public policy measures to support new technology-based firms in the European Union', *Research Policy*, **26**(9), 1037–57.

Stough, R.R., R. Stimson and B. Roberts (1997), 'Merging quantitative and expert response data in setting regional economic development policy: methodology and application', paper presented at the 19th annual research conference of the Association for Public Policy Analysis and Management, Washington, DC.

Stuart, T. and O. Sorenson (2003), 'The geography of opportunity: spatial heterogeneity in founding rates and the performance of biotechnology firms', *Research Policy*, **32**(2), 229–53.

Sumell, A., P. Stephan and J. Adams (2003), 'Capturing knowledge: the location decision of new PhDs working in industry', preliminary draft.

Systems Planning Corporation (1999), 'MEMS 1999: emerging applications and markets', Systems Planning Corporation, Arlington, VA.

Taylor, M. (2004), 'Just-in-time funding – congressional budgeters approve emergency funding for popular program for manufacturers', *Inc magazine*, 7 October.

Thursby, J. and M. Thursby (2000), 'Industry perspectives on licensing university technologies: sources and problems', *Journal of the Association of University Technology Managers*, **12**.

Thursby, J.G. and Thursby, M.C. (2002), 'Who is selling the ivory tower? Sources of growth in university licensing', *Management Science*, **48**(1), 90–104.

Thursby, J., R. Jensen and M. Thursby (2001), 'Objectives, characteristics and outcomes of university licensing: a survey of major US universities', *Journal of Technology Transfer*, **26**, 59–72.

Tibbetts, R. (1999), 'The small business innovation research program and NSF SBIR commercialization results', in C. Wessner (ed.), *The Small Business Innovation Research Program, Challenges and Opportunities*, Washington, DC: National Academy Press, pp. 129–67.

Todd, W.F. (1992), 'History of and rationales for the Reconstruction Finance Corporation', *Federal Reserve Bank of Cleveland Economic Review*, 4th Quarter, 22–35.

Tornatzky, L., P. Waugaman and D. Gray (2002), 'Innovation U, new university roles in a knowledge economy', Southern Growth Policies Board.

Tornatzky, L., P. Waugaman, L. Casson, S. Crowell, C. Spahr and F. Wong (1995), 'Benchmarking best practices for university–industry technology transfer: working with start-up companies', a report of the Southern Technology Council, Atlanta.

Traxler, H. and M. Luger (2000), 'Business and the Internet: implications for firm consequences of IT for location and clustering', *Comparative Journal of Policy Analysis*, **2**(3), 279–300.

US Census Bureau (1997), 'Black 1997', *Economic Census Survey of Minority-Owned Business Enterprises*', company statistics series, Washington, DC: US Department of Commerce.

US Congress, Office of Technology Assessment (1990), 'Making things better: competing in manufacturing', OTA-ITE-443, US Government Printing Office, Washington, DC.

US Department of Commerce (2001), 'US businesses owned by Hispanics top 1 million', US Census Bureau, Public Information Office.

US Department of Education, National Center for Education Statistics, Integrated Postsecondary Education Data System (IPEDS) (1998), Residence of first-time students survey.

US Department of the Census (2002), *Asian and Pacific Islander-Owned Businesses Number 9000+*, Washington, DC: US Government Printing Office.

US News & World Report (2004), 'America's best colleges'.

Varian, H. and C. Shapiro (1998), *Information Rules: A Strategic Guide to The Network Economy*, Boston, MA: Harvard Business School Press.

Vernon, R. (1960), *Metropolis 1985*, Cambridge, MA: Harvard University Press.

Veugelers, R. and B. Cassiman (2004), 'Foreign subsidiaries as a channel of international technology diffusion: some direct firm level evidence from Belgium', *European Economic Review*, **48**(2), 455–76.

Vohora, A., M. Wright and A. Lockett (2004), 'Critical junctures in the development of university high-tech spinout companies', *Research Policy*, **33**(1), 147–75.

von Hippel, E. (1988), *The Sources of Innovation*, New York: Oxford University Press.

Wallenstein, S. (2000), 'The effects of government–industry R&D programs on private R&D, the case of the small business innovation program', *Rand Journal of Economics*, **31**.

Wallmark, J. (1997), 'Inventions and patents at universities: the case of Chalmers University of Technology', *Technovation*, **17**(3), 127–39.

Walsh, J. and W. Cohen (2004), 'Does the golden goose travel? A comparative analysis of the influence of public research on industrial R&D in the US and Japan', working paper, University of Tokyo.

Walton, G. and J. Shepherd (1979), *The Economic Rise of Early America*, London: Cambridge University Press.

Washington, B.T. (1911), 'Durham North Carolina: a city of negro enterprises', *Independent*, **70**, 30 March, 642–51.

Weber, A. (1929), *Theory of the Location of Industries*, Chicago: University of Chicago Press, trans. C.J. Friedrich.

Wessner, C. (ed.) (1999), *The Small Business Innovation Research Program*, Washington, DC: National Academy Press.

Whitford, J. and J. Zeitlin (2004), 'Governing decentralized production: institutions, public policy, and the prospects for inter-firm collaboration in US manufacturing', *Industry and Innovation*, **11**(1–2), 11–44.

Wiarda, E. and D. Luria (1989), 'Fixing what's broke where it counts: agglomeration in the core industrial economy', *TechnEcon* **1**(2), 1–13.

Wickstead, S. (1985), *The Cambridge Phenomenon*, Thetford, UK: Thetford Press.

Wildavsky, A. (1976), 'If planning is everything, maybe it's nothing', *Policy Sciences*, **4**(3).

Winter, S. (1984), 'Schumpeterian competition in alternative technological regimes', *Journal of Economic Behavior and Organization*, **5**, 287–320.

Witsil, A. and D. Winfield (RTI International) (2003), *R&D inventory and growth opportunity analysis*, for the Research Triangle Regional Partnership, July.

Wright, M., A. Vohora and A. Lockett (2002), 'Annual UNICO-NUBS survey on university commercialisation activities: financial year 2001', Nottingham University Business School, Nottingham, UK.

Zacks, R. (2000), 'The TR university research scoreboard', *Technology Review*, July/August, 88–90.

Zhou, M. (1992), *Chinatown: The Socioeconomic Potential of an Urban Enclave*, Philadelphia: Temple University Press.

Zucker, L. and M. Darby (2001), 'Capturing technological opportunity via Japan's star scientists: evidence from Japanese firms' biotech patents and products', *Journal of Technology Transfer*, **26**, 37–58.

Index